REASON
IN COMMON SENSE

REASON
IN COMMON SENSE

Volume One of "The Life of Reason"

GEORGE SANTAYANA

ἡ γὰρ νοῦ ἐνέργεια ζωή

Dover Publications, Inc.
New York

Published in Canada by General Publishing Company, Ltd., 30 Lesmill Road, Don Mills, Toronto, Ontario.

Published in the United Kingdom by Constable and Company, Ltd., 10 Orange Street, London WC2H 7EG.

This Dover edition, first published in 1980, is an unabridged republication of volume one of *The Life of Reason; or the Phases of Human Progress,* originally published by Charles Scribner's Sons in 1905. This volume contains the general introduction to the entire five-volume series. Dover Publications will subsequently publish the other four volumes in the series.

International Standard Book Number: 0-486-23919-5
Library of Congress Catalog Card Number: 79-55842

Manufactured in the United States of America
Dover Publications, Inc.
180 Varick Street
New York, N.Y. 10014

CONTENTS

INTRODUCTION

THE SUBJECT OF THIS WORK, ITS METHOD AND ANTE-
CEDENTS

Progress is relative to an ideal which reflection creates.
—Efficacious reflection is reason.—The Life of Reason a
name for all practical thought and all action justified
by its fruits in consciousness.—It is the sum of Art.—It
has a natural basis which makes it definable.—Modern
philosophy not helpful.—Positivism no positive ideal.—
Christian philosophy mythical: it misrepresents facts and
conditions.—Liberal theology a superstitious attitude
toward a natural world.—The Greeks thought straight
in both physics and morals.—Heraclitus and the immediate.—Democritus and the naturally intelligible.—
Socrates and the autonomy of mind.—Plato gave the
ideal its full expression.—Aristotle supplied its natural
basis.—Philosophy thus complete, yet in need of restatement.—Plato's myths in lieu of physics.—Aristotle's
final causes.—Modern science can avoid such expedients.—Transcendentalism true but inconsequential.—
Verbal ethics.—Spinoza and the Life of Reason.—Modern and classic sources of inspiration.......Pages 1–32

REASON IN COMMON SENSE

CHAPTER I

THE BIRTH OF REASON

Existence always has an Order, called Chaos when
incompatible with a chosen good.—Absolute order, or
truth, is static, impotent, indifferent.—In experience
order is relative to interests which determine the moral

status of all powers.—The discovered conditions of reason
not its beginning.—The flux first.—Life the fixation of
interests.—Primary dualities.—First gropings.—Instinct
the nucleus of reason.—Better and worse the fundamental
categories .... Pages 35–47

CHAPTER II

FIRST STEPS AND FIRST FLUCTUATIONS

Dreams before thoughts.—The mind vegetates uncontrolled save by physical forces.—Internal order supervenes.—Intrinsic pleasure in existence.—Pleasure a good,
but not pursued or remembered unless it suffuses an
object.—Subhuman delights.—Animal living.—Causes at
last discerned.—Attention guided by bodily impulse.
                                        Pages 48–63

CHAPTER III

THE DISCOVERY OF NATURAL OBJECTS

Nature man's home.—Difficulties in conceiving nature.
—Transcendental qualms.—Thought an aspect of life and
transitive.—Perception cumulative and synthetic.—No
identical agent needed.—Example of the sun.—His primitive divinity.—Causes and essences contrasted.—Voracity
of intellect.—Can the transcendent be known?—Can the
immediate be meant?—Is thought a bridge from sensation to sensation?—*Mens naturaliter platonica.*—Identity
and independence predicated of things..... Pages 64–83

CHAPTER IV

ON SOME CRITICS OF THIS DISCOVERY

Psychology as a solvent.—Misconceived rôle of intelligence.—All criticism dogmatic.—A choice of hypotheses.—Critics disguised enthusiasts.—Hume's gratuitous
scepticism.—Kant's substitute for knowledge.—False subjectivity attributed to reason.—Chimerical reconstruction.—The Critique a work on mental architecture.—
Incoherences.—Nature the true system of conditions.—

Artificial pathos in subjectivism.—Berkeley's algebra of perception.—Horror of physics.—Puerility in morals.—Truism and sophism.—Reality is the practical made intelligible.—Vain "realities" and trustworthy "fictions" .... Pages 84–117

CHAPTER V

NATURE UNIFIED AND MIND DISCERNED

Man's feeble grasp of nature.—Its unity ideal and discoverable only by steady thought.—Mind the erratic residue of existence.—Ghostly character of mind.—Hypostasis and criticism both need control.—Comparative constancy in objects and in ideas.—Spirit and sense defined by their relation to nature.—Vague notions of nature involve vague notions of spirit.—Sense and spirit the life of nature, which science redistributes but does not deny.

Pages 118–136

CHAPTER VI

DISCOVERY OF FELLOW-MINDS

Another background for current experience may be found in alien minds.—Two usual accounts of this conception criticised: analogy between bodies, and dramatic dialogue in the soul.—Subject and object empirical, not transcendental, terms.—Objects originally soaked in secondary and tertiary qualities.—Tertiary qualities transposed.—Imputed mind consists of the tertiary qualities of perceived body —"Pathetic fallacy" normal, yet ordinarily fallacious.—Case where it is not a fallacy.—Knowledge succeeds only by accident.—Limits of insight.—Perception of character.—Conduct divined, consciousness ignored.—Consciousness untrustworthy.—Metaphorical mind.—Summary.................. Pages 137–160

CHAPTER VII

CONCRETIONS IN DISCOURSE AND IN EXISTENCE

So-called abstract qualities primary.—General qualities prior to particular things.—Universals are concretions in discourse.—Similar reactions, merged in one habit of reproduction, yield an idea.—Ideas are ideal.—So-called abstractions complete facts.—Things concretions of concretions.—Ideas prior in the order of knowledge, things in the order of nature.—Aristotle's compromise.—Empirical bias in favour of contiguity.—Artificial divorce of logic from practice.—Their mutual involution.—Rationalistic suicide.—Complementary character of essence and existence .... Pages 161–183

CHAPTER VIII

ON THE RELATIVE VALUE OF THINGS AND IDEAS

Moral tone of opinions derived from their logical principle.—Concretions in discourse express instinctive reactions.—Idealism rudimentary.—Naturalism sad.—The soul akin to the eternal and ideal.—Her inexperience.—Platonism spontaneous.—Its essential fidelity to the ideal.—Equal rights of empiricism.—Logic dependent on fact for its importance, and for its subsistence.—Reason and docility.—Applicable thought and clarified experience.............................. Pages 184–204

CHAPTER IX

HOW THOUGHT IS PRACTICAL

Functional relations of mind and body.—They form one natural life.—Artifices involved in separating them.—Consciousness expresses vital equilibrium and docility.—Its worthlessness as a cause and value as an expression.—Thought's march automatic and thereby implicated in events.—Contemplative essence of action.—Mechanical efficacy alien to thought's essence.—Consciousness transcendental and transcendent.—It is the seat of value.—Apparent utility of pain.—Its real impotence.—Preformations involved.—Its untoward significance.—Perfect function not unconscious.—Inchoate ethics.—Thought the entelechy of being.—Its exuberance.... Pages 205–235

CHAPTER X

THE MEASURE OF VALUES IN REFLECTION

Honesty in hedonism.—Necessary qualifications.—The will must judge.—Injustice inherent in representation.—Æsthetic and speculative cruelty.—Imputed values: their

inconstancy.—Methods of control.—Example of fame.—
Disproportionate interest in the æsthetic.—Irrational
religious allegiance.—Pathetic idealisations.—Inevitable
impulsiveness in prophecy.—The test a controlled present
ideal ....Pages 236-255

CHAPTER XI

SOME ABSTRACT CONDITIONS OF THE IDEAL

The ultimate end a resultant.—Demands the substance
of ideals.—Discipline of the will.—Demands made practical and consistent.—The ideal natural.—Need of unity
and finality.—Ideals of nothing.—Darwin on moral sense.
—Conscience and reason compared.—Reason imposes no
new sacrifice.—Natural goods attainable and compatible
in principle.—Harmony the formal and intrinsic demand
of reason ....Pages 256-268

CHAPTER XII

FLUX AND CONSTANCY IN HUMAN NATURE

Respectable tradition that human nature is fixed.—
Contrary currents of opinion.—Pantheism.—Instability
in existences does not dethrone their ideals.—Absolutist
philosophy human and halting.—All science a deliverance
of momentary thought.—All criticism likewise.—Origins
inessential.—Ideals functional.—They are transferable to
similar beings.—Authority internal.—Reason autonomous.
—Its distribution.—Natural selection of minds.—Living
stability.—Continuity necessary to progress.—Limits of
variation. Spirit a heritage.—Perfectibility.—Nature and
human nature.—Human nature formulated.—Its concrete
description reserved for the sequel .... Pages 269-291

Introduction to
"The Life of Reason"

Progress is relative to an ideal which reflection creates. Whatever forces may govern human life, if they are to be recognised by man, must betray themselves in human experience. Progress in science or religion, no less than in morals and art, is a dramatic episode in man's career, a welcome variation in his habit and state of mind; although this variation may often regard or propitiate things external, adjustment to which may be important for his welfare. The importance of these external things, as well as their existence, he can establish only by the function and utility which a recognition of them may have in his life. The entire history of progress is a moral drama, a tale man might unfold in a great autobiography, could his myriad heads and countless scintillas of consciousness conspire, like the seventy Alexandrian sages, in a single version of the truth committed to each for interpretation. What themes would prevail in such an examination of heart? In what order and with what emphasis would they be recounted? In which of its adventures would

1

the human race, reviewing its whole experience, acknowledge a progress and a gain? To answer these questions, as they may be answered speculatively and provisionally by an individual, is the purpose of the following work.

Efficacious reflection is reason.
A philosopher could hardly have a higher ambition than to make himself a mouth-piece for the memory and judgment of his race. Yet the most casual consideration of affairs already involves an attempt to do the same thing. Reflection is pregnant from the beginning with all the principles of synthesis and valuation needed in the most comprehensive criticism. So soon as man ceases to be wholly immersed in sense, he looks before and after, he regrets and desires; and the moments in which prospect or retrospect takes place constitute the reflective or representative part of his life, in contrast to the unmitigated flux of sensations in which nothing ulterior is regarded. Representation, however, can hardly remain idle and merely speculative. To the ideal function of envisaging the absent, memory and reflection will add (since they exist and constitute a new complication in being) the practical function of modifying the future. Vital impulse, however, when it is modified by reflection and veers in sympathy with judgments pronounced on the past, is properly called reason. Man's rational life consists in those moments in which reflection not only occurs but proves efficacious. What is absent then works in

the present, and values are imputed where they cannot be felt. Such representation is so far from being merely speculative that its presence alone can raise bodily change to the dignity of action. Reflection gathers experiences together and perceives their relative worth; which is as much as to say that it expresses a new attitude of will in the presence of a world better understood and turned to some purpose. The limits of reflection mark those of concerted and rational action; they circumscribe the field of cumulative experience, or, what is the same thing, of profitable living.

The Life of Reason a name for all practical thought and all action justified by its fruits in consciousness. Thus if we use the word life in a eulogistic sense to designate the happy maintenance against the world of some definite ideal interest, we may say with Aristotle that life is reason in operation. The *Life of Reason* will then be a name for that part of experience which perceives and pursues ideals—all conduct so controlled and all sense so interpreted as to perfect natural happiness.

Without reason, as without memory, there might still be pleasures and pains in existence. To increase those pleasures and reduce those pains would be to introduce an improvement into the sentient world, as if a devil suddenly died in hell or in heaven a new angel were created. Since the beings, however, in which these values would reside, would, by hypothesis, know nothing of one another, and since the betterment would take place

unprayed-for and unnoticed, it could hardly be
called a progress; and certainly not a progress in
man, since man, without the ideal continuity given
by memory and reason, would have no moral being.
In human progress, therefore, reason is not a
casual instrument, having its sole value in its service to sense; such a betterment in sentience
would not be progress unless it were a progress in
reason, and the increasing pleasure revealed some
object that could please; for without a picture of
the situation from which a heightened vitality
might flow, the improvement could be neither remembered nor measured nor desired. The Life
of Reason is accordingly neither a mere means nor
a mere incident in human progress; it is the total
and embodied progress itself, in which the pleasures of sense are included in so far as they can
be intelligently enjoyed and pursued. To recount
man's rational moments would be to take an in-
ventory of all his goods; for he is not himself (as
we say with unconscious accuracy) in the others.
If he ever appropriates them in recollection or
prophecy, it is only on the ground of some physical relation which they may have to his being.

Reason is as old as man and as prevalent as
human nature; for we should not recognise an
animal to be human unless his instincts were to
some degree conscious of their ends and rendered
his ideas in that measure relevant to conduct.
Many sensations, or even a whole world of dreams,
do not amount to intelligence until the images in

the mind begin to represent in some way, however symbolic, the forces and realities confronted in action. There may well be intense consciousness in the total absence of rationality. Such consciousness is suggested in dreams, in madness, and may be found, for all we know, in the depths of universal nature. Minds peopled only by desultory visions and lusts would not have the dignity of human souls even if they seemed to pursue certain objects unerringly; for that pursuit would not be illumined by any vision of its goal. Reason and humanity begin with the union of instinct and ideation, when instinct becomes enlightened, establishes values in its objects, and is turned from a process into an art, while at the same time consciousness becomes practical and cognitive, beginning to contain some symbol or record of the co-ordinate realities among which it arises.

Reason accordingly requires the fusion of two types of life, commonly led in the world in wellnigh total separation, one a life of impulse expressed in affairs and social passions, the other a life of reflection expressed in religion, science, and the imitative arts. In the Life of Reason, if it were brought to perfection, intelligence would be at once the universal method of practice and its continual reward. All reflection would then be applicable in action and all action fruitful in happiness. Though this be an ideal, yet everyone gives it from time to time a partial embodiment when he practises useful arts, when his passions happily lead him to enlightenment, or when his fancy breeds visions pertinent to his ultimate good. Everyone leads the Life of Reason in so far as he finds a steady light behind the world's glitter and a clear residuum of joy beneath pleasure or success. No experience not to be repented of falls without its sphere. Every solution to a doubt, in so far as it is not a new error, every practical achievement not neutralised by a second maladjustment consequent upon it, every consolation not the seed of another greater sorrow, may be gathered together and built into this edifice. The Life of Reason is the happy marriage of two elements—impulse and ideation—which if wholly divorced would reduce man to a brute or to a maniac. The rational animal is generated by the union of these two monsters. He is constituted by ideas which have ceased to be visionary and actions which have ceased to be vain.

Thus the Life of Reason is another name for what, in the widest sense of the word, might be called Art. Operations become arts when their purpose is conscious and their method teachable. In perfect art the whole idea is creative and exists only to be embodied, while every part of the product is rational and gives delightful expression to that idea. Like art, again, the Life of Reason is not a power but a result, the spontaneous expression of liberal genius in a favouring environment. Both art and

It is the sum of Art.

reason have natural sources and meet with natural checks; but when a process is turned successfully into an art, so that its issues have value and the ideas that accompany it become practical and cognitive, reflection, finding little that it cannot in some way justify and understand, begins to boast that it directs and has created the world in which it finds itself so much at home. Thus if art could extend its sphere to include every activity in nature, reason, being everywhere exemplified, might easily think itself omnipotent. This ideal, far as it is from actual realisation, has so dazzled men, that in their religion and mythical philosophy they have often spoken as if it were already actual and efficient. This anticipation amounts, when taken seriously, to a confusion of purposes with facts and of functions with causes, a confusion which in the interests of wisdom and progress it is important to avoid; but these speculative fables, when we take them for what they are—poetic expressions of the ideal—help us to see how deeply rooted this ideal is in man's mind, and afford us a standard by which to measure his approaches to the rational perfection of which he dreams. For the Life of Reason, being the sphere of all human art, is man's imitation of divinity.

It has a natural basis which makes it definable. To study such an ideal, dimly expressed though it be in human existence, is no prophetic or visionary undertaking. Every genuine ideal has a natural basis; anyone may understand and safely interpret it who is attentive to the life from which it springs. To decipher the Life of Reason nothing is needed but an analytic spirit and a judicious love of man, a love quick to distinguish success from failure in his great and confused experiment of living. The historian of reason should not be a romantic poet, vibrating impotently to every impulse he finds afoot, without a criterion of excellence or a vision of perfection. Ideals are free, but they are neither more numerous nor more variable than the living natures that generate them. Ideals are legitimate, and each initially envisages a genuine and innocent good; but they are not realisable together, nor even singly when they have no deep roots in the world. Neither is the philosopher compelled by his somewhat judicial office to be a satirist or censor, without sympathy for those tentative and ingenuous passions out of which, after all, his own standards must arise. He is the chronicler of human progress, and to measure that progress he should be equally attentive to the impulses that give it direction and to the circumstances amid which it stumbles toward its natural goal.

Modern philosophy not helpful. There is unfortunately no school of modern philosophy to which a critique of human progress can well be attached. Almost every school, indeed, can furnish something useful to the critic, sometimes a physical theory, sometimes a piece of logical analysis. We shall need to borrow from current science and speculation the picture they draw of man's conditions and environment, his history and mental habits. These may furnish a theatre and properties for our drama; but they offer no hint of its plot and meaning. A great imaginative apathy has fallen on the mind. One-half the learned world is amused in tinkering obsolete armour, as Don Quixote did his helmet; deputing it, after a series of catastrophes, to be at last sound and invulnerable. The other half, the naturalists who have studied psychology and evolution, look at life from the outside, and the processes of Nature make them forget her uses.

Positivism no positive ideal. Bacon indeed had prized science for adding to the comforts of life, a function still commemorated by positivists in their eloquent moments. Habitually, however, when they utter the word progress it is, in their mouths, a synonym for inevitable change, or at best for change in that direction which they conceive to be on the whole predominant. If they combine with physical speculation some elements of morals, these are usually purely formal, to the effect that happiness is to be pursued (probably, alas! because to do so is a psychological law); but what happiness consists in we gather only from casual observations or by putting together their national prejudices and party saws.

The truth is that even this radical school, emancipated as it thinks itself, is suffering from the after-effects of supernaturalism. Like children escaped from school, they find their whole happiness in freedom. They are proud of what they have rejected, as if a great wit were required to do so; but they do not know what they want. If you astonish them by demanding what is their positive ideal, further than that there should be a great many people and that they should be all alike, they will say at first that what ought to be is obvious, and later they will submit the matter to a majority vote. They have discarded the machinery in which their ancestors embodied the ideal; they have not perceived that those symbols stood for the Life of Reason and gave fantastic and embarrassed expression to what, in itself, is pure humanity; and they have thus remained entangled in the colossal error that ideals are something adventitious and unmeaning, not having a soil in mortal life nor a possible fulfilment there.

The profound and pathetic ideas which inspired Christianity were attached in the beginning to ancient myths and soon crystallised into many new ones. The mythical manner pervades Christian philosophy; but myth succeeds in expressing ideal life only by misrepresenting its history and conditions. This method was indeed not original with the Fathers; they borrowed it from Plato, who appealed to parables himself in an open and harmless fashion, yet with disastrous consequences to his school. Nor was he the first; for the instinct to regard

Christian philosophy mythical: it misrepresents facts and conditions.

poetic fictions as revelations of supernatural facts is as old as the soul's primitive incapacity to distinguish dreams from waking perceptions, sign from thing signified, and inner emotions from external powers. Such confusions, though in a way they obey moral forces, make a rational estimate of things impossible. To misrepresent the conditions and consequences of action is no merely speculative error; it involves a false emphasis in character and an artificial balance and co-ordination among human pursuits. When ideals are hypostasised into powers alleged to provide for their own expression, the Life of Reason cannot be conceived; in theory its field of operation is preempted and its function gone, while in practice its inner impulses are turned awry by artificial stimulation and repression.

The Patristic systems, though weak in their foundations, were extraordinarily wise and comprehensive in their working out; and while they inverted life they preserved it. Dogma added to the universe fabulous perspectives; it interpolated also innumerable incidents and powers which gave a new dimension to experience. Yet the old world remained standing in its strange setting, like the Pantheon in modern Rome; and, what is more important, the natural springs of human action were still acknowledged, and if a supernatural discipline was imposed, it was only because experience and faith had disclosed a situation in which the pursuit of earthly happiness seemed hopeless.

Nature was not destroyed by its novel appendages,
nor did reason die in the cloister: it hibernated
there, and could come back to its own in due season, only a little dazed and weakened by its long
confinement. Such, at least, is the situation in
Catholic regions, where the Patristic philosophy
has not appreciably varied. Among Protestants
Christian dogma has taken a new and ambiguous
direction, which has at once minimised its disturb-
ing effect in practice and isolated its primary illusion. The symptoms have been cured and the
disease driven in.

Liberal the-
ology a su-
perstitious
attitude
toward a
natural world.

The tenets of Protestant bodies are
notoriously varied and on principle
subject to change. There is hardly a
combination of tradition and spontaneity which has not been tried in some
quarter. If we think, however, of
broad tendencies and ultimate issues, it appears
that in Protestantism myth, without disappear-
ing, has changed its relation to reality: instead of
being an extension to the natural world myth has
become its substratum. Religion no longer reveals divine personalities, future rewards, and ten-
derer Elysian consolations; nor does it seriously
propose a heaven to be reached by a ladder nor a
purgatory to be shortened by prescribed devotions.
It merely gives the real world an ideal status and
teaches men to accept a natural life on supernatural grounds. The consequence is that the
most pious can give an unvarnished description of

things. Even immortality and the idea of God are submitted, in liberal circles, to scientific treatment. On the other hand, it would be hard to conceive a more inveterate obsession than that which keeps the attitude of these same minds inappropriate to the objects they envisage. They have accepted natural conditions; they will not accept natural ideals. The Life of Reason has no existence for them, because, although its field is clear, they will not tolerate any human or finite standard of value, and will not suffer extant interests, which can alone guide them in action or judgment, to define the worth of life.

The after-effects of Hebraism are here contrary to its foundations; for the Jews loved the world so much that they brought themselves, in order to win and enjoy it, to an intense concentration of purpose; but this effort and discipline, which had of course been mythically sanctioned, not only failed of its object, but grew far too absolute and sublime to think its object could ever have been earthly; and the supernatural machinery which was to have secured prosperity, while that still enticed, now had to furnish some worthier object for the passion it had artificially fostered. Fanaticism consists in redoubling your effort when you have forgotten your aim.

An earnestness which is out of proportion to any knowledge or love of real things, which is therefore dark and inward and thinks itself deeper than the earth's foundations—such an earnestness, until culture turns it into intelligent interests, will naturally breed a new mythology. It will try to place some world of Afrites and shadowy giants behind the constellations, which it finds too distinct and constant to be its companions or supporters; and it will assign to itself vague and infinite tasks, for which it is doubtless better equipped than for those which the earth now sets before it. Even these, however, since they are parts of an infinite whole, the mystic may (histrionically, perhaps, yet zealously) undertake; but as his eye will be perpetually fixed on something invisible beyond, and nothing will be done for its own sake or enjoyed in its own fugitive presence, there will be little art and little joy in existence. All will be a tossing servitude and illiberal mist, where the parts will have no final values and the whole no pertinent direction.

The Greeks thought straight in both physics and morals. In Greek philosophy the situation is far more auspicious. The ancients led a rational life and envisaged the various spheres of speculation as men might whose central interests were rational. In physics they leaped at once to the conception of a dynamic unity and general evolution, thus giving that background to human life which shrewd observation would always have descried, and which modern science has laboriously rediscovered. Two great systems offered, in two legitimate directions, what are doubtless the final and radical accounts of physical being. Heraclitus, describing the immediate, found it to be in constant and pervasive change: no substances, no forms, no identities

Heraclitus and the immediate. could be arrested there, but as in the human soul, so in nature, all was instability, contradiction, reconstruction, and oblivion. This remains the empirical fact; and we need but to rescind the artificial division which Descartes has taught us to make between nature and life, to feel again the absolute aptness of Heraclitus's expressions. These were thought obscure only because they were so disconcertingly penetrating and direct. The immediate is what nobody sees, because convention and reflection turn existence, as soon as they can, into ideas; a man who discloses the immediate seems profound, yet his depth is nothing but innocence recovered and a sort of intellectual abstention. Mysticism, scepticism, and transcendentalism have all in their various ways tried to fall back on the immediate; but none of them has been ingenuous enough. Each has added some myth, or sophistry, or delusive artifice to its direct observation. Heraclitus remains the honest prophet of immediacy: a mystic without raptures or bad rhetoric, a sceptic who does not rely for his results on conventions unwittingly adopted, a transcendentalist without false pretensions or incongruous dogmas.

The immediate is not, however, a good subject for discourse, and the expounders of Heraclitus were not unnaturally blamed for monotony. All they could do was to iterate their master's maxim, and declare everything to be in flux. In suggesting laws of recurrence and a reason in which what is common to many might be expressed, Heraclitus had opened the door into another region: had he passed through, his philosophy would have been greatly modified, for permanent forms would have forced themselves on his attention no less than shifting materials. Such a Heraclitus would have anticipated Plato; but the time for such a synthesis had not yet arrived.

Democritus and the naturally intelligible. At the opposite pole from immediacy lies intelligibility. To reduce phenomena to constant elements, as similar and simple as possible, and to conceive their union and separation to obey constant laws, is what a natural philosopher will inevitably do so soon as his interest is not merely to utter experience but to understand it. Democritus brought this scientific ideal to its ultimate expression. By including psychic existence in his atomic system, he indicated a problem which natural science has since practically abandoned but which it may some day be compelled to take up. The atoms of Democritus seem to us gross, even for chemistry, and their quality would have to undergo great transformation if they were to support intelligibly psychic being as well; but that very grossness and false simplicity had its merits, and science must be for ever grateful to the man who at its inception could so clearly formulate its mechanical ideal. That the world is not so intelligible as we could wish is not to be wondered at. In other respects also it fails to respond to our ideals; yet our hope must be to find it more propitious to the intellect as well as to all the arts in proportion as we learn better how to live in it.

The atoms of what we call hydrogen or oxygen may well turn out to be worlds, as the stars are which make atoms for astronomy. Their inner organisation might be negligible on our rude plane of being; did it disclose itself, however, it would be intelligible in its turn only if constant parts and constant laws were discernible within each system. So that while atomism at a given level may not be a final or metaphysical truth, it will describe, on every level, the practical and efficacious structure of the world. We owe to Democritus this ideal of practical intelligibility; and he is accordingly an eternal spokesman of reason. His system, long buried with other glories of the world, has been partly revived; and although it cannot be verified in haste, for it represents an ultimate ideal, every advance in science reconstitutes it in some particular. Mechanism is not one principle of explanation among others. In natural philosophy, where to explain means to discover origins, transmutations, and laws, mechanism is explanation itself.

Heraclitus had the good fortune of having his physics absorbed by Plato. It is a pity that Democritus' physics was not absorbed by Aristotle. For with the flux observed, and mechanism conceived to explain it, the theory of existence is complete; and had a complete physical theory been incorporated into the Socratic philosophy, wisdom would have lacked none of its parts. Democritus, however, appeared too late, when ideal science had overrun the whole field and initiated a verbal and dialectical physics; so that Aristotle, for all his scientific temper and studies, built his natural philosophy on a lamentable misunderstanding, and condemned thought to confusion for two thousand years.

Socrates and the autonomy of mind.   If the happy freedom of the Greeks from religious dogma made them the first natural philosophers, their happy political freedom made them the first moralists. It was no accident that Socrates walked the Athenian agora; it was no petty patriotism that made him shrink from any other scene. His science had its roots there, in the personal independence, intellectual vivacity, and clever dialectic of his countrymen. Ideal science lives in discourse; it consists in the active exercise of reason, in signification, appreciation, intent, and self-expression. Its sum total is to know oneself, not as psychology or anthropology might describe a man, but to know, as the saying is, one's own mind. Nor is he who knows his own mind forbidden to change it; the dialectician has nothing to do with future possibilities or with the opinion of anyone but the man addressed. This kind of truth is but adequate veracity; its only object is its own

intent. Having developed in the spirit the consciousness of its meanings and purposes, Socrates
rescued logic and ethics for ever from authority.
With his friends the Sophists, he made man the
measure of all things, after bidding him measure
himself, as they neglected to do, by his own ideal.
That brave humanity which had first raised its
head in Hellas and had endowed so many things
in heaven and earth, where everything was
hitherto monstrous, with proportion and use, so
that man's works might justify themselves to his
mind, now found in Socrates its precise definition; and it was naturally where the Life of Reason had been long cultivated that it came finally
to be conceived.

Plato gave the ideal its full expression. Socrates had, however, a plebeian
strain in his humanity, and his utili-
tarianism, at least in its expression,
hardly did justice to what gives utility to life.
His condemnation for atheism—if we choose to
take it symbolically—was not altogether unjust:
the gods of Greece were not honoured explicitly
enough in his philosophy. Human good appeared
there in its principle; you would not set a pilot to
mend shoes, because you knew your own purpose;
but what purposes a civilised soul might harbour,
and in what highest shapes the good might appear,
was a problem that seems not to have attracted
his genius. It was reserved to Plato to bring the
Socratic ethics to its sublimest expression and to
elicit from the depths of the Greek conscience

those ancestral ideals which had inspired its legislators and been embodied in its sacred civic traditions. The owl of Minerva flew, as Hegel says,
in the dusk of evening; and it was horror at the
abandonment of all creative virtues that brought
Plato to conceive them so sharply and to preach
them in so sad a tone. It was after all but the
love of beauty that made him censure the poets;
for like a true Greek and a true lover he wished
to see beauty flourish in the real world. It was
love of freedom that made him harsh to his ideal
citizens, that they might be strong enough to
preserve the liberal life. And when he broke
away from political preoccupations and turned to
the inner life, his interpretations proved the absolute sufficiency of the Socratic method; and he
left nothing pertinent unsaid on ideal love and
ideal immortality.

Beyond this point no rendering of the
Life of Reason has ever been carried.
Aristotle improved the detail, and gave
breadth and precision to many a part.

Aristotle supplied its natural basis.

If Plato possessed greater imaginative splendour
and more enthusiasm in austerity, Aristotle had
perfect sobriety and adequacy, with greater fidelity to the common sentiments of his race. Plato,
by virtue of his scope and plasticity, together
with a certain prophetic zeal, outran at times the
limits of the Hellenic and the rational; he saw
human virtue so surrounded and oppressed by
physical dangers that he wished to give it mythi-

cal sanctions, and his fondness for transmigra-
tion and nether punishments was somewhat more
than playful. If as a work of imagination his
philosophy holds the first place, Aristotle's has the
decisive advantage of being the unalloyed expression of reason. In Aristotle the conception of
human nature is perfectly sound; everything ideal
has a natural basis and everything natural an
ideal development. His ethics, when thoroughly
digested and weighed, especially when the meagre
outlines are filled in with Plato's more discursive
expositions, will seem therefore entirely final.
The Life of Reason finds there its classic explication.

Philosophy thus complete, yet in need of restate- ment. As it is improbable that there will
soon be another people so free from
preoccupations, so gifted, and so fortunate as the Greeks, or capable in
consequence of so well exemplifying humanity, so
also it is improbable that a philosopher will soon
arise with Aristotle's scope, judgment, or authority, one knowing so well how to be both reasonable and exalted. It might seem vain, therefore,
to try to do afresh what has been done before with
unapproachable success; and instead of writing
inferior things at great length about the Life of
Reason, it might be simpler to read and to propa-
gate what Aristotle wrote with such immortal just-
ness and masterly brevity. But times change;
and though the principles of reason remain the
same the facts of human life and of human con-

science alter. A new background, a new basis of application, appears for logic, and it may be useful to restate old truths in new words, the better to prove their eternal validity. Aristotle is, in his morals, Greek, concise, and elementary. As a Greek, he mixes with the ideal argument illustrations, appreciations, and conceptions which are not inseparable from its essence. In themselves, no doubt, these accessories are better than what in modern times would be substituted for them, being less sophisticated and of a nobler stamp; but to our eyes they disguise what is profound and universal in natural morality by embodying it in images which do not belong to our life. Our direst struggles and the last sanctions of our morality do not appear in them. The pagan world, because its maturity was simpler than our crudeness, seems childish to us. We do not find there our sins and holiness, our love, charity, and honour.

The Greek too would not find in our world the things he valued most, things to which he surrendered himself, perhaps, with a more constant self-sacrifice—piety, country, friendship, and beauty; and he might add that his ideals were rational and he could attain them, while ours are extravagant and have been missed. Yet even if we acknowledged his greater good fortune, it would be impossible for us to go back and become like him. To make the attempt would show no sense of reality and little sense of humour. We must dress in our own clothes, if we do not wish to substitute a masquerade for practical existence. What we can adopt from Greek morals is only the abstract principle of their development; their foundation in all the extant forces of human nature and their effort toward establishing a perfect harmony among them. These forces themselves have perceptibly changed, at least in their relative power. Thus we are more conscious of wounds to stanch and wrongs to fight against, and less of goods to attain. The movement of conscience has veered; the centre of gravity lies in another part of the character.

Another circumstance that invites a restatement of rational ethics is the impressive illustration of their principle which subsequent history has afforded. Mankind has been making extraordinary experiments of which Aristotle could not dream; and their result is calculated to clarify even his philosophy. For in some respects it needed experiments and clarification. He had been led into a systematic fusion of dialectic with physics, and of this fusion all pretentious modern philosophy is the aggravated extension. Socrates' pupils could not abandon his ideal principles, yet they could not bear to abstain from physics altogether; they therefore made a mock physics in moral terms, out of which theology was afterward developed. Plato, standing nearer to Socrates and being no naturalist by disposition, never carried the fatal experiment beyond the mythical stage. He accordingly remained the purer moralist, much as Aristotle's judgment may be preferred in many particulars. Their relative position may be roughly indicated by saying that Plato had no physics and that Aristotle's physics was false; so that ideal science in the one suffered from want of environment and control, while in the other it suffered from misuse in a sphere where it had no application.

Plato's myths in lieu of physics.   What had happened was briefly this: Plato, having studied many sorts of philosophy and being a bold and universal genius, was not satisfied to leave all physical questions pending, as his master had done. He adopted, accordingly, Heraclitus's doctrine of the immediate, which he now called the realm of phenomena; for what exists at any instant, if you arrest and name it, turns out to have been an embodiment of some logical essence, such as discourse might define; in every fact some idea makes its appearance, and such an apparition of the ideal is a phenomenon. Moreover, another philosophy had made a deep impression on Plato's mind and had helped to develop Socratic definitions: Parmenides had called the concept of pure Being the only reality; and to satisfy the strong dialectic by which this doctrine was supported and at the same time to bridge the infinite chasm between one formless substance and many appearances irrelevant to it, Plato substituted the many Socratic ideas, all of which were relevant to appearance, for the one concept of Parmenides. The ideas thus acquired what is called metaphysical subsistence; for they stood in the place of the Eleatic Absolute, and at the same time were the realities that phenomena manifested.

The technique of this combination is much to be admired; but the feat is technical and adds nothing to the significance of what Plato has to say on any concrete subject. This barren triumph was, however, fruitful in misunderstandings. The characters and values a thing possessed were now conceived to subsist apart from it, and might even have preceded it and caused its existence; a mechanism composed of values and definitions could thus be placed behind phenomena to constitute a substantial physical world. Such a dream could not be taken seriously, until good sense was wholly lost and a bevy of magic spirits could be imagined peopling the infinite and yet carrying on the business of earth. Aristotle rejected the metaphysical subsistence of ideas, but thought they might still be essences operative in nature, if only they were identified with the life or form of particular things. The dream thus lost its frank wildness, but none of its inherent incongruity: for the sense in which characters and values make a thing what it is, is purely dialectical. They give it its status in the ideal world; but the appearance of these characters and values here and now is what needs explanation in physics, an explanation which can be

furnished, of course, only by the physical concatenation and distribution of causes.

Aristotle's
final causes.
Modern sci-
ence can
avoid such
expedients.
Aristotle himself did not fail to
make this necessary distinction between efficient cause and formal essence; but as his science was only
natural history, and mechanism had no
plausibility in his eyes, the efficiency
of the cause was always due, in his view, to its
ideal quality; as in heredity the father's human
character, not his physical structure, might seem
to warrant the son's humanity. Every ideal,
before it could be embodied, had to pre-exist in
some other embodiment; but as when the ultimate purpose of the cosmos is considered it seems
to lie beyond any given embodiment, the highest
ideal must somehow exist disembodied. It must
pre-exist, thought Aristotle, in order to supply, by
way of magic attraction, a physical cause for perpetual movement in the world.

It must be confessed, in justice to this consum-
mate philosopher, who is not less masterly in the
use of knowledge than unhappy in divination, that
the transformation of the highest good into a
physical power is merely incidental with him, and
due to a want of faith (at that time excusable)
in mechanism and evolution. Aristotle's deity is
always a moral ideal and every detail in its definition is based on discrimination between the better
and the worse. No accommodation to the ways
of nature is here allowed to cloud the kingdom of

heaven; this deity is not condemned to do whatever happens nor to absorb whatever exists. It is mythical only in its physical application; in moral philosophy it remains a legitimate conception.

Truth certainly exists, if existence be not too mean an attribute for that eternal realm which is tenanted by ideals; but truth is repugnant to physical or psychical being. Moreover, truth may very well be identified with an impassible intellect, which should do nothing but possess all truth, with no point of view, no animal warmth, and no transitive process. Such an intellect and truth are expressions having a different metaphorical background and connotation, but, when thought out, an identical import. They both attempt to evoke that ideal standard which human thought proposes to itself. This function is their effective essence. It insures their eternal fixity, and this property surely endows them with a very genuine and sublime reality. What is fantastic is only the dynamic function attributed to them by Aristotle, which obliges them to inhabit some fabulous extension to the physical world. Even this physical efficacy, however, is spiritualised as much as possible, since deity is said to move the cosmos only as an object of love or an object of knowledge may move the mind. Such efficacy is imputed to a hypostasised end, but evidently resides in fact in the functioning and impulsive spirit that conceives and pursues an ideal, endowing it with whatever attraction it may seem to have. The absolute intellect described by Aristotle remains, therefore, as pertinent to the Life of Reason as Plato's idea of the good. Though less comprehensive (for it abstracts from all animal interests, from all passion and mortality), it is more adequate and distinct in the region it dominates. It expresses sublimely the goal of speculative thinking; which is none other than to live as much as may be in the eternal and to absorb and be absorbed in the truth.

The rest of ancient philosophy belongs to the decadence and rests in physics on eclecticism and in morals on despair. That creative breath which had stirred the founders and legislators of Greece no longer inspired their descendants. Helpless to control the course of events, they took refuge in abstention or in conformity, and their ethics became a matter of private economy and sentiment, no longer aspiring to mould the state or give any positive aim to existence. The time was approaching when both speculation and morals were to regard the other world; reason had abdicated the throne, and religion, after that brief interregnum, resumed it for long ages.

Such are the threads which tradition puts into the hands of an observer who at the present time might attempt to knit the Life of Reason ideally together. The problem is to unite a trustworthy conception of the conditions under which man lives with an adequate conception of his inter-

ests. Both conceptions, fortunately, lie before
us. Heraclitus and Democritus, in systems
easily seen to be complementary, gave long
ago a picture of nature such as all later
observation, down to our own day, has done nothing but fill out and confirm. Psychology and
physics still repeat their ideas, often with richer
detail, but never with a more radical or prophetic
glance. Nor does the transcendental philosophy,
in spite of its self-esteem, add anything essential.

It was a thing taken for granted in
ancient and scholastic philosophy that
a being dwelling, like man, in
the immediate, whose moments are in
flux, needed constructive reason to interpret his
experience and paint in his unstable consciousness
some symbolic picture of the world. To have
reverted to this constructive process and studied
its stages is an interesting achievement; but the
construction is already made by common-sense
and science, and it was visionary insolence in the
Germans to propose to make that construction otherwise. Retrospective self-consciousness is
dearly bought if it inhibits the intellect and em-
barrasses the inferences which, in its spontaneous
operation, it has known perfectly how to make.
In the heat of scientific theorising or dialectical
argument it is sometimes salutary to be reminded
that we are men thinking; but, after all, it is
no news. We know that life is a dream, and how
should thinking be more? Yet the thinking must

*Transcen-
dentalism
true but in-
consequential.*

go on, and the only vital question is to what practical or poetic conceptions it is able to lead us.

Similarly the Socratic philosophy affords a
noble and genuine account of what goods may
be realised by living. Modern theory has not
done so much to help us here, however, as it has
in physics. It seldom occurs to modern moralists
that theirs is the science of all good and the art
of its attainment; they think only of
Verbal ethics. some set of categorical precepts or some
theory of moral sentiments, abstracting altogether
from the ideals reigning in society, in science, and
in art. They deal with the secondary question
What ought I to do? without having answered
the primary question, What ought to be? They
attach morals to religion rather than to politics,
and this religion unhappily long ago ceased to be
wisdom expressed in fancy in order to become
superstition overlaid with reasoning. They divide
man into compartments and the less they leave
in the one labelled "morality" the more sublime they think their morality is; and sometimes
pedantry and scholasticism are carried so far that
nothing but an abstract sense of duty remains in
the broad region which should contain all human
goods.

Such trivial sanctimony in morals is doubtless
due to artificial views about the conditions of welfare; the basis is laid in authority rather than in
human nature, and the goal in salvation rather
than in happiness. One great modern philoso-

pher, however, was free from these preconceptions, and might have reconstituted the Life of Reason had he had a sufficient interest in culture. Spinoza brought man back into nature, and made him the nucleus of all moral values, showing how he may recognise his environment and how he may master it. But Spinoza's sympathy with mankind fell short of imagination; any noble political or poetical ideal eluded him. Everything impassioned seemed to him insane, everything human necessarily petty. Man was to be a pious tame animal, with the stars shining above his head. Instead of imagination Spinoza cultivated mysticism, which is indeed an alternative. A prophet in speculation, he remained a levite in sentiment. Little or nothing would need to be changed in his system if the Life of Reason, in its higher ranges, were to be grafted upon it; but such affiliation is not necessary, and it is rendered unnatural by the lack of sweep and generosity in Spinoza's practical ideals.

Spinoza and the Life of Reason.

For moral philosophy we are driven back, then, upon the ancients; but not, of course, for moral inspiration. Industrialism and democracy, the French Revolution, the Renaissance, and even the Catholic system, which in the midst of ancient illusions enshrines so much tenderness and wisdom, still live in the world, though forgotten by philosophers, and point unmistakably toward their several

Modern and classic sources of inspiration.

goals. Our task is not to construct but only to interpret ideals, confronting them with one another and with the conditions which, for the most part, they alike ignore. There is no need of refuting anything, for the will which is behind all ideals and behind most dogmas cannot itself be refuted; but it may be enlightened and led to reconsider its intent, when its satisfaction is seen to be either naturally impossible or inconsistent with better things. The age of controversy is past; that of interpretation has succeeded.

Here, then, is the programme of the following work: Starting with the immediate flux, in which all objects and impulses are given, to describe the Life of Reason; that is, to note what facts and purposes seem to be primary, to show how the conception of nature and life gathers around them, and to point to the ideals of thought and action which are approached by this gradual mastering of experience by reason. A great task, which it would be beyond the powers of a writer in this age either to execute or to conceive, had not the Greeks drawn for us the outlines of an ideal culture at a time when life was simpler than at present and individual intelligence more resolute and free.

REASON IN COMMON SENSE

CHAPTER I

THE BIRTH OF REASON

Whether Chaos or Order lay at the beginning of things is a question once much debated in the schools but afterward long in abeyance, not so much because it had been solved as because one party had been silenced by social pressure. The question is bound to recur in an age when observation and dialectic again freely confront each other. Naturalists look back to chaos since they observe everything growing from seeds and shifting its character in regeneration. The order now established in the world may be traced back to a situation in which it did not appear. Dialecticians, on the other hand, refute this presumption by urging that every collocation of things must have been preceded by another collocation in itself no less definite and precise; and further that some principle of transition or continuity must always have obtained, else successive states would stand in no relation to one another, notably not in the relation of cause and effect, expressed in a natural law, which is presupposed in this instance. Potentiali-

Existence always has an Order, called Chaos when incompatible with a chosen good.

35

ties are dispositions, and a disposition involves an order, as does also the passage from any specific potentiality into act. Thus the world, we are told, must always have possessed a structure.

The two views may perhaps be reconciled if we take each with a qualification. Chaos doubtless has existed and will return—nay, it reigns now, very likely, in the remoter and inmost parts of the universe—if by chaos we understand a nature containing none of the objects we are wont to distinguish, a nature such that human life and human thought would be impossible in its bosom; but this nature must be presumed to have an order, an order directly importing, if the tendency of its movement be taken into account, all the complexities and beauties, all the sense and reason which exist now. Order is accordingly continual; but only when order means not a specific arrangement, favourable to a given form of life, but any arrangement whatsoever. The process by which an arrangement which is essentially unstable gradually shifts cannot be said to aim at every stage which at any moment it involves. For the process passes beyond. It presently abolishes all the forms which may have arrested attention and generated love; its initial energy defeats every purpose which we may fondly attribute to it. Nor is it here necessary to remind ourselves that to call results their own causes is always preposterous; for in this case even the mythical sense which might be attached to such language is inapplicable. Here the process, taken in the gross, does not, even by mechanical necessity, support the value which is supposed to guide it. That value is realised for a moment only; so that if we impute to Cronos any intent to beget his children we must also impute to him an intent to devour them.

Absolute order, or truth, is static, impotent, indifferent. Of course the various states of the world, when we survey them retrospectively, constitute another and now static order called historic truth. To this absolute and impotent order every detail is essential. If we wished to abuse language so much as to speak of will in an " Absolute " where change is excluded, so that nothing can be or be conceived beyond it, we might say that the Absolute willed everything that ever exists, and that the eternal order terminated in every fact indiscriminately; but such language involves an afterimage of motion and life, of preparation, risk, and subsequent accomplishment, adventures all presupposing refractory materials and excluded from eternal truth by its very essence. The only function those traditional metaphors have is to shield confusion and sentimentality. Because Jehovah once fought for the Jews, we need not continue to say that the truth is solicitous about us, when it is only we that are fighting to attain it. The universe can wish particular things only in so far as particular beings wish them; only in its relative capacity can it find things good, and only in its relative capacity can it be good for anything.

The efficacious or physical order which exists at any moment in the world and out of which the next moment's order is developed, may accordingly be termed a relative chaos: a chaos, because the values suggested and supported by the second moment could not have belonged to the first; but merely a relative chaos, first because it probably carried values of its own which rendered it an order in a moral and eulogistic sense, and secondly because it was potentially, by virtue of its momentum, a basis for the second moment's values as well.

Human life, when it begins to possess intrinsic value, is an incipient order in the midst of what seems a vast though, to some extent, a vanishing chaos. This reputed chaos can be deciphered and appreciated by man only in proportion as the order in himself is confirmed and extended. For man's consciousness is evidently practical; it clings to his fate, registers, so to speak, the higher and lower temperature of his fortunes, and, so far as it can, represents the agencies on which those fortunes depend. When this dramatic vocation of consciousness has not been fulfilled at all, consciousness is wholly confused; the world it envisages seems consequently a chaos. Later, if .experience has fallen into shape, and there are settled categories and constant objects in human discourse, the inference is drawn that the original dis-

In experience order is relative to interests, which determine the moral status of all powers.

position of things was also orderly and indeed
mechanically conducive to just those feats of
instinct and intelligence which have been since
accomplished. A theory of origins, of substance,
and of natural laws may thus be framed and
accepted, and may receive confirmation in the
further march of events. It will be observed, however, that what is credibly asserted about the past
is not a report which the past was itself able to
make when it existed nor one it is now able, in
some oracular fashion, to formulate and to impose
upon us. The report is a rational construction
based and seated in present experience; it has no
cogency for the inattentive and no existence for
the ignorant. Although the universe, then, may
not have come from chaos, human experience certainly has begun in a private and dreamful chaos
of its own, out of which it still only partially and
momentarily emerges. The history of this awa-
kening is of course not the same as that of
the environing world ultimately discovered; it is
the history, however, of that discovery itself, of the
knowledge through which alone the world can be
revealed. We may accordingly dispense ourselves
from preliminary courtesies to the real universal
order, nature, the absolute, and the gods. We
shall make their acquaintance in due season and
better appreciate their moral status, if we strive
merely to recall our own experience, and to retrace
the visions and reflections out of which those apparitions have grown.

The discovered conditions of reason not its beginning.

To revert to primordial feeling is an exercise in mental disintegration, not a feat of science. We might, indeed, as in animal psychology, retrace the situations in which instinct and sense seem first to appear and write, as it were, a genealogy of reason based on circumstantial evidence. Reason was born, as it has since discovered, into a world already wonderfully organised, in which it found its precursor in what is called life, its seat in an animal body of unusual plasticity, and its function in rendering that body's volatile instincts and sensations harmonious with one another and with the outer world on which they depend. It did not arise until the will or conscious stress, by which any modification of living bodies' inertia seems to be accompanied, began to respond to represented objects, and to maintain that inertia not absolutely by resistance but only relatively and indirectly through labour. Reason has thus supervened at the last stage of an adaptation which had long been carried on by irrational and even unconscious processes. Nature preceded, with all that fixation of impulses and conditions which gives reason its tasks and its *point-d'appui*. Nevertheless, such a matrix or cradle for reason belongs only externally to its life. The description of conditions involves their previous discovery and a historian equipped with many data and many analogies of thought. Such scientific resources are absent in those first moments of

rational living which we here wish to recall; the
first chapter in reason's memoirs would no more
entail the description of its real environment than
the first chapter in human history would include
true accounts of astronomy, psychology, and animal evolution.

The flux   In order to begin at the beginning
first.   we must try to fall back on uninter-
preted feeling, as the mystics aspire to do. We
need not expect, however, to find peace there, for
the immediate is in flux. Pure feeling rejoices
in a logical nonentity very deceptive to dialectical
minds. They often think, when they fall back on
elements necessarily indescribable, that they have
come upon true nothingness. If they are mystics, distrusting thought and craving the large-
ness of indistinction, they may embrace this
alleged nothingness with joy, even if it seem posi-
tively painful, hoping to find rest there through
self-abnegation. If on the contrary they are
rationalists they may reject the immediate with
scorn and deny that it exists at all, since in their
books they cannot define it satisfactorily. Both
mystics and rationalists, however, are deceived by
their mental agility; the immediate exists, even if
dialectic cannot explain it. What the rationalist
calls nonentity is the substrate and locus of all
ideas, having the obstinate reality of matter, the
crushing irrationality of existence itself; and one
who attempts to override it becomes to that extent
an irrelevant rhapsodist, dealing with thin after-

images of being. Nor has the mystic who sinks into the immediate much better appreciated the situation. This immediate is not God but chaos; its nothingness is pregnant, restless, and brutish; it is that from which all things emerge in so far as they have any permanence or value, so that to lapse into it again is a dull suicide and no salvation. Peace, which is after all what the mystic seeks, lies not in indistinction but in perfection. If he reaches it in a measure himself, it is by the traditional discipline he still practises, not by his heats or his languors.

The seed-bed of reason lies, then, in the immediate, but what reason draws thence is momentum and power to rise above its source. It is the perturbed immediate itself that finds or at least seeks its peace in reason, through which it comes in sight of some sort of ideal permanence. When the flux manages to form an eddy and to maintain by breathing and nutrition what we call a life, it affords some slight foothold and object for thought and becomes in a measure like the ark in the desert, a moving habitation for the eternal. Life begins to have some value and continuity so soon as there is something definite that lives and something definite to live for. The primacy of will, as Fichte and Schopenhauer conceived it, is a mythical way of designating this situation. Of course a will can have no being in the absence of realities or ideas marking its direction and contrast-

Life the fixation of interests.

ing the eventualities it seeks with those it flies
from; and tendency, no less than movement, needs
an organised medium to make it possible, while
aspiration and fear involve an ideal world. Yet
a principle of choice is not deducible from mere
ideas, and no interest is involved in the formal
relations of things. All survey needs an arbitrary
starting-point; all valuation rests on an irrational
bias. The absolute flux cannot be physically arrested; but what arrests it ideally is the fixing of
some point in it from which it can be measured
and illumined. Otherwise it could show no form
and maintain no preference; it would be impossible to approach or recede from a represented
state, and to suffer or to exert will in view of
events. The irrational fate that lodges the transcendental self in this or that body, inspires it
with definite passions, and subjects it to particular
buffets from the outer world—this is the prime
condition of all observation and inference, of all
failure or success.

Primary dualities. Those sensations in which a transition is contained need only analysis to
yield two ideal and related terms—two points in
space or two characters in feeling. Hot and cold,
here and there, good and bad, now and then, are
dyads that spring into being when the flux accen-
tuates some term and so makes possible a discrimination of parts and directions in its own
movement. An initial attitude sustains incipient
interests. What we first discover in ourselves,

before the influence we obey has given rise to any
definite idea, is the working of instincts already
in motion. Impulses to appropriate and to reject
first teach us the points of the compass, and space
itself, like charity, begins at home.

First grop-   The guide in early sensuous educa-
ings. In-   tion is the same that conducts the
stinct the
nucleus of   whole Life of Reason, namely, impulse
reason.   checked by experiment, and experiment judged again by impulse. What teaches the
child to distinguish the nurse's breast from sundry
blank or disquieting presences? What induces
him to arrest that image, to mark its associates,
and to recognise them with alacrity? The discomfort of its absence and the comfort of its
possession. To that image is attached the chief
satisfaction he knows, and the force of that
satisfaction disentangles it before all other images
from the feeble and fluid continuum of his life.
What first awakens in him a sense of reality is
what first is able to appease his unrest.

Had the group of feelings, now welded together
in fruition, found no instinct in him to awaken
and become a signal for, the group would never
have persisted; its loose elements would have
been allowed to pass by unnoticed and would
not have been recognised when they recurred.
Experience would have remained absolute inexperience, as foolishly perpetual as the gurglings
of rivers or the flickerings of sunlight in a grove.
But an instinct was actually present, so formed as

to be aroused by a determinate stimulus; and the image produced by that stimulus, when it came, could have in consequence a meaning and an individuality. It seemed by divine right to signify something interesting, something real, because by natural contiguity it flowed from something pertinent and important to life. Every accompanying sensation which shared that privilege, or in time was engrossed in that function, would ultimately become a part of that conceived reality, a quality of that thing.

The same primacy of impulses, irrational in themselves but expressive of bodily functions, is observable in the behaviour of animals, and in those dreams, obsessions, and primary passions which in the midst of sophisticated life sometimes lay bare the obscure groundwork of human nature. Reason's work is there undone. We can observe sporadic growths, disjointed fragments of rationality, springing up in a moral wilderness. In the passion of love, for instance, a cause unknown to the sufferer, but which is doubtless the spring-flood of hereditary instincts accidentally let loose, suddenly checks the young man's gayety, dispels his random curiosity, arrests perhaps his very breath; and when he looks for a cause to explain his suspended faculties, he can find it only in the presence or image of another being, of whose character, possibly, he knows nothing and whose beauty may not be remarkable; yet that image pursues him everywhere, and he is dominated by an unac-

customed tragic earnestness and a new capacity
for suffering and joy. If the passion be strong
there is no previous interest or duty that will be
remembered before it; if it be lasting the whole
life may be reorganised by it; it may impose new
habits, other manners, and another religion. Yet
what is the root of all this idealism? An irrational instinct, normally intermittent, such as all
dumb creatures share, which has here managed to
dominate a human soul and to enlist all the mental powers in its more or less permanent service,
upsetting their usual equilibrium. This madness,
however, inspires method; and for the first time,
perhaps, in his life, the man has something to
live for. The blind affinity that like a magnet
draws all the faculties around it, in so uniting
them, suffuses them with an unwonted spiritual
light.

Better and worse the fundamental categories. Here, on a small scale and on a precarious foundation, we may see clearly
illustrated and foreshadowed that Life
of Reason which is simply the unity given to all
existence by a mind *in love with the good*. In the
higher reaches of human nature, as much as in
the lower, rationality depends on distinguishing
the excellent; and that distinction can be made,
in the last analysis, only by an irrational impulse.
As life is a better form given to force, by which
the universal flux is subdued to create and
serve a somewhat permanent interest, so reason is a better form given to interest itself, by

which it is fortified and propagated, and ultimately, perhaps, assured of satisfaction. The substance to which this form is given remains irrational; so that rationality, like all excellence, is something secondary and relative, requiring a natural being to possess or to impute it. When definite interests are recognised and the values of things are estimated by that standard, action at the same time veering in harmony with that estimation, then reason has been born and a moral world has arisen.

CHAPTER II

FIRST STEPS AND FIRST FLUCTUATIONS

Dreams before thoughts. Consciousness is a born hermit. Though subject, by divine dispensation, to spells of fervour and apathy, like a singing bird, it is at first quite unconcerned about its own conditions or maintenance. To acquire a notion of such matters, or an interest in them, it would have to lose its hearty simplicity and begin to reflect; it would have to forget the present with its instant joys in order laboriously to conceive the absent and the hypothetical. The body may be said to make for self-preservation, since it has an organic equilibrium which, when not too rudely disturbed, restores itself by growth and co-operative action; but no such principle appears in the soul. Foolish in the beginning and generous in the end, consciousness thinks of nothing so little as of its own interests. It is lost in its objects; nor would it ever acquire even an indirect concern in its future, did not love of things external attach it to their fortunes. Attachment to ideal terms is indeed what gives consciousness its continuity; its parts have no relevance or relation to one another save what they

48

acquire by depending on the same body or representing the same objects. Even when consciousness grows sophisticated and thinks it cares for itself, it really cares only for its ideals; the world it pictures seems to it beautiful, and it may incidentally prize itself also, when it has come to regard itself as a part of that world. Initially, however, it is free even from that honest selfishness; it looks straight out; it is interested in the movements it observes; it swells with the represented world, suffers with its commotion, and subsides, no less willingly, in its interludes of calm.

Natural history and psychology arrive at consciousness from the outside, and consequently give it an artificial articulation and rationality which are wholly alien to its essence. These sciences infer feeling from habit or expression; so that only the expressible and practical aspects of feeling figure in their calculation. But these aspects are really peripheral; the core is an irresponsible, ungoverned, irrevocable dream. Psychologists have discussed perception *ad nauseam* and become horribly entangled in a combined idealism and physiology; for they must perforce approach the subject from the side of matter, since all science and all evidence is external; nor could they ever reach consciousness at all if they did not observe its occasions and then interpret those occasions dramatically. At the same time, the inferred mind they subject to examination will yield nothing but ideas, and it is a marvel how such a dream can regard those natural objects from which the psychologist has inferred it. Perception is in fact no primary phase of consciousness; it is an ulterior practical function acquired by a dream which has become symbolic of its conditions, and therefore relevant to its own destiny. Such relevance and symbolism are indirect and slowly acquired; their status cannot be understood unless we regard them as forms of imagination happily grown significant. In imagination, not in perception, lies the substance of experience, while knowledge and reason are but its chastened and ultimate form.

The mind vegetates uncontrolled save by physical forces.
Every actual animal is somewhat dull and somewhat mad. He will at times miss his signals and stare vacantly when he might well act, while at other times he will run off into convulsions and raise a dust in his own brain to no purpose. These imperfections are so human that we should hardly recognise ourselves if we could shake them off altogether. Not to retain any dulness would mean to possess untiring attention and universal interests, thus realising the boast about deeming nothing human alien to us; while to be absolutely without folly would involve perfect self-knowledge and self-control. The intelligent man known to history flourishes within a dullard and holds a lunatic in leash. He is encased in a protective shell of ignorance and insensibility which keeps him from being exhausted and confused by this too complicated world; but that integument

blinds him at the same time to many of his near‹
est and highest interests. He is amused by the
antics of the brute dreaming within his breast;
he gloats on his passionate reveries, an amuse-
ment which sometimes costs him very dear. Thus
the best human intelligence is still decidedly barbarous; it fights in heavy armour and keeps a fool
at court.

If consciousness could ever have the function
of guiding conduct better than instinct can, in the
beginning it would be most incompetent for that
office. Only the routine and equilibrium which
healthy instinct involves keep thought and will at
all within the limits of sanity. The predeter-
mined interests we have as animals
fortunately focus our attention on
practical things, pulling it back, like a
ball with an elastic cord, within the radius of
pertinent matters. Instinct alone compels us to
neglect and seldom to recall the irrelevant infinity
of ideas. Philosophers have sometimes said that
all ideas come from experience; they never could
have been poets and must have forgotten that they
were ever children. The great difficulty in education is to get experience out of ideas. Shame,
conscience, and reason continually disallow and
ignore what consciousness presents; and what are
they but habit and latent instinct asserting themselves and forcing us to disregard our midsum-
mer madness? Idiocy and lunacy are merely
reversions to a condition in which present con-

Internal order supervenes.

sciousness is in the ascendant and has escaped the
control of unconscious forces. We speak of people
being "out of their senses," when they have in
fact fallen back into them; or of those who have
"lost their mind," when they have lost merely that
habitual control over consciousness which pre-
vented it from flaring into all sorts of obsessions
and agonies. Their bodies having become de-
ranged, their minds, far from correcting that
derangement, instantly share and betray it. A
dream is always simmering below the conventional
surface of speech and reflection. Even in the
highest reaches and serenest meditations of science
it sometimes breaks through. Even there we are
seldom constant enough to conceive a truly natural
world; somewhere passionate, fanciful, or magic
elements will slip into the scheme and baffle
rational ambition.

A body seriously out of equilibrium, either with
itself or with its environment, perishes outright.
Not so a mind. Madness and suffering can set
themselves no limit; they lapse only when the
corporeal frame that sustains them yields to circumstances and changes its habit. If they are
unstable at all, it is because they ordinarily correspond to strains and conjunctions which a vig-
orous body overcomes, or which dissolve the body
altogether. A pain not incidental to the play of
practical instincts may easily be recurrent, and it
might be perpetual if even the worst habits were
not intermittent and the most useless agitations

exhausting. Some respite will therefore ensue upon pain, but no magic cure. Madness, in like manner, if pronounced, is precarious, but when speculative enough to be harmless or not strong enough to be debilitating, it too may last for ever.

An imaginative life may therefore exist parasitically in a man, hardly touching his action or environment. There is no possibility of exorcising these apparitions by their own power. A nightmare does not dispel itself; it endures until the organic strain which caused it is relaxed either by natural exhaustion or by some external influence. Therefore human ideas are still for the most part sensuous and trivial, shifting with the chance currents of the brain, and representing nothing, so to speak, but personal temperature. Personal temperature, moreover, is sometimes tropical. There are brains like a South American jungle, as there are others like an Arabian desert, strewn with nothing but bones. While a passionate sultriness prevails in the mind there is no end to its luxuriance. Languages intricately articulate, flaming mythologies, metaphysical perspectives lost in infinity, arise in remarkable profusion. In time, however, there comes a change of climate and the whole forest disappears.

It is easy, from the stand-point of acquired practical competence, to deride a merely imaginative life. Derision, however, is not interpretation, and

the better method of overcoming erratic ideas is
to trace them out dialectically and see if they will
not recognise their own fatuity. The most irresponsible vision has certain principles of order and
valuation by which it estimates itself; and in these
principles the Life of Reason is already broached,
however halting may be its development. We
should lead ourselves out of our dream, as the
Israelites were led out of Egypt, by the promise
and eloquence of that dream itself. Otherwise we
might kill the goose that lays the golden egg, and
by proscribing imagination abolish science.

Intrinsic
pleasure in
existence.

Visionary experience has a first
value in its possible pleasantness.
Why any form of feeling should be delightful is not to be explained transcendentally:
a physiological law may, after the fact, render
every instance predictable; but no logical affinity
between the formal quality of an experience and
the impulse to welcome it will thereby be disclosed.
We find, however, that pleasure suffuses certain
states of mind and pain others; which is another
way of saying that, for no reason, we love the
first and detest the second. The polemic which
certain moralists have waged against pleasure and
in favour of pain is intelligible when we remember that their chief interest is edification, and that
ability to resist pleasure and pain alike is a val-
uable virtue in a world where action and renunciation are the twin keys to happiness. But to
deny that pleasure is a good and pain an evil

is a grotesque affectation: it amounts to giving
"good" and " evil " artificial definitions and there-
Pleasure a   by reducing ethics to arbitrary verbi-
good,   age. Not only is good that adherence
of the will to experience of which pleasure is the
basal example, and evil the corresponding rejection which is the very essence of pain, but when
we pass from good and evil in sense to their highest embodiments, pleasure remains eligible and
pain something which it is a duty to prevent. A
man who without necessity deprived any person of
a pleasure or imposed on him a pain, would be a
contemptible knave, and the person so injured
would be the first to declare it, nor could the highest celestial tribunal, if it was just, reverse that
sentence. For it suffices that one being, however
weak, loves or abhores anything, no matter how
slightly, for that thing to acquire a proportionate
value which no chorus of contradiction ringing
through all the spheres can ever wholly abolish.
An experience good or bad in itself remains so
for ever, and its inclusion in a more general order
of things can only change that totality propor-
tionately to the ingredient absorbed, which will
infect the mass, so far as it goes, with its own
colour. The more pleasure a universe can yield,
other things being equal, the more beneficent and
generous is its general nature; the more pains its
constitution involves, the darker and more malign
is its total temper. To deny this would seem impossible, yet it is done daily; for there is nothing

people will not maintain when they are slaves to
superstition; and candour and a sense of justice
are, in such a case, the first things lost.

but not pur-
sued or re-
membered
unless it
suffuses an
object.
Pleasures differ sensibly in intensity; but the intensest pleasures are
often the blindest, and it is hard to
recall or estimate a feeling with which
no definite and complex object is
conjoined. The first step in making pleasure
intelligible and capable of being pursued is to make
it pleasure in something. The object it suffuses
acquires a value, and gives the pleasure itself a
place in rational life. The pleasure can now be
named, its variations studied in reference to
changes in its object, and its comings and goings
foreseen in the order of events. The more articulate the world that produces emotion the more
controllable and recoverable is the emotion itself.
Therefore diversity and order in ideas makes the
life of pleasure richer and easier to lead. A voluminous dumb pleasure might indeed outweigh the
pleasure spread thin over a multitude of tame
perceptions, if we could only weigh the two in one
scale; but to do so is impossible, and in memory
and prospect, if not in experience, diversified
pleasure must needs carry the day.

Subhuman
delights.
Here we come upon a crisis in
human development which shows
clearly how much the Life of Reason is a natural
thing, a growth that a different course of events
might well have excluded. Laplace is reported to

have said on his death-bed that science was mere
trifling and that nothing was real but love. Love,
for such a man, doubtless involved objects and
ideas: it was love of persons. The same revulsion
of feeling may, however, be carried further.
Lucretius says that passion is a torment because
its pleasures are not pure, that is, because they are
mingled with longing and entangled in vexatious
things. Pure pleasure would be without ideas.
Many a man has found in some moment of his
life an unutterable joy which made all the rest of
it seem a farce, as if a corpse should play it was
living. Mystics habitually look beneath the Life
of Reason for the substance and infinity of happiness. In all these revulsions, and many others,
there is a certain justification, inasmuch as systematic living is after all an experiment, as is the
formation of animal bodies, and the inorganic
pulp out of which these growths have come may
very likely have had its own incommunicable values, its absolute thrills, which we vainly try to
remember and to which, in moments of dissolution, we may half revert. Protoplasmic pleasures
and strains may be the substance of consciousness;
and as matter seeks its own level, and as the sea
and the flat waste to which all dust returns have
a certain primordial life and a certain sublimity,
so all passions and ideas, when spent, may re-
join the basal note of feeling, and enlarge their
volume as they lose their form. This loss of form
may not be unwelcome, if it is the formless that,

by anticipation, speaks through what is surrendering its being. Though to acquire or impart form is delightful in art, in thought, in generation, in government, yet a euthanasia of finitude is also known. All is not affectation in the poet who says, "Now more than ever seems it rich to die"; and, without any poetry or affectation, men may love sleep, and opiates, and every luxurious escape from humanity.

The step by which pleasure and pain are attached to ideas, so as to be predictable and to become factors in action, is therefore by no means irrevocable. It is a step, however, in the direction of reason; and though reason's path is only one of innumerable courses perhaps open to existence, it is the only one that we are tracing here; the only one, obviously, which human discourse is competent to trace.

Animal living. When consciousness begins to add diversity to its intensity, its value is no longer absolute and inexpressible. The felt variations in its tone are attached to the observed movement of its objects; in these objects its values are imbedded. A world loaded with dramatic values may thus arise in imagination; terrible and delightful presences may chase one another across the void; life will be a kind of music made by all the senses together. Many animals probably have this form of experience; they are not wholly submerged in a vegetative stupor; they can discern what they love or fear. Yet all this is still a

disordered apparition that reels itself off amid
sporadic movements, efforts, and agonies. Now
gorgeous, now exciting, now indifferent, the landscape brightens and fades with the day. If a dog,
while sniffing about contentedly, sees afar off his
master arriving after long absence, the change in
the animal's feeling is not merely in the quantity
of pure pleasure; a new circle of sensations appears, with a new principle governing interest and
desire; instead of waywardness subjection, instead
of freedom love. But the poor brute asks for no
reason why his master went, why he has come
again, why he should be loved, or why presently while lying at his feet you forget him and
begin to grunt and dream of the chase—all that
is an utter mystery, utterly unconsidered. Such
experience has variety, scenery, and a certain vital
rhythm; its story might be told in dithyrambic
verse. It moves wholly by inspiration; every
event is providential, every act unpremeditated.
Absolute freedom and absolute helplessness have
met together: you depend wholly on divine favour,
yet that unfathomable agency is not distinguishable from your own life. This is the condition
to which some forms of piety invite men to return;
and it lies in truth not far beneath the level of
ordinary human consciousness.

Causes at last discerned. The story which such animal experience contains, however, needs only to
be better articulated in order to disclose its underlying machinery. The figures even

of that disordered drama have their exits and their
entrances; and their cues can be gradually discovered by a being capable of fixing his attention and
retaining the order of events.   Thereupon a third
step is made in imaginative experience.   As pleasures and pains were formerly distributed among
objects, so objects are now marshalled into a world.
Felix qui potuit rerum cognoscere causas, said a
poet who stood near enough to fundamental
human needs and to the great answer which art
and civilisation can make to them, to value the
Life of Reason and think it sublime.   To discern
causes is to turn vision into knowledge and motion
into action.   It is to fix the associates of things,
so that their respective transformations are col-
lated, and they become significant of one another.
In proportion as such understanding advances
each moment of experience becomes consequential and prophetic of the rest.   The calm places
in life are filled with power and its spasms with
resource.   No emotion can overwhelm the mind,
for of none is the basis or issue wholly hidden;
no event can disconcert it altogether, because it
sees beyond.   Means can be looked for to escape
from the worst predicament; and whereas each
moment had been formerly filled with nothing but
its own adventure and surprised emotion, each now
makes room for the lesson of what went before
and surmises what may be the plot of the whole.

At the threshold of reason there is a kind of
choice.   Not all impressions contribute equally to

the new growth; many, in fact, which were formerly equal in rank to the best, now grow obscure.
Attention ignores them, in its haste to arrive at
what is significant of something more. Nor are
the principles of synthesis, by which the aristo-
cratic few establish their oligarchy, themselves unequivocal. The first principles of logic are like
the senses, few but arbitrary. They might have
been quite different and yet produced, by a now
unthinkable method, a language no less significant
than the one we speak. Twenty-six letters may
suffice for a language, but they are a wretched
minority among all possible sounds. So the
forms of perception and the categories of thought,
which a grammarian's philosophy might think
primordial necessities, are no less casual than
words or their syntactical order. Why, we may
ask, did these forms assert themselves here?
What principles of selection guide mental growth?

To give a logical ground for such a selection is
evidently impossible, since it is logic itself that is
to be accounted for. A natural ground is, in
strictness, also irrelevant, since natural connections, where thought has not reduced them to a
sort of equivalence and necessity, are mere data
and juxtapositions. Yet it is not necessary to
leave the question altogether unanswered. By
using our senses we may discover, not indeed why
each sense has its specific quality or exists at all,
but what are its organs and occasions. In like
manner we may, by developing the Life of Reason,

come to understand its conditions. When consciousness awakes the body has, as we long after-

Attention
guided by
bodily im-
pulse.

ward discover, a definite organisation.
Without guidance from reflection bodily processes have been going on, and
most precise affinities and reactions have been set
up between its organs and the surrounding objects.

On these affinities and reactions sense and intellect are grafted. The plants are of different
nature, yet growing together they bear excellent
fruit. It is as the organs receive appropriate
stimulations that attention is riveted on definite
sensations. It is as the system exercises its
natural activities that passion, will, and meditation possess the mind. No syllogism is needed to
persuade us to eat, no prophecy of happiness to
teach us to love. On the contrary, the living
organism, caught in the act, informs us how to
reason and what to enjoy. The soul adopts the
body's aims; from the body and from its instincts
she draws a first hint of the right means to those
accepted purposes. Thus reason enters into part-
nership with the world and begins to be respected
there; which it would never be if it were not expressive of the same mechanical forces that are to
preside over events and render them fortunate or
unfortunate for human interests. Reason is significant in action only because it has begun by
taking, so to speak, the body's side; that sympathetic bias enables her to distinguish events pertinent to the chosen interests, to compare im-

pulse with satisfaction, and, by representing a new
and circular current in the system, to preside over
the formation of better habits, habits expressing
more instincts at once and responding to more
opportunities.

CHAPTER III

THE DISCOVERY OF NATURAL OBJECTS

Nature man's home. At first sight it might seem an idle observation that the first task of intelligence is to represent the environing reality, a reality actually represented in the notion, universally prevalent among men, of a cosmos in space and time, an animated material engine called nature. In trying to conceive nature the mind lisps its first lesson; natural phenomena are the mother tongue of imagination no less than of science and practical life. Men and gods are not conceivable otherwise than as inhabitants of nature. Early experience knows no mystery which is not somehow rooted in transformations of the natural world, and fancy can build no hope which would not be expressible there. But we are grown so accustomed to this ancient apparition that we may be no longer aware how difficult was the task of conjuring it up. We may even have forgotten the possibility that such a vision should never have arisen at all. A brief excursion into that much abused subject, the psychology of perception, may here serve to remind us of the great

work which the budding intellect must long ago
have accomplished unawares.

**Difficulties
in conceiv-
ing nature.** Consider how the shocks out of
which the notion of material things is
to be built first strike home into the
soul. Eye and hand, if we may neglect the other
senses, transmit their successive impressions, all
varying with the position of outer objects and with
the other material conditions. A chaos of multitudinous impressions rains in from all sides at all
hours. Nor have the external or cognitive senses
an original primacy. The taste, the smell, the
alarming sounds of things are continually distract-
ing attention. There are infinite reverberations in
memory of all former impressions, together with
fresh fancies created in the brain, things at first in
no wise subordinated to external objects. All these
incongruous elements are mingled like a witches'
brew. And more: there are indications that inner
sensations, such as those of digestion, have an
overpowering influence on the primitive mind,
which has not learned to articulate or distinguish
permanent needs. So that to the whirl of outer
sensations we must add, to reach some notion of
what consciousness may contain before the advent
of reason, interruptions and lethargies caused by
wholly blind internal feelings; trances such as fall
even on comparatively articulate minds in rage,
lust, or madness. Against all these bewildering
forces the new-born reason has to struggle; and we
need not wonder that the costly experiments and

disillusions of the past have not yet produced a complete enlightenment.

The onslaught made in the last century by the transcendental philosophy upon empirical traditions is familiar to everybody: it seemed a pertinent attack, yet in the end proved quite trifling and unavailing. Thought, we are told rightly enough, cannot be accounted for by enumerating its conditions. A number of detached sensations, being each its own little world, cannot add themselves together nor conjoin themselves in the void. Again, experiences having an alleged common cause would not have, merely for that reason, a common object. Nor would a series of successive perceptions, no matter how quick, logically involve a sense of time nor a notion of succession. Yet, in point of fact, when such a succession occurs and a living brain is there to acquire some structural modification by virtue of its own passing states, a memory of that succession and its terms may often supervene. It is quite true also that the simultaneous presence or association of images belonging to different senses does not carry with it by intrinsic necessity any fusion of such images nor any notion of an object having them for its qualities. Yet, in point of fact, such a group of sensations does often merge into a complex image; instead of the elements originally perceptible in isolation, there arises a familiar term, a sort of personal presence. To this felt presence, certain instinctive reactions are attached, and the sensations that may be involved in that apparition, when each for any reason becomes emphatic, are referred to it as its qualities or its effects.

Such complications of course involve the gift of memory, with capacity to survey at once vestiges of many perceptions, to feel their implication and absorption in the present object, and to be carried, by this sense of relation, to the thought that those perceptions have a representative function. And this is a great step. It manifests the mind's powers. It illustrates those transformations of consciousness the principle of which, when abstracted, we call intelligence. We must accordingly proceed with caution, for we are digging at the very roots of reason.

Thought an aspect of life and transitive. The chief perplexity, however, which besets this subject and makes discussions of it so often end in a cloud, is quite artificial. Thought is not a mechanical calculus, where the elements and the method exhaust the fact. Thought is a form of life, and should be conceived on the analogy of nutrition, generation, and art. Reason, as Hume said with profound truth, is an unintelligible instinct. It could not be otherwise if reason is to remain something transitive and existential; for transition is unintelligible, and yet is the deepest characteristic of existence. Philosophers, however, having perceived that the function of thought is to fix static terms and reveal eternal relations, have inadver-

tently transferred to the living act what is true
only of its ideal object; and they have expected
to find in the process, treated psychologically, that
luminous deductive clearness which belongs to the
ideal world it tends to reveal. The intelligible,
however, lies at the periphery of experience, the
surd at its core; and intelligence is but one centrif-
ugal ray darting from the slime to the stars.
Thought must execute a metamorphosis; and
while this is of course mysterious, it is one of those
familiar mysteries, like motion and will, which
are more natural than dialectical lucidity itself;
for dialectic grows cogent by fulfilling intent, but
intent or meaning is itself vital and inexplicable.

Perception cumula-tive and syn-thetic. The process of counting is perhaps
as simple an instance as can be found
of a mental operation on sensible data.
The clock, let us say, strikes two: if the sensorium
were perfectly elastic and after receiving the first
blow reverted exactly to its previous state, retaining absolutely no trace of that momentary oscil-
lation and no altered habit, then it is certain that
a sense for number or a faculty of counting could
never arise. The second stroke would be re-
sponded to with the same reaction which had met
the first. There would be no summation of effects,
no complication. However numerous the successive impressions might come to be, each would
remain fresh and pure, the last being identical in
character with the first. One, one, one, would be
the monotonous response for ever. Just so gen-

erations of ephemeral insects that succeeded one
another without transmitting experience might
repeat the same round of impressions—an ever-
lasting progression without a shadow of progress.
Such, too, is the idiot's life: his liquid brain
transmits every impulse without resistance and
retains the record of no impression.

Intelligence is accordingly conditioned by a
modification of both structure and consciousness
by dint of past events. To be aware that a
second stroke is not itself the first, I must retain
something of the old sensation. The first must
reverberate still in my ears when the second ar-
rives, so that this second, coming into a consciousness still filled by the first, is a different experience from the first, which fell into a mind
perfectly empty and unprepared. Now the new-
comer finds in the subsisting One a sponsor to
christen it by the name of Two. The first stroke
was a simple 1. The second is not simply another
1, a mere iteration of the first. It is 1^1, where
the coefficient represents the reverberating first
stroke, still persisting in the mind, and forming a
background and perspective against which the new
stroke may be distinguished. The meaning of
" two," then, is " this after that " or " this again,"
where we have a simultaneous sense of two things
which have been separately perceived but are identified as similar in their nature. Repetition must
cease to be pure repetition and become cumulative
before it can give rise to the consciousness of
repetition.

The first condition of counting, then, is that the sensorium should retain something of the first impression while it receives the second, or (to state the corresponding mental fact) that the second sensation should be felt together with a survival of the first from which it is distinguished in point of existence and with which it is identified in point of character.

Now, to secure this, it is not enough **No identical agent needed.** that the sensorium should be materially continuous, or that a " spiritual substance " or a " transcendental ego " should persist in time to receive the second sensation after having received and registered the first. A perfectly elastic sensorium, a wholly unchanging soul, or a quite absolute ego might remain perfectly identical with itself through various experiences without collating them. It would then remain, in fact, more truly and literally identical than if it were modified somewhat by those successive shocks. Yet a sensorium or a spirit thus unchanged would be incapable of memory, unfit to connect a past perception with one present or to become aware of their relation. It is not identity in the substance impressed, but growing complication in the phenomenon presented, that makes possible a sense of diversity and relation between things. The identity of substance or spirit, if it were absolute, would indeed prevent comparison, because it would exclude modifications, and it is the survival of past modifications within the present that makes comparisons possible. We may impress any number of forms successively on the same water, and the identity of the substance will not help those forms to survive and accumulate their effects. But if we have a surface that retains our successive stampings we may change the substance from wax to plaster and from plaster to bronze, and the effects of our labour will survive and be superimposed upon one another. It is the actual plastic form in both mind and body, not any unchanging substance or agent, that is efficacious in perpetuating thought and gathering experience.

Were not Nature and all her parts such models of patience and pertinacity, they never would have succeeded in impressing their existence on something so volatile and irresponsible as thought is. **Example of the sun.** A sensation needs to be violent, like the sun's blinding light, to arrest attention, and keep it taut, as it were, long enough for the system to acquire a respectful attitude, and grow predisposed to resume it. A repetition of that sensation will thereafter meet with a prepared response which we call recognition; the concomitants of the old experience will form themselves afresh about the new one and by their convergence give it a sort of welcome and interpretation. The movement, for instance, by which the face was raised toward the heavens was perhaps one element which added to the first sensation, brightness, a concomitant sensation, height; the

brightness was not bright merely, but high. Now
when the brightness reappears the face will more
quickly be lifted up; the place where the brightness shone will be looked for; the brightness will
have acquired a claim to be placed somewhere.
The heat which at the same moment may have
burned the forehead will also be expected and,
when felt, projected into the brightness, which will
now be hot as well as high. So with whatever
other sensations time may associate with this
group. They will all adhere to the original impression, enriching it with an individuality which
will render it before long a familiar complex in
experience, and one easy to recognise and to complete in idea.

In the case of so vivid a thing as
His prim-
itive divinity. the sun's brightness many other sensations beside those out of which science
draws the qualities attributed to that heavenly
body adhere in the primitive mind to the phenomenon. Before he is a substance the sun is a god.
He is beneficent and necessary no less than bright
and high; he rises upon all happy opportunities
and sets upon all terrors. He is divine, since all
life and fruitfulness hang upon his miraculous
revolutions. His coming and going are life and
death to the world. As the sensations of light and
heat are projected upward together to become
attributes of his body, so the feelings of pleasure,
safety, and hope which he brings into the soul are
projected into his spirit; and to this spirit, more

than to anything else, energy, independence, and substantiality are originally attributed. The emotions felt in his presence being the ultimate issue and term of his effect in us, the counterpart or shadow of those emotions is regarded as the first and deepest factor in his causality. It is his divine life, more than aught else, that underlies his apparitions and explains the influences which he propagates. The substance or independent existence attributed to objects is therefore by no means only or primarily a physical notion. What is conceived to support the physical qualities is a pseudo-psychic or vital force. It is a moral and living object that we construct, building it up out of all the materials, emotional, intellectual, and sensuous, which lie at hand in our consciousness to be synthesised into the hybrid reality which we are to fancy confronting us. To discriminate and redistribute those miscellaneous physical and psychical elements, and to divorce the god from the material sun, is a much later problem, arising at a different and more reflective stage in the Life of Reason.

Causes and essences contrasted.   When reflection, turning to the comprehension of a chaotic experience, busies itself about recurrences, when it seeks to normalise in some way things coming and going, and to straighten out the causes of events, that reflection is inevitably turned toward something dynamic and independent, and can have no successful issue except in mechanical science.

When on the other hand reflection stops to challenge and question the fleeting object, not so much to prepare for its possible return as to conceive its present nature, this reflection is turned no less unmistakably in the direction of ideas, and will terminate in logic or the morphology of being. We attribute independence to things in order to normalise their recurrence. We attribute essences to them in order to normalise their manifestations or constitution. Independence will ultimately turn out to be an assumed constancy in material processes, essence an assumed constancy in ideal meanings or points of reference in discourse. The one marks the systematic distribution of objects, the other their settled character.

Voracity of intellect. We talk of recurrent perceptions, but materially considered no perception recurs. Each recurrence is one of a finite series and holds for ever its place and number in that series. Yet human attention, while it can survey several simultaneous impressions and find them similar, cannot keep them distinct if they grow too numerous. The mind has a native bias and inveterate preference for form and identification. Water does not run down hill more persistently than attention turns experience into constant terms. The several repetitions of one essence given in consciousness will tend at once to be neglected, and only the essence itself—the character shared by those sundry perceptions—will stand and become a term in mental discourse. After a few strokes of the clock, the reiterated impressions merge and cover one another; we lose count and perceive the quality and rhythm but not the number of the sounds. If this is true of so abstract and mathematical a perception as is counting, how emphatically true must it be of continuous and infinitely varied perceptions flowing in from the whole spatial world. Glimpses of the environment follow one another in quick succession, like a regiment of soldiers in uniform; only now and then does the stream take a new turn, catch a new ray of sunlight, or arrest our attention at some break.

The senses in their natural play revert constantly to familiar objects, gaining impressions which differ but slightly from one another. These slight differences are submerged in apperception, so that sensation comes to be not so much an addition of new items to consciousness as a reburnishing there of some imbedded device. Its character and relations are only slightly modified at each fresh rejuvenation. To catch the passing phenomenon in all its novelty and idiosyncrasy is a work of artifice and curiosity. Such an exercise does violence to intellectual instinct and involves an æsthetic power of diving bodily into the stream of sensation, having thrown overboard all rational ballast and escaped at once the inertia and the momentum of practical life. Normally every datum of sense is at once devoured by a hungry intellect and digested for the sake of its vital

juices. The result is that what ordinarily remains in memory is no representative of particular moments or shocks—though sensation, as in
dreams, may be incidentally recreated from within
—but rather a logical possession, a sense of acquaintance with a certain field of reality, in a
word, a consciousness of *knowledge*.

Can the
transcendent
be known?
But what, we may ask, is this reality, which we boast to know? May not
the sceptic justly contend that nothing
is so unknown and indeed unknowable as this pre-
tended object of knowledge? The sensations
which reason treats so cavalierly were at least
something actual while they lasted and made good
their momentary claim to our interest; but what
is this new ideal figment, unseizable yet ever
present, invisible but indispensable, unknowable
yet alone interesting or important? Strange that
the only possible object or theme of our knowledge
should be something we cannot know.

Can the im-
mediate be
meant?
An answer to these doubts will perhaps appear if we ask ourselves what
sort of contact with reality would satisfy us, and in what terms we expect or desire to
possess the subject-matter of our thoughts. Is it
simply corroboration that we look for? Is it a
verification of truth in sense? It would be un-
reasonable, in that case, after all the evidence we
demand has been gathered, to complain that the
ideal term thus concurrently suggested, the super-
sensible substance, reality, or independent object,

does not itself descend into the arena of immediate
sensuous presentation. Knowledge is not eating,
and we cannot expect to devour and possess *what
we mean*. Knowledge is recognition of something absent; it is a salutation, not an embrace.
It is an advance on sensation precisely because it
is representative. The terms or goals of thought
have for their function to subtend long tracts of
sensuous experience, to be ideal links between fact
and fact, invisible wires behind the scenes, threads
along which inference may run in making phenomena intelligible and controllable. An idea
that should become an image would cease to be
ideal; a principle that is to remain a principle can
never become a fact. A God that you could see
with the eyes of the body, a heaven you might
climb into by a ladder planted at Bethel, would
be parts of this created and interpretable world,
not terms in its interpretation nor objects in a
spiritual sphere. Now external objects are
thought to be principles and sources of experience; they are accordingly conceived realities on
an ideal plane. We may look for all the evidence
we choose before we declare our inference to be
warranted; but we must not ask for something
more than evidence, nor expect to know realities
without inferring them anew. They are revealed
only to understanding. We cannot cease to think
and still continue to know.

It may be said, however, that principles and
external objects are interesting only because they

symbolise further sensations, that thought is an expedient of finite minds, and that representation

Is thought a bridge from sensation to sensation? is a ghostly process which we crave to materialise into bodily possession. We may grow sick of inferring truth and long rather to become reality. Intelligence is after all no compulsory possession; and while some of us would gladly have more of it, others find that they already have too much. The tension of thought distresses them and to represent what they cannot and would not be is not a natural function of their spirit. To such minds experience that should merely corroborate ideas would prolong dissatisfaction. The ideas must be realised; they must pass into immediacy. If reality (a word employed generally in a eulogistic sense) is to mean this desired immediacy, no ideal of thought can be real. All intelligible objects and the whole universe of mental discourse would then be an unreal and conventional structure, impinging ultimately on sense from which it would derive its sole validity.

There would be no need of quarrelling with such a philosophy, were not its use of words rather misleading. Call experience in its existential and immediate aspect, if you will, the sole reality; that will not prevent reality from having an ideal dimension. The intellectual world will continue to give beauty, meaning, and scope to those bubbles of consciousness on which it is painted. Reality would not be, in that case, what thought aspires

to reach. Consciousness is the least ideal of things
when reason is taken out of it. Reality would then
need thought to give it all those human values of
which, in its substance, it would have been wholly
deprived; and the ideal would still be what lent
music to throbs and significance to being.

The equivocation favoured by such language at
once begins to appear. Is not thought with all
its products a part of experience? Must not
sense, if it be the only reality, be sentient sometimes of the ideal? What the site is to a city that is
immediate experience to the universe of discourse.
The latter is all held materially within the limits defined by the former; but if immediate experience be the seat of the moral world, the moral
world is the only interesting possession of immediate experience. When a waste is built on, however, it is a violent paradox to call it still a waste;
and an immediate experience that represents the
rest of sentience, with all manner of ideal harmonies read into the whole in the act of representing it, is an immediate experience raised to
its highest power: it is the Life of Reason. In
vain, then, will a philosophy of intellectual abstention limit so Platonic a
term as reality to the immediate aspect
of existence, when it is the ideal aspect that endows existence with character and value, together
with representative scope and a certain lien upon
eternity.

Mens naturaliter platonica.

More legitimate, therefore, would be the assertion that knowledge reaches reality when it touches its ideal goal. Reality is known when, as in mathematics, a stable and unequivocal object is developed by thinking. The locus or material embodiment of such a reality is no longer in view; these questions seem to the logician irrelevant. If necessary ideas find no illustration in sense, he deems the fact an argument against the importance and validity of sensation, not in the least a disproof of his ideal knowledge. If no site be found on earth for the Platonic city, its constitution is none the less recorded and enshrined in heaven; nor is that the only true ideal that has not where to lay its head. What in the sensualistic or mystical system was called reality will now be termed appearance, and what there figured as an imaginary construction borne by the conscious moment will now appear to be a prototype for all existence and an eternal standard for its estimation.

It is this rationalistic or Platonic system (little as most men may suspect the fact) that finds a first expression in ordinary perception. When you distinguish your sensations from their cause and laugh at the idealist (as this kind of sceptic is called) who says that chairs and tables exist only in your mind, you are treating a figment of reason as a deeper and truer thing than the moments of life whose blind experience that reason has come to illumine. What you call the evidence of sense is pure confidence in reason. You will

not be so idiotic as to make no inferences from
your sensations; you will not pin your faith so
unimaginatively on momentary appearance as to
deny that the world exists when you stop thinking
about it.   You feel that your intellect has wider
scope and has discovered many a thing that goes
on behind the scenes, many a secret that would
escape a stupid and gaping observation.   It is the
fool that looks to look and stops at the barely
visible: you not only look but *see;* for you understand.

Identity and   Now the practical burden of such
independence understanding, if you take the trouble
predicated of
things.   to analyse it, will turn out to be what
the sceptic says it is: assurance of eventual sensations.   But as these sensations, in memory and
expectation, are numerous and indefinitely variable, you are not able to hold them clearly before
the mind; indeed, the realisation of all the potentialities which you vaguely feel to lie in the future
is a task absolutely beyond imagination.   Yet
your present impressions, dependent as they are
on your chance attitude and disposition and on a
thousand trivial accidents, are far from representing adequately all that might be discovered
or that is actually known about the object before
you.   This object, then, to your apprehension, is
not identical with any of the sensations that reveal it, nor is it exhausted by all these sensations
when they are added together; yet it contains
nothing assignable but what they might conceiv-

ably reveal. As it lies in your fancy, then, this object, the reality, is a complex and elusive entity, the sum at once and the residuum of all particular impressions which, underlying the present one, have bequeathed to it their surviving linkage in discourse and consequently endowed it with a large part of its present character. With this hybrid object, sensuous in its materials and ideal in its locus, each particular glimpse is compared, and is recognised to be but a glimpse, an aspect which the object presents to a particular observer. Here are two identifications. In the first place various sensations and felt relations, which cannot be kept distinct in the mind, fall together into one term of discourse, represented by a sign, a word, or a more or less complete sensuous image. In the second place the new perception is referred to that ideal entity of which it is now called a manifestation and effect.

Such are the primary relations of reality and appearance. A reality is a term of discourse based on a psychic complex of memories, associations, and expectations, but constituted in its ideal independence by the assertive energy of thought. An appearance is a passing sensation, recognised as belonging to that group of which the object itself is the ideal representative, and accordingly regarded as a manifestation of that object.

Thus the notion of an independent and permanent world is an ideal term used to mark and as it were to justify the cohesion in space and the recurrence in time of recognisable groups of sensations. This coherence and recurrence force the intellect, if it would master experience at all or understand anything, to frame the idea of such a reality. If we wish to defend the use of such an idea and prove to ourselves its necessity, all we need do is to point to that coherence and recurrence in external phenomena. That brave effort and flight of intelligence which in the beginning raised man to the conception of reality, enabling him to discount and interpret appearance, will, if we retain our trust in reason, raise us continually anew to that same idea, by a no less spontaneous and victorious movement of thought.

CHAPTER IV

ON SOME CRITICS OF THIS DISCOVERY

Psychology as a solvent. The English psychologists who first disintegrated the idea of substance, and whose traces we have in general followed in the above account, did not study the question wholly for its own sake or in the spirit of a science that aims at nothing but a historical analysis of mind. They had a more or less malicious purpose behind their psychology. They thought that if they could once show how metaphysical ideas are made they would discredit those ideas and banish them for ever from the world. If they retained confidence in any notion—as Hobbes in body, Locke in matter and in God, Berkeley in spirits, and Kant, the inheritor of this malicious psychology, in the thing-in-itself and in heaven— it was merely by inadvertence or want of courage. The principle of their reasoning, where they chose to apply it, was always this, that ideas whose materials could all be accounted for in consciousness and referred to sense or to the operations of mind were thereby exhausted and deprived of further validity. Only the unaccountable, or rather the uncriticised, could be true. Consequently the

advance of psychology meant, in this school, the
retreat of reason; for as one notion after another
was clarified and reduced to its elements it was
ipso facto deprived of its function.

So far were these philosophers from conceiving
that validity and truth are ideal relations, accruing
to ideas by virtue of dialectic and use, that while on
the one hand they pointed out vital affinities and
pragmatic sanctions in the mind's economy they
confessed on the other that the outcome of their
philosophy was sceptical; for no idea could be
found in the mind which was not a phenomenon
there, and no inference could be drawn from these
phenomena not based on some inherent "tendency
to feign." The analysis which was in truth legiti-
mising and purifying knowledge seemed to them
absolutely to blast it, and the closer they came to
the bed-rock of experience the more incapable they
felt of building up anything upon it. Self-
knowledge meant, they fancied, self-detection; the
representative value of thought decreased as
thought grew in scope and elaboration. It became
impossible to be at once quite serious and quite
intelligent; for to use reason was to indulge in
subjective fiction, while conscientiously to abstain
from using it was to sink back upon inarticulate
and brutish instinct.

In Hume this sophistication was frankly
avowed. Philosophy discredited itself; but a man
of parts, who loved intellectual games even better
than backgammon, might take a hand with the

wits and historians of his day, until the clock
struck twelve and the party was over.   Even
in Kant, though the mood was more cramped and
earnest, the mystical sophistication was quite the
same.   Kant, too, imagined that the bottom had
been knocked out of the world; that in comparison
with some unutterable sort of truth empirical
truth was falsehood, and that validity for all possible experience was weak validity, in comparison
with validity of some other and unmentionable
sort.   Since space and time could not repel the
accusation of being the necessary forms of perception, space and time were not to be much thought
of; and when the sad truth was disclosed that
causality and the categories were instruments by
which the idea of nature had to be constructed, if
such an idea was to exist at all, then nature and
causality shrivelled up and were dishonoured
together; so that, the soul's occupation being
gone, she must needs appeal to some mysterious
oracle, some abstract and irrelevant omen within
the breast, and muster up all the stern courage
of an accepted despair to carry her through this
world of mathematical illusion into some green
and infantile paradise beyond.

Misconceived rôle of intelligence.   What idea, we may well ask ourselves, did these modern philosophers
entertain regarding the pretensions of
ancient and mediæval metaphysics?   What understanding had they of the spirit in which the
natural organs of reason had been exercised and

developed in those schools? Frankly, very little; for they accepted from ancient philosophy and from common-sense the distinction between reality and appearance, but they forgot the function of that distinction and dislocated its meaning, which was nothing but to translate the chaos of perception into the regular play of stable natures and objects congenial to discursive thought and valid in the art of living. Philosophy had been the natural science of perception raised to the reflective plane, the objects maintaining themselves on this higher plane being styled realities, and those still floundering below it being called appearances or mere ideas. The function of envisaging reality, ever since Parmenides and Heraclitus, had been universally attributed to the intellect. When the moderns, therefore, proved anew that it was the mind that framed that idea, and that what we call reality, substance, nature, or God, can be reached only by an operation of reason, they made no very novel or damaging discovery.

Of course, it is possible to disregard the suggestions of reason in any particular case and it is quite possible to believe, for instance, that the hypothesis of an external material world is an erroneous one. But that this hypothesis is erroneous does not follow from the fact that it is a hypothesis. To discard it on that ground would be to discard all reasoned knowledge and to deny altogether the validity of thought. If intelligence is assumed to be an organ of cognition and a vehicle for truth, a given

hypothesis about the causes of perception can only
be discarded when a better hypothesis on the same
subject has been supplied. To be better such a
hypothesis would have to meet the multiplicity of
phenomena and their mutations with a more intelligible scheme of comprehension and a more useful
instrument of control.

All criticism   Scepticism is always possible while
dogmatic.   it is partial. It will remain the privilege and resource of a free mind that has elasticity enough to disintegrate its own formations
and to approach its experience from a variety of
sides and with more than a single method. But
the method chosen must be coherent in itself and
the point of view assumed must be adhered to
during that survey; so that whatever reconstruction the novel view may produce in science will
be science still, and will involve assumptions and
dogmas which must challenge comparison with
the dogmas and assumptions they would supplant.
People speak of dogmatism as if it were a method
to be altogether outgrown and something for which
some non-assertive philosophy could furnish a substitute. But dogmatism is merely a matter of
degree. Some thinkers and some systems retreat
further than others into the stratum beneath current conventions and make us more conscious of
the complex machinery which, working silently in
the soul, makes possible all the rapid and facile
operations of reason. The deeper this retrospective glance the less dogmatic the philosophy. A

primordial constitution or tendency, however, must
always remain, having structure and involving a
definite life; for if we thought to reach some
wholly vacant and indeterminate point of origin,
we should have reached something wholly impotent
and indifferent, a blank pregnant with nothing
that we wished to explain or that actual experience presented. When, starting with the inevitable preformation and constitutional bias, we
sought to build up a simpler and nobler edifice of
thought, to be a palace and fortress rather than a
prison for experience, our critical philosophy
would still be dogmatic, since it would be built
upon inexplicable but actual data by a process of
inference underived but inevitable.

A choice of   No doubt Aristotle and the scholas-
hypotheses.   tics were often uncritical. They were
too intent on building up and buttressing their
system on the broad human or religious foundations which they had chosen for it. They nursed
the comfortable conviction that whatever their
thought contained was eternal and objective truth,
a copy of the divine intellect or of the world's intelligible structure. A sceptic may easily deride that
confidence of theirs; their system may have been
their system and nothing more. But the way to
proceed if we wish to turn our shrewd suspicions
and our sense of insecurity into an articulate conviction and to prove that they erred, is to build
another system, a more modest one, perhaps, which
will grow more spontaneously and inevitably in

the mind out of the data of experience. Obviously
the rival and critical theory will make the same
tacit claim as the other to absolute validity. If
all our ideas and perceptions conspire to reinforce
the new hypothesis, this will become inevitable
and necessary to us. We shall then condemn the
other hypothesis, not indeed for having been a
hypothesis, which is the common fate of all
rational and interpretative thought, but for having
been a hypothesis artificial, misleading, and false;
one not following necessarily nor intelligibly out
of the facts, nor leading to a satisfactory reaction
upon them, either in contemplation or in practice.

Critics dis-guised enthu-siasts. Now this is in truth exactly the conviction which those malicious psycholo-
gists secretly harboured. Their critical
scruples and transcendental qualms covered a
robust rebellion against being fooled by authority.
They rose to abate abuses among which, as
Hobbes said, "the frequency of insignificant speech
is one." Their psychology was not merely a
cathartic, but a gospel. Their young criticism was
sent into the world to make straight the path of
a new positivism, as now, in its old age, it is invoked to keep open the door to superstition. Some
of those reformers, like Hobbes and Locke, had at
heart the interests of a physical and political
mechanism, which they wished to substitute for
the cumbrous and irritating constraints of tradition. Their criticism stopped at the frontiers of
their practical discontent; they did not care to ask

how the belief in matter, space, motion, God, or whatever else still retained their allegiance, could withstand the kind of psychology which, as they conceived, had done away with individual essences and nominal powers. Berkeley, whose interests lay in a different quarter, used the same critical method in support of a different dogmatism; armed with the traditional pietistic theory of Providence he undertook with a light heart to demolish the whole edifice which reason and science had built upon spatial perception. He wished the lay intellect to revert to a pious idiocy in the presence of Nature, lest consideration of her history and laws should breed " mathematical atheists "; and the outer world being thus reduced to a sensuous dream and to the blur of immediate feeling, intelligence and practical faith would be more unremittingly employed upon Christian mythology. Men would be bound to it by a necessary allegiance, there being no longer any rival object left for serious or intelligent consideration.

The psychological analysis on which these partial or total negations were founded was in a general way admirable; the necessary artifices to which it had recourse in distinguishing simple and complex ideas, principles of association and inference, were nothing but premonitions of what a physiological psychology would do in referring the mental process to its organic and external supports; for experience has no other divisions than those it creates in itself by distinguishing its objects and its organs. Reference to external conditions, though seldom explicit in these writers, who imagined they could appeal to an introspection not revealing the external world, was pervasive in them; as, for instance, where Hume made his fundamental distinction between impressions and ideas, where the discrimination was based nominally on relative vividness and priority in time, but really on causation respectively by outer objects or by spontaneous processes in the brain.

Hume's gratuitous scepticism. Hume it was who carried this psychological analysis to its goal, giving it greater simplicity and universal scope; and he had also the further advantage of not nursing any metaphysical changeling of his own to substitute for the legitimate offspring of human understanding. His curiosity was purer and his scepticism more impartial, so that he laid bare the natural habits and necessary fictions of thought with singular lucidity, and sufficient accuracy for general purposes. But the malice of a psychology intended as a weapon against superstition here recoils on science itself. Hume, like Berkeley, was extremely young, scarce five-and-twenty, when he wrote his most incisive work; he was not ready to propose in theory that test of ideas by their utility which in practice he and the whole English school have instinctively adopted. An ulterior test of validity would not have seemed to him satisfactory, for though inclined to rebellion and positivism he was still the pupil of that mythical philosophy which attributed the value of things to their origin rather than to their uses, because it had first, in its parabolic way, erected the highest good into a First Cause. Still breathing, in spite of himself, this atmosphere of materialised Platonism, Hume could not discover the true origin of anything without imagining that he had destroyed its value. A natural child meant for him an illegitimate one; his philosophy had not yet reached the wisdom of that French lady who asked if all children were not natural. The outcome of his psychology and criticism seemed accordingly to be an inhibition of reason; he was left free to choose between the distractions of backgammon and "sitting down in a forlorn scepticism."

In his first youth, while disintegrating reflection still overpowered the active interests of his mind, Hume seems to have had some moments of genuine suspense and doubt: but with years and prosperity the normal habits of inference which he had so acutely analysed asserted themselves in his own person and he yielded to the " tendency to feign " so far at least as to believe languidly in the histories he wrote, the compliments he received, and the succulent dinners he devoured. There is a kind of courtesy in scepticism. It would be an offence against polite conventions to press our doubts too far and question the permanence of our estates, our neighbours' independent existence, or even the justification of a good

bishop's faith and income. Against metaphysicians, and even against bishops, sarcasm was not
without its savour; but the line must be drawn
somewhere by a gentleman and a man of the
world. Hume found no obstacle in his speculations to the adoption of all necessary and useful
conceptions in the sphere to which he limited his
mature interests. That he never extended this
liberty to believe into more speculative and comprehensive regions was due simply to a voluntary
superficiality in his thought. Had he been interested in the rationality of things he would have
laboured to discover it, as he laboured to discover
that historical truth or that political utility to
which his interests happened to attach.

Kant's substi-
tute for
knowledge.
Kant, like Berkeley, had a private
mysticism in reserve to raise upon the
ruins of science and common-sense.
Knowledge was to be removed to make way for
faith. This task is ambiguous, and the equivocation involved in it is perhaps the deepest of those
confusions with which German metaphysics has
since struggled, and which have made it waver
between the deepest introspection and the dreari-
est mythology. To substitute faith for knowledge might mean to teach the intellect humility,
to make it aware of its theoretic and transitive
function as a faculty for hypothesis and rational
fiction, building a bridge of methodical inferences
and ideal unities between fact and fact, between
endeavour and satisfaction. It might be to remind

us, sprinkling over us, as it were, the Lenten ashes of an intellectual contrition, that our thoughts are air even as our bodies are dust, momentary vehicles and products of an immortal vitality in God and in nature, which fosters and illumines us for a moment before it lapses into other forms.

Had Kant proposed to humble and concentrate into a practical faith *the same natural ideas* which had previously been taken for absolute knowledge, his intention would have been innocent, his conclusions wise, and his analysis free from venom and *arrière-pensée*. Man, because of his finite and propulsive nature and because he is a pilgrim and a traveller throughout his life, is obliged to have faith: the absent, the hidden, the eventual, is the necessary object of his concern. But what else shall his faith rest in except in what the necessary forms of his perception present to him and what the indispensable categories of his understanding help him to conceive? What possible objects are there for faith except objects of a possible experience? What else should a practical and moral philosophy concern itself with, except the governance and betterment of the real world? It is surely by using his only possible forms of perception and his inevitable categories of understanding that man may yet learn, as he has partly learned already, to live and prosper in the universe. Had Kant's criticism amounted simply to such a confession of the tentative, practical, and hypothetical nature of human reason,

it would have been wholly acceptable to the wise;
and its appeal to faith would have been nothing
but an expression of natural vitality and courage,
just as its criticism of knowledge would have been
nothing but a better acquaintance with self. This
faith would have called the forces of impulse and
passion to reason's support, not to its betrayal.
Faith would have meant faith in the intellect, a
faith naturally expressing man's practical and
ideal nature, and the only faith yet sanctioned by
its fruits.

False
subjectivity
attributed
to reason.
Side by side with this reinstatement
of reason, however, which was not
absent from Kant's system in its critical phase and in its application to science, there
lurked in his substitution of faith for knowledge
another and sinister intention. He wished to
blast as insignificant, because "subjective," the
whole structure of human intelligence, with all the
lessons of experience and all the triumphs of
human skill, and to attach absolute validity
instead to certain echoes of his rigoristic religious
education. These notions were surely just as subjective, and far more local and transitory, than the
common machinery of thought; and it was actually
proclaimed to be an evidence of their sublimity
that they remained entirely without practical sanction in the form of success or of happiness. The
"categorical imperative" was a shadow of the ten
commandments; the postulates of practical reason
were the minimal tenets of the most abstract

Protestantism. These fossils, found unaccountably imbedded in the old man's mind, he regarded as the evidences of an inward but supernatural revelation.

Chimerical reconstruction. Only the quaint severity of Kant's education and character can make intelligible to us the restraint he exercised in making supernatural postulates. All he asserted was his inscrutable moral imperative and a God to reward with the pleasures of the next world those who had been Puritans in this. But the same principle could obviously be applied to other cherished imaginations: there is no superstition which it might not justify in the eyes of men accustomed to see in that superstition the sanction of their morality. For the "practical" proofs of freedom, immortality, and Providence—of which all evidence in reason or experience had previously been denied—exceed in perfunctory sophistry anything that can be imagined. Yet this lamentable epilogue was in truth the guiding thought of the whole investigation. Nature had been proved a figment of human imagination so that, once rid of all but a mock allegiance to her facts and laws, we might be free to invent any world we chose and believe it to be absolutely real and independent of our nature. Strange prepossession, that while part of human life and mind was to be an avenue to reality and to put men in relation to external and eternal things, the whole of human life and mind should not be able to do so! Conceptions

rooted in the very elements of our being, in our
senses, intellect, and imagination, which had
shaped themselves through many generations
under a constant fire of observation and disillusion, these were to be called subjective, not only
in the sense in which all knowledge must obviously be so, since it is knowledge that someone
possesses and has gained, but subjective in a dis-
paraging sense, and in contrast to some better
form of knowledge. But what better form of
knowledge is this? If it be a knowledge of things
as they really are and not as they appear, we must
remember that reality means what the intellect
infers from the data of sense; and yet the principles of such inference, by which the distinction
between appearance and reality is first instituted,
are precisely the principles now to be discarded
as subjective and of merely empirical validity.

"Merely empirical" is a vicious phrase: what is
other than empirical is less than empirical, and
what is not relative to eventual experience is
something given only in present fancy. The gods
of genuine religion, for instance, are terms in a
continual experience: the pure in heart may see
God. If the better and less subjective principle
be said to be the moral law, we must remember
that the moral law which has practical importance
and true dignity deals with facts and forces of
the natural world, that it expresses interests and
aspirations in which man's fate in time and space,
with his pains, pleasures, and all other empirical

feelings, is concerned. This was not the moral
law to which Kant appealed, for this is a part of
the warp and woof of nature. His moral law was
a personal superstition, irrelevant to the impulse
and need of the world. His notions of the supernatural were those of his sect and generation, and
did not pass to his more influential disciples:
what was transmitted was simply the contempt for
sense and understanding and the practice, author-
ised by his modest example, of building air-castles
in the great clearing which the Critique was supposed to have made.

It is noticeable in the series of philosophers
from Hobbes to Kant that as the metaphysical
residuum diminished the critical and psychological machinery increased in volume and value. In
Hobbes and Locke, with the beginnings of empirical psychology, there is mixed an abstract materialism; in Berkeley, with an extension of analytic
criticism, a popular and childlike theology, entirely without rational development; in Hume,
with a completed survey of human habits of ideation, a withdrawal into practical conventions; and
in Kant, with the conception of the creative understanding firmly grasped and elaborately worked
out, a flight from the natural world altogether.
The Critique a   The Critique, in spite of some arti-
work on   ficialities and pedantries in arrange-
mental
architecture.   ment, presented a conception never
before attained of the rich architecture of reason.
It revealed the intricate organisation, comparable

to that of the body, possessed by that fine web of
intentions and counter-intentions whose pulsations
are our thoughts. The dynamic logic of intelligence was laid bare, and the hierarchy of ideas, if
not always correctly traced, was at least manifested in its principle. It was as great an enlarge-
ment of Hume's work as Hume's had been of
Locke's or Locke's of Hobbes's. And the very
fact that the metaphysical residuum practically
disappeared—for the weak reconstruction in the
second Critique may be dismissed as irrelevant
—renders the work essentially valid, essentially a
description of something real. It is therefore a
great source of instruction and a good compendium or store-house for the problems of mind.
But the work has been much overestimated. It
is the product of a confused though laborious
mind. It contains contradictions not merely incidental, such as any great novel work must retain
(since no man can at once remodel his whole
vocabulary and opinions) but contradictions absolutely fundamental and inexcusable, like that
between the transcendental function of intellect
and its limited authority, or that between the
efficacy of things-in-themselves and their un-
knowability. Kant's assumptions and his conclusions, his superstitions and his wisdom, alternate
without neutralising each other.

Incoherences. That experience is a product of two
factors is an assumption made by Kant.
It rests on a psychological analogy, namely on the

fact that organ and stimulus are both necessary to
sensation. That experience is the substance or matter of nature, which is a construction in thought,
is Kant's conclusion, based on intrinsic logical
analysis. Here experience is evidently viewed as
something uncaused and without conditions, being
itself the source and condition of all thinkable
objects. The relation between the transcendental function of experience and its empirical
causes Kant never understood. The transcendentalism which—if we have it at all—must be fundamental, he made derivative; and the realism,
which must then be derivative, he made absolute.
Therefore his metaphysics remained fabulous and
his idealism sceptical or malicious.

Ask what can be meant by " conditions of experience " and Kant's bewildering puzzle solves
itself at the word. Condition, like cause, is a
term that covers a confusion between dialectical
and natural connections. The conditions of experience, in the dialectical sense, are the characteristics a thing must have to deserve the name of
experience; in other words, its conditions are its
nominal essence. If experience be used in a loose
sense to mean any given fact or consciousness in
general, the condition of experience is merely immediacy. If it be used, as it often is in empirical
writers, for the shock of sense, its conditions are
two: a sensitive organ and an object capable of
stimulating it. If finally experience be given its

highest and most pregnant import and mean a fund of knowledge gathered by living, the condition of experience is intelligence. Taking the word in this last sense, Kant showed in a confused but essentially conclusive fashion that only by the application of categories to immediate data could knowledge of an ordered universe arise; or, in other language, that knowledge is a vista, that it has a perspective, since it is the presence to a given thought of a diffused and articulated landscape. The categories are the principles of interpretation by which the flat datum acquires this perspective in thought and becomes representative of a whole system of successive or collateral existences.

The circumstance that experience, in the second sense, is a term reserved for what has certain natural conditions, namely, for the spark flying from the contact of stimulus and organ, led Kant to shift his point of view, and to talk half the time about conditions in the sense of natural causes or needful antecedents. Intelligence is not an antecedent of thought and knowledge but their character and logical energy. Synthesis is not a natural but only a dialectical condition of pregnant experience; it does not introduce such experience but constitutes it. Nevertheless, the whole skeleton and dialectical mould of experience came to figure, in Kant's mythology, as machinery behind the scenes, as a system of non-natural efficient forces, as a partner in a marriage

the issue of which was human thought. The idea
could thus suggest itself—favoured also by remembering inopportunely the actual psychological
situation—that all experience, in every sense of the
word, had supernatural antecedents, and that the
dialectical conditions of experience, in the highest
sense, were efficient conditions of experience in
the lowest.

It is hardly necessary to observe that absolute
experience can have no natural conditions. Existence in the abstract can have no cause; for
every real condition would have to be a factor in
absolute experience, and every cause would be
something existent. Of course there is a modest
and non-exhaustive experience—that is, any particular sensation, thought, or life—which it would
be preposterous to deny was subject to natural
conditions. Saint Lawrence's experience of being
roasted, for instance, had conditions; some of
them were the fire, the decree of the court, and his
own stalwart Christianity. But these conditions
are other parts or objects of conceivable experience which, as we have learned, fall into a system
with the part we say they condition. In our grop-
ing and inferential thought one part
Nature the may become a ground for expecting or
true system supposing the other. Nature is then
of conditions. the sum total of its own conditions; the whole
object, the parts observed *plus* the parts interpolated, is the self-existent fact. The mind, in its
empirical flux, is a part of this complex; to say it

is its own condition or that of the other objects
is a grotesque falsehood. A babe's casual sensation of light is a condition neither of his own
existence nor of his mother's. The true conditions are those other parts of the world without
which, as we find by experience, sensations of
light do not appear.

Had Kant been trained in a better school of philosophy he might have felt that the phrase "subjective conditions " is a controdiction in terms. When
we find ourselves compelled to go behind the actual
and imagine something antecedent or latent to
pave the way for it, we are *ipso facto* conceiving
the potential, that is, the " objective " world. All
antecedents, by transcendental necessity, are therefore objective and all conditions natural. An
imagined potentiality that holds together the episodes which are actual in consciousness is the very
definition of an object or thing. Nature is the
sum total of things potentially observable, some
observed actually, others interpolated hypotheti-
cally; and common-sense is right as against Kant's
subjectivism in regarding nature as the condition
of mind and not mind as the condition of nature.
This is not to say that experience and feeling are
not the only given existence, from which the material part of nature, something essentially dynamic
and potential, must be intelligently inferred. But
are not " conditions " inferred? Are they not, in
their deepest essence, potentialities and powers?
Kant's fabled conditions also are inferred; but

they are inferred illegitimately since the "subjective" ones are dialectical characters turned into
antecedents, while the thing-in-itself is a natural
object without a natural function. Experience
alone being given, it is the ground from which its
conditions are inferred: its conditions, therefore,
are empirical. The secondary position of nature
goes with the secondary position of all causes,
objects, conditions, and ideals. To have made the
conditions of experience metaphysical, and prior
in the order of knowledge to experience itself, was
simply a piece of surviving Platonism. The form
was hypostasised into an agent, and mythical
machinery was imagined to impress that form on
whatever happened to have it.

All this was opposed to Kant's own discovery
and to his critical doctrine which showed that the
world (which is the complex of those conditions
which experience assigns to itself as it develops
and progresses in knowledge) is not before experience in the order of knowledge, but after it. His
fundamental oversight and contradiction lay in
not seeing that the concept of a set of conditions
was the precise and exact concept of nature, which
he consequently reduplicated, having one nature
before experience and another after. The first
thus became mythical and the second illusory: for
the first, said to condition experience, was a set
of verbal ghosts, while the second, which alone
could be observed or discovered scientifically, was
declared fictitious. The truth is that the single

nature or set of conditions for experience which the intellect constructs is the object of our thoughts and perceptions ideally completed. This is neither mythical nor illusory. It is, strictly speaking, in its system and in many of its parts, hypothetical; but the hypothesis is absolutely safe. At whatever point we test it, we find the experience we expect, and the inferences thence made by the intellect are verified in sense at every moment of existence.

Artificial pathos in subjectivism. The ambiguity in Kant's doctrine makes him a confusing representative of that criticism of perception which malicious psychology has to offer. When the mind has made its great discovery; when it has recognised independent objects, and thus taken a first step in its rational life, we need to know unequivocally whether this step is a false or a true one. If it be false, reason is itself misleading, since a hypothesis indispensable in the intellectual mastery of experience is a false hypothesis and the detail of experience has no substructure. Now Kant's answer was that the discovery of objects was a true and valid discovery in the field of experience; there were, scientifically speaking, causes for perception which could be inferred from perception by thought. But this inference was not true absolutely or metaphysically because there was a real world beyond possible experience, and there were oracles, not intellectual, by which knowledge of that unrealisable world might be obtained. This mysticism undid the intellectualism which characterised Kant's system in its scientific and empirical application; so that the justification for the use of such categories as that of cause and substance (categories by which the idea of reality is constituted) was invalidated by the counter-assertion that empirical reality was not true reality but, being an object reached by inferential thought, was merely an idea. Nor was the true reality appearance itself in its crude immediacy, as sceptics would think; it was a realm of objects present to a supposed intuitive thought, that is, to a non-inferential inference or non-discursive discourse.

So that while Kant insisted on the point, which hardly needed pressing, that it is mind that discovers empirical reality by making inferences from the data of sense, he admitted at the same time that such use of understanding is legitimate and even necessary, and that the idea of nature so framed his empirical truth. There remained, however, a sense that this empirical truth was somehow insufficient and illusory. Understanding was a superficial faculty, and we might by other and oracular methods arrive at a reality that was not empirical. Why any reality—such as God, for instance—should not be just as empirical as the other side of the moon, if experience suggested it and reason discovered it, or why, if not suggested by experience and discovered by reason, anything should be called a reality at all or should hold for a moment a man's waking attention—that is what Kant never tells us and never himself knew.

Clearer upon this question of perception is the position of Berkeley; we may therefore take him as a fair representative of those critics who seek to invalidate the discovery of material objects.

Our ideas, said Berkeley, were in our minds; the material world was patched together out of our ideas; it therefore existed only in our minds. To the suggestion that the idea of the external world is of course in our minds, but that our minds have constructed it by treating sensations as effects of a permanent substance distributed in a permanent space, he would reply that this means nothing, bcause " substance," " permanence," and " space " are non-existent ideas, *i.e.*, they are not images in sense. They might, however, be " notions " like that of " spirit," which Berkeley ingenuously admitted into his system, to be, mysteriously enough, *that which has* ideas. Or they might be (what would do just as well for our purpose) that which he elsewhere called them, algebraic signs used to facilitate the operations of thought. This is, indeed, what they are, if we take the word algebraic in a loose enough sense. They are like algebraic signs in being, in respect of their object or signification, not concrete images but terms in a mental process, elements in a method of inference. Why, then, denounce them? They could be used

Berkeley's algebra of perception.

with all confidence to lead us back to the concrete
values for which they stood and to the relations
which they enabled us to state and discover. Experience would thus be furnished with an intelligible structure and articulation, and a psychological analysis would be made of knowledge into
its sensuous material and its ideal objects. What,
then, was Berkeley's objection to these algebraic
methods of inference and to the notions of space,
matter, independent existence, and efficient causality which these methods involve?

Horror of physics. What he abhorred was the belief
that such methods of interpreting experience were ultimate and truly valid, and that
by thinking after the fashion of "mathematical
atheists" we could understand experience as well
as it can be understood. If the flux of ideas had
no other key to it than that system of associations
and algebraic substitutions which is called the
natural world we should indeed know just as well
what to expect in practice and should receive the
same education in perception and reflection; but
what difference would there be between such an
idealist and the most pestilential materialist, save
his even greater wariness and scepticism? Berkeley at this time—long before days of "Siris" and
tar-water—was too ignorant and hasty to understand how inane all spiritual or poetic ideals would
be did they not express man's tragic dependence
on nature and his congruous development in her
bosom. He lived in an age when the study and

dominion of external things no longer served directly spiritual uses. The middle-men had appeared, those spirits in whom the pursuit of the true and the practical never leads to possession of the good, but loses itself, like a river in sand, amid irrational habits and passions. He was accordingly repelled by whatever philosophy was in him, no less than by his religious prejudices, from submergence in external interests, and he could see no better way of vindicating the supremacy of moral goods than to deny the reality of matter, the finality of science, and the constructive powers of reason altogether. With honest English empiricism he saw that science had nothing absolute or sacrosanct about it, and rightly placed the value of theory in its humane uses; but the complementary truth escaped him altogether that only the free and contemplative expression of reason, of which science is a chief part, can render anything else humane, useful, or practical. He was accordingly a party man in philosophy, where partisanship is treason, and opposed the work of reason in the theoretical field, hoping thus to advance it in the moral.

Of the moral field he had, it need hardly be added, a quite childish and perfunctory conception. There the prayer-book and the catechism could solve every problem. He lacked the feeling, possessed by all large and mature minds, that there would be no intelligibility or value in things divine were they not inter-

Puerility in morals.

pretations and sublimations of things natural.
To master the real world was an ancient and not
too promising ambition: it suited his youthful
radicalism better to exorcise or to cajole it. He
sought to refresh the world with a water-spout of
idealism, as if to change the names of things could
change their values. Away with all arid investigation, away with the cold algebra of sense and
reason, and let us have instead a direct conversation with heaven, an unclouded vision of the purposes and goodness of God; as if there were any
other way of understanding the sources of human
happiness than to study the ways of nature and
man.

Converse with God has been the life of many
a wiser and sadder philosopher than Berkeley;
but they, like Plato, for instance, or Spinoza,
have made experience the subject as well as
the language of that intercourse, and have thus
given the divine revelation some degree of pertinence and articulation. Berkeley in his positive
doctrine was satisfied with the vaguest generalities; he made no effort to find out how the consciousness that God is the direct author of our
incidental perceptions is to help us to deal with
them; what other insights and principles are to be
substituted for those that disclose the economy of
nature; how the moral difficulties incident to an
absolute providentialism are to be met, or how the
existence and influence of fellow-minds is to be
defended. So that to a piety inspired by con-

ventional theology and a psychology that refused
to pass, except grudgingly and unintelligently,
beyond the sensuous stratum, Berkeley had nothing to add by way of philosophy. An insignificant repetition of the truism that ideas are all
" in the mind " constituted his total wisdom. To
be was to be perceived. That was the great maxim
by virtue of which we were asked, if not to refrain
from conceiving nature at all, which was perhaps
impossible at so late a stage in human development, at least to refrain from regarding our necessary thoughts on nature as true or rational. Intelligence was but a false method of imagination
by which God trained us in action and thought;
for it was apparently impossible to endow us with
a true method that would serve that end. And
what shall we think of the critical acumen or practical wisdom of a philosopher who dreamed of
some other criterion of truth than necessary implication in thought and action?

Truism and   In the melodramatic fashion so com-
sophism.   mon in what is called philosophy we
may delight ourselves with such flashes of lightning as this: *esse est percipi*. The truth of this
paradox lies in the fact that through perception
alone can we get at being—a modest and familiar
notion which makes, as Plato's " Theætetus" shows,
not a bad point of departure for a serious theory of
knowledge. The sophistical intent of it, however,
is to deny our right to make a distinction which
in fact we do make and which the speaker him-

self is making as he utters the phrase; for he would not be so proud of himself if he thought he was thundering a tautology. If a thing were never perceived, or inferred from perception, we should indeed never know that it existed; but once perceived or inferred it may be more conducive to comprehension and practical competence to regard it as existing independently of our perception; and our ability to make this supposition is registered in the difference between the two words *to be* and *to be perceived*—words which are by no means synonymous but designate two very different relations of things in thought. Such idealism at one fell swoop, through a collapse of assertive intellect and a withdrawal of reason into self-consciousness, has the puzzling character of any clever pun, that suspends the fancy between two incompatible but irresistible meanings. The art of such sophistry is to choose for an axiom some ambiguous phrase which taken in one sense is a truism and taken in another is an absurdity; and then, by showing the truth of that truism, to give out that the absurdity has also been proved. It is a truism to say that I am the only seat or locus of my ideas, and that whatever I know is known by me; it is an absurdity to say that I am the only object of my thought and perception.

Reality is the practical made intelligible. To confuse the instrument with its function and the operation with its meaning has been a persistent foible in modern philosophy. It could thus come about that the function of intelligence should be altogether misconceived and in consequence denied, when it was discovered that figments of reason could never become elements of sense but must always remain, as of course they should, ideal and regulative objects, and therefore objects to which a practical and energetic intellect will tend to give the name of realities. Matter is a reality to the practical intellect because it is a necessary and ideal term in the mastery of experience; while negligible sensations, like dreams, are called illusions by the same authority because, though actual enough while they last, they have no sustained function and no right to practical dominion.

Let us imagine Berkeley addressing himself to that infant or animal consciousness which first used the category of substance and passed from its perceptions to the notion of an independent thing. "Beware, my child," he would have said, "you are taking a dangerous step, one which may hereafter produce a multitude of mathematical atheists, not to speak of cloisterfuls of scholastic triflers. Your ideas can exist only in your mind; if you suffer yourself to imagine them materialised in mid-air and subsisting when you do not perceive them, you will commit a great impiety. If you unthinkingly believe that when you shut your eyes the world continues to exist until you open them again, you will inevitably be hurried into an infinity of metaphysical quibbles about the discrete and the continuous, and you will be so bewildered and deafened by perpetual controversies that the clear light of the gospel will be extinguished in your soul." "But," that tender Peripatetic might answer, "I cannot forget the things about me when I shut my eyes: I know and almost feel their persistent presence, and I always find them again, upon trial, just as they were before, or just in that condition to which the operation of natural causes would have brought them in my absence. If I believe they remain and suffer steady and imperceptible transformation, I know what to expect, and the event does not deceive me; but if I had to resolve upon action before knowing whether the conditions for action were to exist or no, I should never understand what sort of a world I lived in."

"Ah, my child," the good Bishop would reply, "you misunderstand me. You may indeed, nay, you must, live and think *as if* everything remained independently real. That is part of your education for heaven, which God in his goodness provides for you in this life. He will send into your soul at every moment the impressions needed to verify your necessary hypotheses and support your humble and prudent expectations. Only you must not attribute that constancy to the things themselves which is due to steadfastness in the designs of Providence. *Think and act* as if a material world existed, but do not for a moment *believe* it to exist."

Vain "reali-
ties" and
trustworthy
"fictions." With this advice, coming reassuringly from the combined forces of scepticism and religion, we may leave the embryonic mind to its own devices, satisfied that even according to the most malicious psychologists its first step toward the comprehension of experience is one it may congratulate itself on having taken and which, for the present at least, it is not called upon to retrace. The Life of Reason is not concerned with speculation about unthinkable and gratuitous "realities"; it seeks merely to attain those conceptions which are necessary and appropriate to man in his acting and thinking. The first among these, underlying all arts and philosophies alike, is the indispensable conception of permanent external objects, forming in their congeries, shifts, and secret animation the system and life of nature.

NOTE—There is a larger question raised by Berkeley's arguments which I have not attempted to discuss here, namely, whether knowledge is possible at all, and whether any mental representation can be supposed to inform us about anything. Berkeley of course assumed this power in that he continued to believe in God, in other spirits, in the continuity of experience, and in its discoverable laws. His objection to material objects, therefore, could not consistently be that they are objects of knowledge rather than absolute feelings, exhausted by their momentary possession in consciousness. It could only be that they are unthinkable and invalid objects, in which the materials of sense are given a mode of existence inconsistent with their nature. But if the only criticism to which material objects were obnoxious were a dialectical criticism, such as that contained in Kant's antinomies, the royal road to idealism coveted by

Berkeley would be blocked; to be an idea in the mind
would not involve lack of cognitive and representative value
in that idea.   The fact that material objects were represented
or conceived would not of itself prove that they could not
have a real existence.   It would be necessary, to prove their
unreality, to study their nature and function and to compare
them with such conceptions as those of Providence and a
spirit-world in order to determine their relative validity.
Such a critical comparison would have augured ill for
Berkeley's prejudices ; what its result might have been we
can see in Kant's Critique of Pure Reason.   In order to
escape such evil omens and prevent the collapse of his
mystical paradoxes, Berkeley keeps in reserve a much
more insidious weapon, the sceptical doubt as to the representative character of anything mental, the possible illusive-
ness of all knowledge.   This doubt he invokes in all those
turns of thought and phrase in which he suggests that if an idea
is in the mind it cannot have its counterpart elsewhere, and
that a given cognition exhausts and contains its object.
There are, then, two separate maxims in his philosophy, one
held consistently, viz., that nothing can be known which is
different in character or nature from the object present to
the thinking mind; the other, held incidentally and incon-
sistently, since it is destructive of all predication and knowledge, viz., that nothing can exist beyond the mind which is
similar in nature or character to the " ideas " within it; or,
to put the same thing in other words, that nothing can be revealed by an idea which is different from that idea in point
of existence.   The first maxim does not contradict the existence of external objects in space; the second contradicts
every conception that the human mind can ever form, the
most airy no less than the grossest.   No idealist can go so
far as to deny that his memory represents his past experience
by inward similarity and conscious intention, or, if he pre-
fers this language, that the moments or aspects of the divine
mind represent one another and their general system.   Else
the idealist's philosophy itself would be an insignificant and
momentary illusion.

CHAPTER V

NATURE UNIFIED AND MIND DISCERNED

Man's feeble grasp of nature. When the mind has learned to distinguish external objects and to attribute to them a constant size, shape, and potency, in spite of the variety and intermittence ruling in direct experience, there yet remains a great work to do before attaining a clear, even if superficial, view of the world. An animal's customary habitat may have constant features and their relations in space may be learned by continuous exploration; but probably many other landscapes are also within the range of memory and fancy that stand in no visible relation to the place in which we find ourselves at a given moment. It is true that, at this day, we take it for granted that all real places, as we call them, lie in one space, in which they hold definite geometric relations to one another; and if we have glimpses of any region for which no room can be found in the single map of the universe which astronomy has drawn, we unhesitatingly relegate that region to the land of dreams. Since the Elysian Fields and the Coast of Bohemia have no assignable latitude and longitude, we call these

118

places imaginary, even if in some dream we remember to have visited them and dwelt there with no less sense of reality than in this single and geometrical world of commerce. It belongs to sanity and common-sense, as men now possess them, to admit no countries unknown to geography and filling no part of the conventional space in three dimensions. All our waking experience is understood to go on in some part of this space, and no court of law would admit evidence relating to events in some other sphere.

This principle, axiomatic as it has become, is in no way primitive, since primitive experience is sporadic and introduces us to detached scenes separated by lapses in our senses and attention. These scenes do not hang together in any local contiguity. To construct a chart of the world is a difficult feat of synthetic imagination, not to be performed without speculative boldness and a heroic insensibility to the claims of fancy. Even now most people live without topographical ideas and have no clear conception of the spatial relations that keep together the world in which they move. They feel their daily way about like animals, following a habitual scent, without dominating the range of their instinctive wanderings. Reality is rather a story to them than a system of objects and forces, nor would they think themselves mad if at any time their experience should wander into a fourth dimension. Vague dramatic and moral laws, when they find any casual ap-

plication, seem to such dreaming minds more
notable truths, deeper revelations of efficacious
reality, than the mechanical necessities of the case,
which they scarcely conceive of; and in this primordial prejudice they are confirmed by superstitious affinities often surviving in their religion
and philosophy. In the midst of cities and affairs
they are like landsmen at sea, incapable of an intellectual conception of their position: nor have
they any complete confidence in their principles
of navigation. They know the logarithms by rote
merely, and if they reflect are reduced to a stupid
wonder and only half believe they are in a known
universe or will ever reach an earthly port. It
would not require superhuman eloquence in some
prophetic passenger to persuade them to throw
compass and quadrant overboard and steer enthu-
siastically for El Dorado. The theory of navigation is essentially as speculative as that of salvation, only it has survived more experiences of the
judgment and repeatedly brought those who trust
in it to their promised land.

Its unity ideal   The theory that all real objects and
and discover-   places lie together in one even and
able only by
steady   homogeneous space, conceived as simi-
thought.   lar in its constitution to the parts of
extension of which we have immediate intuition, is
a theory of the greatest practical importance and
validity. By its light we carry on all our affairs,
and the success of our action while we rely upon it
is the best proof of its truth. The imaginative

parsimony and discipline which such a theory involves are balanced by the immense extension and certitude it gives to knowledge. It is at once an act of allegiance to nature and a Magna Charta which mind imposes on the tyrannous world, which in turn pledges itself before the assembled faculties of man not to exceed its constitutional privilege and to harbour no magic monsters in unattainable lairs from which they might issue to disturb human labours. Yet that spontaneous intelligence which first enabled men to make this genial discovery and take so fundamental a step toward taming experience should not be laid by after this first victory; it is a weapon needed in many subsequent conflicts. To conceive that all nature makes one system is only a beginning: the articulation of natural life has still to be discovered in detail and, what is more, a similar articulation has to be given to the psychic world which now, by the very act that constitutes Nature and makes her consistent, appears at her side or rather in her bosom.

That the unification of nature is eventual and theoretical is a point useful to remember: else the relation of the natural world to poetry, metaphysics, and religion will never become intelligible. Lalande, or whoever it was, who searched the heavens with his telescope and could find no God, would not have found the human mind if he had searched the brain with a microscope. Yet God existed in man's apprehension long before mathe-

matics or even, perhaps, before the vault of
heaven; for the objectification of the whole mind,
with its passions and motives, naturally precedes
that abstraction by which the idea of a material
world is drawn from the chaos of experience, an
abstraction which culminates in such atomic and
astronomical theories as science is now familiar
with. The sense for life in things, be they small
or great, is not derived from the abstract idea of
their bodies but is an ancient concomitant to that
idea, inseparable from it until it became abstract.
Truth and materiality, mechanism and ideal interests, are collateral projections from one rolling
experience, which shows up one aspect or the other
as it develops various functions and dominates
itself to various ends. When one ore is abstracted
and purified, the residuum subsists in that primeval quarry in which it originally lay. The failure
to find God among the stars, or even the attempt
to find him there, does not indicate that human
experience affords no avenue to the idea of God—
for history proves the contrary—but indicates
rather the atrophy in this particular man of the
imaginative faculty by which his race had attained
to that idea. Such an atrophy might indeed
become general, and God would in that case disappear from human experience as music would disappear if universal deafness attacked the race.
Such an event is made conceivable by the loss of
allied imaginative habits, which is observable in
historic times. Yet possible variations in human

faculty do not involve the illegitimacy of such faculties as actually subsist; and the abstract world known to science, unless it dries up the ancient fountains of ideation by its habitual presence in thought, does not remove those parallel dramatisations or abstractions which experience may have suggested to men.

What enables men to perceive the unity of nature is the unification of their own wills. A man half-asleep, without fixed purposes, without intellectual keenness or joy in recognition, might graze about like an animal, forgetting each satisfaction in the next and banishing from his frivolous mind the memory of every sorrow; what had just failed to kill him would leave him as thoughtless and unconcerned as if it had never crossed his path. Such irrational elasticity and innocent improvidence would never put two and two together. Every morning there would be a new world with the same fool to live in it. But let some sobering passion, some serious interest, lend perspective to the mind, and a point of reference will immediately be given for protracted observation; then the laws of nature will begin to dawn upon thought. Every experiment will become a lesson, every event will be remembered as favourable or unfavourable to the master-passion. At first, indeed, this keen observation will probably be animistic and the laws discovered will be chiefly habits, human or divine, special favours or envious punishments and warnings. But the same

constancy of aim which discovers the dramatic conflicts composing society, and tries to read nature
in terms of passion, will, if it be long sustained,
discover behind this glorious chaos a deeper
mechanical order.   Men's thoughts, like the
weather, are not so arbitrary as they seem and the
true master in observation, the man guided by a
steadfast and superior purpose, will see them re-
volving about their centres in obedience to quite
calculable instincts, and the principle of all their
flutterings will not be hidden from his eyes.
Belief in indeterminism is a sign of indetermina-
tion.   No commanding or steady intellect flirts
with so miserable a possibility, which in so far as
it actually prevailed would make virtue impotent
and experience, in its pregnant sense, impossible.

Mind the erratic residue of existence.   We have said that those objects
which cannot be incorporated into the
one space which the understanding
envisages are relegated to another sphere called
imagination.   We reach here a most important
corollary.   As material objects, making a single
system which fills space and evolves in time, are
conceived by abstraction from the flux of sensuous
experience, so, *pari passu,* the rest of experience,
with all its other outgrowths and concretions, falls
out with the physical world and forms the sphere
of mind, the sphere of memory, fancy, and the
passions.   We have in this discrimination the
genesis of mind, not of course in the transcendental sense in which the word mind is extended to

mean the sum total and mere fact of existence—
for mind, so taken, can have no origin and indeed
no specific meaning—but the genesis of mind as
a determinate form of being, a distinguishable part
of the universe known to experience and discourse,
the mind that unravels itself in meditation, inhabits animal bodies, and is studied in psychology.

Mind, in this proper sense of the word, is the
residue of existence, the leavings, so to speak,
and parings of experience when the material world
has been cut out of the whole cloth. Reflection
underlines in the chaotic continuum of sense and
longing those aspects that have practical significance; it selects the efficacious ingredients in the
world. The trustworthy object which is thus retained in thought, the complex of connected
events, is nature, and though so intelligible an
object is not soon nor vulgarly recognised, because
human reflection is perturbed and halting, yet every
forward step in scientific and practical knowledge
is a step toward its clearer definition. At first
much parasitic matter clings to that dynamic
skeleton. Nature is drawn like a sponge heavy
and dripping from the waters of sentience. It is
soaked with inefficacious passions and overlaid
with idle accretions. Nature, in a word, is at first
conceived mythically, dramatically, and retains
much of the unintelligible, sporadic habit of animal experience itself. But as attention awakes
and discrimination, practically inspired, grows
firm and stable, irrelevant qualities are stripped

off, and the mechanical process, the efficacious infallible order, is clearly disclosed beneath. Meantime the incidental effects, the " secondary qualities," are relegated to a personal inconsequential
region; they constitute the realm of appearance,
the realm of mind.

Ghostly character of mind.
Mind is therefore sometimes identified with the unreal. We oppose, in
an antithesis natural to thought and language, the
imaginary to the true, fancy to fact, idea to thing.
But this thing, fact, or external reality is, as we
have seen, a completion and hypostasis of certain
portions of experience, packed into such shapes as
prove cogent in thought and practice. The stuff
of external reality, the matter out of which its idea
is made, is therefore continuous with the stuff and
matter of our own minds. Their common substance is the immediate flux. This living worm
has propagated by fission, and the two halves into
which it has divided its life are mind and nature.
Mind has kept and clarified the crude appearance,
the dream, the purpose that seethed in the mass;
nature has appropriated the order, the constant
conditions, the causal substructure, disclosed in
reflection, by which the immediate flux is explained and controlled. The chemistry of
thought has precipitated these contrasted terms,
each maintaining a recognisable identity and having the function of a point of reference for
memory and will. Some of these terms or objects
of thought we call things and marshal in all their

ideal stability—for there is constancy in their
motions and transformations—to make the intelligible external world of practice and science.
Whatever stuff has not been absorbed in this construction, whatever facts of sensation, ideation, or
will, do not coalesce with the newest conception
of reality, we then call the mind.

Raw experience, then, lies at the basis of the
idea of nature and approves its reality; while an
equal reality belongs to the residue of experience,
not taken up, as yet, into that idea. But this residual sensuous reality often seems comparatively
unreal because what it presents is entirely without
practical force apart from its mechanical associates. This inconsequential character of what
remains over follows of itself from the concretion
of whatever is constant and efficacious into the
external world. If this fact is ever called in question, it is only because the external world is
vaguely conceived, and loose wills and ideas are
thought to govern it by magic. Yet in many ways
falling short of absolute precision people recognise
that thought is not dynamic or, as they call it,
not real. The idea of the physical world is the
first flower or thick cream of practical thinking.
Being skimmed off first and proving so nutri-
cious, it leaves the liquid below somewhat thin and
unsavoury. Especially does this result appear
when science is still unpruned and mythical, so
that what passes into the idea of material nature
is much more than the truly causal network of

forces, and includes many spiritual and moral functions.

The material world, as conceived in the first instance, had not that clear abstractness, nor the spiritual world that wealth and interest, which they have acquired for modern minds. The complex reactions of man's soul had been objectified together with those visual and tactile sensations which, reduced to a mathematical baldness, now furnish terms to natural science. Mind then dwelt in the world, not only in the warmth and beauty with which it literally clothed material objects, as it still does in poetic perception, but in a literal animistic way; for human passion and reflection were attributed to every object and made a fairy-land of the world. Poetry and religion discerned life in those very places in which sense and understanding perceived body; and when so much of the burden of experience took wing into space, and the soul herself floated almost visibly among the forms of nature, it is no marvel that the poor remnant, a mass of merely personal troubles, an uninteresting distortion of things in individual minds, should have seemed a sad and unsubstantial accident. The inner world was all the more ghostly because the outer world was so much alive.

Hypostasis and criticism both need control. This movement of thought, which clothed external objects in all the wealth of undeciphered dreams, has long lost its momentum and yielded to a contrary tendency. Just as the hypostasis of some terms in experience is sanctioned by reason, when the objects so fixed and externalised can serve as causes and explanations for the order of events, so the criticism which tends to retract that hypostasis is sanctioned by reason when the hypostasis has exceeded its function and the external object conceived is loaded with useless ornament. The transcendental and functional secret of such hypostases, however, is seldom appreciated by the headlong mind; so that the ebb no less than the flow of objectification goes on blindly and impulsively, and is carried to absurd extremes. An age of mythology yields to an age of subjectivity; reason being equally neglected and exceeded in both. The reaction against imagination has left the external world, as represented in many minds, stark and bare. All the interesting and vital qualities which matter had once been endowed with have been attributed instead to an irresponsible sensibility in man. And as habits of ideation change slowly and yield only piecemeal to criticism or to fresh intuitions, such a revolution has not been carried out consistently, but instead of a thorough renaming of things and a new organisation of thought it has produced chiefly distress and confusion. Some phases of this confusion may perhaps repay a moment's attention; they may enable us, when seen in their logical sequence, to understand somewhat better the hypostasising intellect that is trying to assert itself and come to the light through all these gropings.

Comparative constancy in objects and in ideas.   What helps in the first place to disclose a permanent object is a permanent sensation. There is a vast and clear difference between a floating and a fixed feeling; the latter, in normal circumstances, is present only when continuous stimulation renews it at every moment. Attention may wander, but the objects in the environment do not cease to radiate their influences on the body, which is thereby not allowed to lose the modification which those influences provoke. The consequent perception is therefore always at hand and in its repetitions substantially identical. Perceptions not renewed in this way by continuous stimulation come and go with cerebral currents; they are rare visitors, instead of being, like external objects, members of the household. Intelligence is most at home in the ultimate, which is the object of intent. Those realities which it can trust and continually recover are its familiar and beloved companions. The mists that may originally have divided it from them, and which psychologists call the mind, are gladly forgotten so soon as intelligence avails to pierce them, and as friendly communication can be established with the real world. Moreover, perceptions not sustained by a constant external stimulus are apt to be greatly changed when they reappear, and to be changed unaccountably, whereas external things show some method and proportion in their variations. Even when not much changed in themselves, mere ideas fall into a new setting, whereas things, unless something else has intervened to move them, reappear in their old places. Finally things are acted upon by other men, but thoughts are hidden from them by divine miracle.

Existence reveals reality when the flux discloses something permanent that dominates it. What is thus dominated, though it is the primary existence itself, is thereby degraded to appearance. Perceptions caused by external objects are, as we have just seen, long sustained in comparison with thoughts and fancies; but the objects are themselves in flux and a man's relation to them may be even more variable; so that very often a memory or a sentiment will recur, almost unchanged in character, long after the perception that first aroused it has become impossible. The brain, though mobile, is subject to habit; its formations, while they lapse instantly, return again and again. These ideal objects may accordingly be in a way more real and enduring than things external. Hence no primitive mind puts all reality, or what is most real in reality, in an abstract material universe. It finds, rather, ideal points of reference by which material mutation itself seems to be controlled. An ideal world is recognised from the beginning and placed, not in the immediate foreground, nearer than material things, but much farther off. It has greater substantiality and independence than material objects are credited with. It is divine.

When agriculture, commerce, or manual crafts have given men some knowledge of nature, the world thus recognised and dominated is far from seeming ultimate. It is thought to lie between two others, both now often called mental, but in their original quality altogether disparate: the world of spiritual forces and that of sensuous appearance. The notions of permanence and independence by which material objects are conceived apply also, of course, to everything spiritual; and while the dominion exercised by spirits may be somewhat precarious, they are as remote as possible from immediacy and sensation. They come and go; they govern nature or, if they neglect to do so, it is from aversion or high indifference; they visit man with obsessions and diseases; they hasten to extricate him from difficulties; and they dwell in him, constituting his powers of conscience and invention. Sense, on the other hand, is a mere effect, either of body or spirit or of both in conjunction. It gives a vitiated personal view of these realities. Its pleasures are dangerous and unintelligent, and it perishes as it goes.

Spirit and sense defined by their relation to nature. Such are, for primitive apperception, the three great realms of being: nature, sense, and spirit. Their frontiers, however, always remain uncertain. Sense, because it is insignificant when made an object, is long neglected by reflection. No attempt is made to describe its processes or ally them systematically to natural changes. Its illusions, when noticed, are regarded as scandals calculated to foster scepticism. The spiritual world is, on the other hand, a constant theme for poetry and speculation. In the absence of ideal science, it can be conceived only in myths, which are naturally as shifting and self-contradictory as they are persistent. They acquire no fixed character until, in dogmatic religion, they are defined with reference to natural events, foretold or reported. Nature is what first acquires a form and then imparts form to the other spheres. Sense admits definition and distribution only as an effect of nature and spirit only as its principle.

Vague notions of nature involve vague notions of spirit. The form nature acquires is, however, itself vague and uncertain and can ill serve, for long ages, to define the other realms which depend on it for definition. Hence it has been common, for instance, to treat the spiritual as a remote or finer form of the natural. Beyond the moon everything seemed permanent; it was therefore called divine and declared to preside over the rest. The breath that escaped from the lips at death, since it took away with it the spiritual control and miraculous life that had quickened the flesh, was itself the spirit. On the other hand, natural processes have been persistently attributed to spiritual causes, for it was not matter that moved itself but intent that moved it. Thus spirit was barbarously taken for a natural substance and a natural force. It was identified with everything in which it was manifested, so long as no natural causes could be assigned for that operation.

Sense and spirit the life of nature, which science redistributes but does not deny. If the unification of nature were complete sense would evidently fall within it; since it is to subtend and sustain the sensible flux that intelligence acknowledges first stray material objects and then their general system. The elements of experience not taken up into the constitution of objects remain attached to them as their life. In the end the dynamic skeleton, without losing its articulation, would be clothed again with its flesh. Suppose my notions of astronomy allowed me to believe that the sun, sinking into the sea, was extinguished every evening, and that what appeared the next morning was his younger brother, hatched in a sun-producing nest to be found in the Eastern regions. My theory would have robbed yesterday's sun of its life and brightness; it would have asserted that during the night no sun existed anywhere; but it would have added the sun's qualities afresh to a matter that did not previously possess them, namely, to the imagined egg that would produce a sun for tomorrow. Suppose we substitute for that astronomy the one that now prevails: we have deprived the single sun—which now exists and spreads its influences without interruption—of its humanity and even of its metaphysical unity. It has become a congeries of chemical substances. The facts revealed to perception have partly changed their locus and been differently deployed throughout nature. Some have become attached to operations in the human brain. Nature has not thereby lost any quality she had ever manifested; these have merely been redistributed so as to secure a more systematic connection between them all. They are the materials of the system, which has been conceived by making existences continuous, whenever this extension of their being was needful to render their recurrences intelligible. Sense, which was formerly regarded as a sad distortion of its objects, now becomes an original and congruent part of nature, from which, as from any other part, the rest of nature might be scientifically inferred.

Spirit is not less closely attached to nature, although in a different manner. Taken existentially it is a part of sense; taken ideally it is the form or value which nature acquires when viewed from the vantage-ground of any interest. Individual objects are recognisable for a time not because the flux is materially arrested but because it somewhere circulates in a fashion which awakens an interest and brings different parts of the surrounding process into definable and prolonged relations with that interest. Particular objects may perish yet others may continue, like the series of suns imagined by Heraclitus, to perform the same office. The function will outlast the particular organ. That interest in reference to which the

function is defined will essentially determine a
perfect world of responsive extensions and conditions.   These ideals will be a spiritual reality;
and they will be expressed in nature in so far as
nature supports that regulative interest.   Many a
perfect and eternal realm, merely potential in existence but definite in constitution, will thus subtend nature and be what a rational philosophy
might call the ideal.   What is called spirit would
be the ideal in so far as it obtained expression in
nature; and the power attributed to spirit would
be the part of nature's fertility by which such
expression was secured.

CHAPTER VI

DISCOVERY OF FELLOW-MINDS

Another background for current experience may be found in alien minds. When a ghostly sphere, containing memory and all ideas, has been distinguished from the material world, it tends to grow at the expense of the latter, until nature is finally reduced to a mathematical skeleton. This skeleton itself, but for the need of a bridge to connect calculably episode with episode in experience, might be transferred to mind and identified with the scientific thought in which it is represented. But a scientific theory inhabiting a few scattered moments of life cannot connect those episodes among which it is itself the last and the least substantial; nor would such a notion have occurred even to the most reckless sceptic, had the world not possessed another sort of reputed reality—the minds of others—which could serve, even after the supposed extinction of the physical world, to constitute an independent order and to absorb the potentialities of being when immediate consciousness nodded. But other men's minds, being themselves precarious and ineffectual, would never have seemed a possible substitute for nature, to be in her stead the back-

ground and intelligible object of experience.
Something constant, omnipresent, infinitely fertile is needed to support and connect the given
chaos. Just these properties, however, are actually attributed to one of the minds supposed to
confront the thinker, namely, the mind of God.
The divine mind has therefore always constituted
in philosophy either the alternative to nature or
her other name: it is *par excellence* the seat of all
potentiality and, as Spinoza said, the refuge of all
ignorance.

Speculative problems would be greatly clarified,
and what is genuine in them would be more easily
distinguished from what is artificial, if we could
gather together again the original sources for the
belief in separate minds and compare these
sources with those we have already assigned to the
conception of nature. But speculative problems
are not alone concerned, for in all social life we
envisage fellow-creatures conceived to share the
same thoughts and passions and to be similarly
affected by events. What is the basis of this conviction? What are the forms it takes, and in what
sense is it a part or an expression of reason?

This question is difficult, and in broaching it we
cannot expect much aid from what philosophers
have hitherto said on the subject. For the most
part, indeed, they have said nothing, as by nature's
kindly disposition most questions which it is
beyond a man's power to answer do not occur to
him at all. The suggestions which have actually

been made in the matter may be reduced to two:
first, that we conceive other men's minds by pro-
jecting into their bodies those feelings
which we immediately perceive to accompany similar operations in our-
selves, that is, we infer alien minds by analogy;
and second, that we are immediately aware of
them and feel them to be friendly or hostile
counterparts of our own thinking and effort, that
is, we evoke them by dramatic imagination.

Two usual ac-
counts of this
conception
criticised:

The first suggestion has the advantage that it escapes solipsism by a reasonable argument, provided the existence of the material world has already been
granted. But if the material world is called back
into the private mind, it is evident that every soul
supposed to inhabit it or to be expressed in it must
follow it thither, as inevitably as the characters
and forces in an imagined story must remain with
it in the inventor's imagination. When, on the
contrary, nature is left standing, it is reasonable to suppose that animals having a similar
origin and similar physical powers should have
similar minds, if any of them was to have a
mind at all. The theory, however, is not satisfactory on other grounds. We do not in reality
associate our own grimaces with the feelings that
accompany them and subsequently, on recognising similar grimaces in another, proceed to attribute emotions to him like those we formerly
experienced. Our own grimaces are not easily

analogy
between
bodies,

perceived, and other men's actions often reveal
passions which we have never had, at least with
anything like their suggested colouring and intensity. This first view is strangely artificial and
mistakes for the natural origin of the belief in
question what may be perhaps its ultimate test.

and dramatic
dialogue in
the soul.
The second suggestion, on the other
hand, takes us into a mystic region.
That we evoke the felt souls of our fel-
lows by dramatic imagination is doubtless true;
but this does not explain how we come to do so,
under what stimulus and in what circumstances.
Nor does it avoid solipsism; for the felt counterparts of my own will are echoes within me, while
if other minds actually exist they cannot have for
their essence to play a game with me in my own
fancy. Such society would be mythical, and while
the sense for society may well be mythical in its
origin, it must acquire some other character if it
is to have practical and moral validity. But practical and moral validity is above all what society
seems to have. This second theory, therefore,
while its feeling for psychological reality is keener,
does not make the recognition of other minds intelligible and leaves our faith in them without
justification.

Subject and
object empiri-
cal, not tran-
scendental,
terms.
In approaching the subject afresh
we should do well to remember that
crude experience knows nothing of the
distinction between subject and object.
This distinction is a division in things, a contrast

established between masses of images which show different characteristics in their modes of existence and relation. If this truth is overlooked, if subject and object are made conditions of experience instead of being, like body and mind, its contrasted parts, the revenge of fate is quick and ironical; either subject or object must immediately collapse and evaporate altogether. All objects must become modifications of the subject or all subjects aspects or fragments of the object.

Objects originally soaked in secondary and tertiary qualities.
Now the fact that crude experience is innocent of modern philosophy has this important consequence: that for crude experience all data whatever lie originally side by side in the same field; extension is passionate, desire moves bodies, thought broods in space and is constituted by a visible metamorphosis of its subject matter. Animism or mythology is therefore no artifice. Passions naturally reside in the object they agitate—our own body, if that be the felt seat of some pang, the stars, if the pang can find no nearer resting-place. Only a long and still unfinished education has taught men to separate emotions from things and ideas from their objects. This education was needed because crude experience is a chaos, and the qualities it jumbles together do not march together in time. Reflection must accordingly separate them, if knowledge (that is, ideas with eventual application and practical transcendence) is to exist at all. In other words, action must be adjusted to

certain elements of experience and not to others, and those chiefly regarded must have a certain interpretation put upon them by trained apperception. The rest must be treated as moonshine and taken no account of except perhaps in idle and poetic revery. In this way crude experience grows reasonable and appearance becomes knowledge of reality.

The fundamental reason, then, why we attribute consciousness to natural bodies is that those bodies, before they are conceived to be merely material, are conceived to possess all the qualities which our own consciousness possesses when we behold them. Such a supposition is far from being a paradox, since only this principle justifies us to this day in believing in whatever we may decide to believe in. The qualities attributed to reality must be qualities found in experience, and if we deny their presence in ourselves (*e.g.,* in the case of omniscience), that is only because the idea of self, like that of matter, has already become special and the region of ideals (in which omniscience lies) has been formed into a third sphere. But before the idea of self is well constituted and before the category of ideals has been conceived at all, every ingredient ultimately assigned to those two regions is attracted into the perceptual vortex for which such qualities as pressure and motion supply a nucleus. The moving image is therefore impregnated not only with secondary qualities—colour, heat, etc.—but with qualities which we may call tertiary, such as pain, fear, joy, malice, feebleness, expectancy. Sometimes these tertiary qualities are attributed to the object in their fulness and just as they are felt. Thus the sun is not only bright and warm in the same way as he is round, but by the same right he is also happy, arrogant, ever-young, and all-seeing; for a suggestion of these tertiary qualities runs through us when we look at him, just as immediately as do his warmth and light. The fact that these imaginative suggestions are not constant does not impede the instant perception that they are actual, and for crude experience whatever a thing possesses in appearance it possesses indeed, no matter how soon that quality may be lost again. The moment when things have most numerous and best defined tertiary qualities is accordingly, for crude experience, the moment when they are most adequately manifested and when their inner essence is best revealed; for it is then that they appear in experience most splendidly arrayed and best equipped for their eventual functions. The sun is a better expression of all his ulterior effects when he is conceived to be an arrogant and all-seeing spirit than when he is stupidly felt to be merely hot; so that the attentive and devout observer, to whom those tertiary qualities are revealed, stands in the same relation to an ordinary sensualist, who can feel only the sun's material attributes, as the sensualist in turn stands in to one born blind, who cannot add the sun's brightness to its warmth except by faith in some happier man's reported intuition. The mythologist or poet, before science exists, is accordingly the man of truest and most adequate vision. His persuasion that he knows the heart and soul of things is no fancy reached by artificial inference or analogy but is a direct report of his own experience and honest contemplation.

Tertiary qualities transposed.
More often, however, tertiary qualities are somewhat transposed in projection, as sound in being lodged in the bell is soon translated into sonority, made, that is, into its own potentiality. In the same way painfulness is translated into malice or wickedness, terror into hate, and every felt tertiary quality into whatever tertiary quality is in experience its more quiescent or potential form. So religion, which remains for the most part on the level of crude experience, attributes to the gods not only happiness—the object's direct tertiary quality—but goodness—its tertiary quality transposed and made potential; for goodness is that disposition which is fruitful in happiness throughout imagined experience. The devil, in like manner, is cruel and wicked as well as tormented. Uncritical science still attributes these transposed tertiary qualities to nature; the mythical notion of force, for instance, being a transposed sensation of effort. In this case we may distinguish two stages or degrees in the transposition: first, before we think of our own pulling, we say the object itself pulls;

in the first transposition we say it pulls against us, its pull is the counterpart or rival of ours but it is still conceived in the same direct terms of effort; and in the second transposition this intermittent effort is made potential or slumbering in what we call strength or force.

It is obvious that the feelings attributed to other men are nothing but the tertiary qualities of their bodies. In beings of the same species, however, these qualities are naturally exceedingly numerous, variable, and precise. Nature has made man man's constant study. His thought, from infancy to the drawing up of his last will and testament, is busy about his neighbour. A smile makes a child happy; a caress, a moment's sympathetic attention, wins a heart and gives the friend's presence a voluminous and poignant value. In youth all seems lost in losing a friend. For the tertiary values, the emotions attached to a given image, the moral effluence emanating from it, pervade the whole present world. The sense of union, though momentary, is the same that later returns to the lover or the mystic, when he feels he has plucked the heart of life's mystery and penetrated to the peaceful centre of things. What the mystic beholds in his ecstasy and loses in his moments of dryness, what the lover pursues and adores, what the child cries for when left alone, is much more a spirit, a person, a haunting mind, than a set of visual sensa-

Imputed mind consists of the tertiary qualities of perceived body.

tions; yet the visual sensations are connected inextricably with that spirit, else the spirit would
not withdraw when the sensations failed. We are
not dealing with an articulate mind whose possessions are discriminated and distributed into a mas-
tered world where everything has its department,
its special relations, its limited importance; we
are dealing with a mind all pulp, all confusion,
keenly sensitive to passing influences and reacting
on them massively and without reserve.

This mind is feeble, passionate, and ignorant.
Its sense for present spirit is no miracle of intelligence or of analogical reasoning; on the contrary,
it betrays a vagueness natural to rudimentary consciousness. Those visual sensations suddenly cut
off cannot there be recognised for what they are.
The consequences which their present disappearance may have for subsequent experience are in
no wise foreseen or estimated, much less are any
inexperienced feelings invented and attached to
that retreating figure, otherwise a mere puppet.
What happens is that by the loss of an absorbing
stimulus the whole chaotic mind is thrown out of
gear; the child cries, the lover faints, the mystic
feels hell opening before him. All this is a present sensuous commotion, a derangement in an
actual dream. Yet just at this lowest plunge of
experience, in this drunkenness of the soul, does
the overwhelming reality and externality of the
other mind dawn upon us. Then we feel that we
are surrounded not by a blue sky or an earth

known to geographers but by unutterable and most
personal hatreds and loves. For then we allow
the half-deciphered images of sense to drag behind
them every emotion they have awakened. We
endow each overmastering stimulus with all its
diffuse effects; and any dramatic potentiality that
our dream acts out under that high pressure—
and crude experience is rich in dreams—becomes
our notion of the life going on before us. We
cannot regard it as our own life, because it is not
felt to be a passion in our own body, but attaches
itself rather to images we see moving about in
the world; it is consequently, without hesitation,
called the life of those images, or those creatures'
souls.

"Pathetic
fallacy" nor-
mal yet or-
dinarily fal-
lacious. The pathetic fallacy is accordingly
what originally peoples the imagined
world. All the feelings aroused by
perceived things are merged in those
things and made to figure as the spiritual and invisible part of their essence, a part, moreover,
quite as well known and as directly perceived as
their motions. To ask why such feelings are
objectified would be to betray a wholly sophisticated view of experience and its articulation.
They do not need to be objectified, seeing they
were objective from the beginning, inasmuch as
they pertain to objects and have never, any more
than those objects, been "subjectified" or localised
in the thinker's body, nor included in that train
of images which as a whole is known to have in

that body its seat and thermometer. The thermometer for these passions is, on the contrary, the
body of another; and the little dream in us, the
quick dramatic suggestion which goes with our
perception of his motions, is our perception of his
thoughts.

A sense for alien thought is accordingly at its
inception a complete illusion. The thought is
one's own, it is associated with an image moving
in space, and is uncritically supposed to be a hidden part of that image, a metaphysical signification attached to its motion and actually existing
behind the scenes in the form of an unheard
soliloquy. A complete illusion this sense remains
in mythology, in animism, in the poetic forms of
love and religion. A better mastery of experience
will in such cases dispel those hasty conceits by
showing the fundamental divergence which at once
manifests itself between the course of phenomena
and the feelings associated with them. It will
appear beyond question that those feelings were
private fancies merged with observation in an un-
digested experience. They indicated nothing in
the object but its power of arousing emotional and
playful reverberations in the mind. Criticism
will tend to clear the world of such poetic distortion; and what vestiges of it may linger will be
avowed fables, metaphors employed merely in conventional expression. In the end even poetic
power will forsake a discredited falsehood: the
poet himself will soon prefer to describe nature in

natural terms and to represent human emotions
in their pathetic humility, not extended beyond
their actual sphere nor fantastically uprooted from
their necessary soil and occasions. He will sing
the power of nature over the soul, the joys of the
soul in the bosom of nature, the beauty visible in
things, and the steady march of natural processes,
so rich in momentous incidents and collocations.
The precision of such a picture will accentuate its
majesty, as precision does in the poems of Lucretius and Dante, while its pathos and dramatic
interest will be redoubled by its truth.

Case where it is not a fallacy. A primary habit producing wide-
spread illusions may in certain cases
become the source of rational knowledge. This
possibility will surprise no one who has studied
nature and life to any purpose. Nature and life
are tentative in all their processes, so that there
is nothing exceptional in the fact that, since in
crude experience image and emotion are inevitably
regarded as constituting a single event, this habit
should usually lead to childish absurdities, but
also, under special circumstances, to rational
insight and morality. There is evidently one case
in which the pathetic fallacy is not fallacious, the
case in which the object observed happens to be an
animal similar to the observer and similarly
affected, as for instance when a flock or herd are
swayed by panic fear. The emotion which each,
as he runs, attributes to the others is, as usual, the
emotion he feels himself; but this emotion, fear,

is the same which in fact the others are then feeling. Their aspect thus becomes the recognised expression for the feeling which really accompanies it. So in hand-to-hand fighting: the intention and passion which each imputes to the other is what he himself feels; but the imputation is probably just, since pugnacity is a remarkably contagious and monotonous passion. It is awakened by the slightest hostile suggestion and is greatly intensified by example and emulation; those we fight against and those we fight with arouse it concurrently and the universal battle-cry that fills the air, and that each man instinctively emits, is an adequate and exact symbol for what is passing in all their souls.

Whenever, then, feeling is attributed to an animal similar to the percipient and similarly employed the attribution is mutual and correct. Contagion and imitation are great causes of feeling, but in so far as they are its causes and set the pathetic fallacy to work they forestall and correct what is fallacious in that fallacy and turn it into a vehicle of true and, as it were, miraculous insight.

Knowledge succeeds only by accident. Let the reader meditate for a moment upon the following point: to know reality is, in a way, an impossible pretension, because knowledge means significant representation, discourse about an existence not contained in the knowing thought, and different in duration or locus from the ideas which repre-

sent it. But if knowledge does not possess its
object how can it intend it? And if knowledge
possesses its object, how can it be knowledge or
have any practical, prophetic, or retrospective
value? Consciousness is not knowledge unless
it indicates or signifies what actually it is not.
This transcendence is what gives knowledge its
cognitive and useful essence, its transitive function and validity. In knowledge, therefore, there
must be some such thing as a justified illusion, an
irrational pretension by chance fulfilled, a chance
shot hitting the mark. For dead logic would stick
at solipsism; yet irrational life, as it stumbles
along from moment to moment, and multiplies
itself in a thousand centres, is somehow amenable
to logic and finds uses for the reason it breeds.

Now, in the relation of a natural being to similar beings in the same habitat there is just the
occasion we require for introducing a miraculous
transcendence in knowledge, a leap out of solipsism which, though not prompted by reason, will
find in reason a continual justification. For tertiary qualities are imputed to objects by psychological or pathological necessity. Something not
visible in the object, something not possibly revealed by any future examination of that object,
is thus united with it, felt to be its core, its metaphysical truth. Tertiary qualities are emotions
or thoughts present in the observer and in his
rudimentary consciousness not yet connected with
their proper concomitants and antecedents, not yet

relegated to his private mind, nor explained by his personal endowment and situation. To take these private feelings for the substance of other beings is evidently a gross blunder; yet this blunder, without ceasing to be one in point of method, ceases to be one in point of fact when the other being happens to be similar in nature and situation to the mythologist himself and therefore actually possesses the very emotions and thoughts which lie in the mythologist's bosom and are attributed by him to his fellow. Thus an imaginary self-transcendence, a rash pretension to grasp an independent reality and to know the unknowable, may find itself accidentally rewarded. Imagination will have drawn a prize in its lottery and the pathological accidents of thought will have begotten knowledge and right reason. The inner and unattainable core of other beings will have been revealed to private intuition.

Limits of insight. This miracle of insight, as it must seem to those who have not understood its natural and accidental origin, extends only so far as does the analogy between the object and the instrument of perception. The gift of intuition fails in proportion as the observer's bodily habit differs from the habit and body observed. Misunderstanding begins with constitutional divergence and deteriorates rapidly into false imputations and absurd myths. The limits of mutual understanding coincide with the limits of similar structure and common occupation, so that the distortion of insight begins very near home. It is hard to understand the minds of children unless we retain unusual plasticity and capacity to play; men and women do not really understand each other, what rules between them being not so much sympathy as habitual trust, idealisation, or satire; foreigners' minds are pure enigmas, and those attributed to animals are a grotesque compound of Æsop and physiology. When we come to religion the ineptitude of all the feelings attributed to nature or the gods is so egregious that a sober critic can look to such fables only for a pathetic expression of human sentiment and need; while, even apart from the gods, each religion itself is quite unintelligible to infidels who have never followed its worship sympathetically or learned by contagion the human meaning of its sanctions and formulas. Hence the stupidity and want of insight commonly shown in what calls itself the history of religions. We hear, for instance, that Greek religion was frivolous, because its mystic awe and momentous practical and poetic truths escape the Christian historian accustomed to a catechism and a religious morality; and similarly Catholic piety seems to the Protestant an æsthetic indulgence, a religion appealing to sense, because such is the only emotion its externals can awaken in him, unused as he is to a supernatural economy reaching down into the incidents and affections of daily life.

Language is an artificial means of establishing

unanimity and transferring thought from one
mind to another. Every symbol or phrase, like
every gesture, throws the observer into an attitude
to which a certain idea corresponded in the
speaker; to fall exactly into the speaker's attitude
is exactly to understand. Every impediment to
contagion and imitation in expression is an impediment to comprehension. For this reason language, like all art, becomes pale with years; words
and figures of speech lose their contagious and
suggestive power; the feeling they once expressed
can no longer be restored by their repetition.
Even the most inspired verse, which boasts not
without a relative justification to be immortal,
becomes in the course of ages a scarcely legible
hieroglyphic; the language it was written in dies,
a learned education and an imaginative effort are
requisite to catch even a vestige of its original
force. Nothing is so irrevocable as mind.

> Unsure the ebb and flood of thought,
> The moon comes back, the spirit not.

Perception of character. There is, however, a wholly different and far more positive method of
reading the mind, or what in a metaphorical sense
is called by that name. This method is to read
character. Any object with which we are familiar
teaches us to divine its habits; slight indications,
which we should be at a loss to enumerate separately, betray what changes are going on and
what promptings are simmering in the organism.

Hence the expression of a face or figure; hence the traces of habit and passion visible in a man and that indescribable something about him which inspires confidence or mistrust. The gift of reading character is partly instinctive, partly a result of experience; it may amount to foresight and is directed not upon consciousness but upon past or eventual action. Habits and passions, however, have metaphorical psychic names, names indicating dispositions rather than particular acts (a disposition being mythically represented as a sort of wakeful and haunting genius waiting to whisper suggestions in a man's ear). We may accordingly delude ourselves into imagining that a pose or a manner which really indicates habit indicates feeling instead. In truth the feeling involved, if conceived at all, is conceived most vaguely, and is only a sort of reverberation or penumbra surrounding the pictured activities.

Conduct divined, consciousness ignored. It is a mark of the connoisseur to be able to read character and habit and to divine at a glance all a creature's potentialities. This sort of penetration characterises the man with an eye for horse-flesh, the dog-fancier, and men and women of the world. It guides the born leader in the judgments he instinctively passes on his subordinates and enemies; it distinguishes every good judge of human affairs or of natural phenomena, who is quick to detect small but telling indications of events past or brewing. As the weather-prophet reads the

heavens so the man of experience reads other men.
Nothing concerns him less than their consciousness; he can allow that to run itself off when he is
sure of their temper and habits. A great master
of affairs is usually unsympathetic. His observation is not in the least dramatic or dreamful, he
does not yield himself to animal contagion or re-
enact other people's inward experience. He is
too busy for that, and too intent on his own purposes. His observation, on the contrary, is
straight calculation and inference, and it sometimes reaches truths about people's character and
destiny which they themselves are very far from
divining. Such apprehension is masterful and
odious to weaklings, who think they know themselves because they indulge in copious soliloquy
(which is the discourse of brutes and madmen),
but who really know nothing of their own capacity,
situation, or fate.

If Rousseau, for instance, after writing those
Confessions in which candour and ignorance of self
are equally conspicuous, had heard some intelligent friend, like Hume, draw up in a few words
an account of their author's true and contemptible
character, he would have been loud in protesta-
tions that no such ignoble characteristics existed
in his eloquent consciousness; and they might not
have existed there, because his consciousness was
a histrionic thing, and as imperfect an expression
of his own nature as of man's. When the mind
is irrational no practical purpose is served by stop-

ping to understand it, because such a mind is irrelevant to practice, and the principles that guide the man's practice can be as well understood by eliminating his mind altogether. So a wise governor ignores his subjects' religion or concerns himself only with its economic and temperamental aspects; if the real forces that control life are understood, the symbols that represent those forces in the mind may be disregarded. But such a government, like that of the British in India, is more practical than sympathetic. While wise men may endure it for the sake of their material interests, they will never love it for itself. There is nothing sweeter than to be sympathised with, while nothing requires a rarer intellectual heroism than willingness to see one's equation written out.

Consciousness untrustworthy. Nevertheless this same algebraic sense for character plays a large part in human friendship. A chief element in friendship is trust, and trust is not to be acquired by reproducing consciousness but only by penetrating to the constitutional instincts which, in determining action and habit, determine consciousness as well. Fidelity is not a property of ideas. It is a virtue possessed pre-eminently by nature, from the animals to the seasons and the stars. But fidelity gives friendship its deepest sanctity, and the respect we have for a man, for his force, ability, constancy, and dignity, is no sentiment evoked by his floating thoughts but an assurance founded

on our own observation that his conduct and character are to be counted upon. Smartness and
vivacity, much emotion and many conceits, are
obstacles both to fidelity and to merit. There is
a high worth in rightly constituted natures independent of incidental consciousness. It consists
in that ingrained virtue which under given circumstances would insure the noblest action and
with that action, of course, the noblest sentiments
and ideas; ideas which would arise spontaneously
and would make more account of their objects
than of themselves.

Metaphorical   The expression of habit in psychic
mind.   metaphors is a procedure known also
to theology. Whenever natural or moral law is
declared to reveal the divine mind, this mind is
a set of formal or ethical principles rather than
an imagined consciousness, re-enacted dramatically. What is conceived is the god's operation,
not his emotions. In this way God's goodness
becomes a symbol for the advantages of life, his
wrath a symbol for its dangers, his commandments a symbol for its laws. The deity spoken
of by the Stoics had exclusively this symbolic character; it could be called a city—dear City of Zeus
—as readily as an intelligence. And that intelligence which ancient and ingenuous philosophers
said they saw in the world was always intelligence
in this algebraic sense, it was intelligible order.
Nor did the Hebrew prophets, in their emphatic
political philosophy, seem to mean much more by

Jehovah than a moral order, a principle giving vice and virtue their appropriate fruits.

Summary. True society, then, is limited to similar beings living similar lives and enabled by the contagion of their common habits and arts to attribute to one another, each out of his own experience, what the other actually endures. A fresh thought may be communicated to one who has never had it before, but only when the speaker so dominates the auditor's mind by the instrumentalities he brings to bear upon it that he compels that mind to reproduce his experience. Analogy between actions and bodies is accordingly the only test of valid inference regarding the existence or character of conceived minds; but this eventual test is far from being the source of such a conception. Its source is not inference at all but direct emotion and the pathetic fallacy. In the beginning, as in the end, what is attributed to others is something directly felt, a dream dreamed through and dramatically enacted, but uncritically attributed to the object by whose motions it is suggested and controlled. In a single case, however, tertiary qualities happen to correspond to an experience actually animating the object to which they are assigned. This is the case in which the object is a body similar in structure and action to the percipient himself, who assigns to that body a passion he has caught by contagion from it and by imitation of its actual attitude. Such are the conditions of intelligible expression and true com-

munion; beyond these limits nothing is possible
save myth and metaphor, or the algebraic desig-
nation of observed habits under the name of moral
dispositions.

CHAPTER VII

CONCRETIONS IN DISCOURSE AND IN EXISTENCE

So-called ab-
stract quali-
ties primary. Ideas of material objects ordinarily absorb the human mind, and their prevalence has led to the rash supposition that ideas of all other kinds are posterior to physical ideas and drawn from the latter by a process of abstraction. The table, people said, was a particular and single reality; its colour, form, and material were parts of its integral nature, qualities which might be attended to separately, perhaps, but which actually existed only in the table itself. Colour, form, and material were therefore abstract elements. They might come before the mind separately and be contrasted objects of attention, but they were incapable of existing in nature except together, in the concrete reality called a particular thing. Moreover, as the same colour, shape, or substance might be found in various tables, these abstract qualities were thought to be general qualities as well; they were universal terms which might be predicated of many individual things. A contrast could then be drawn between these qualities or ideas, which the mind may envisage, and the concrete reality existing

beyond. Thus philosophy could reach the familiar maxim of Aristotle that the particular alone
exists in nature and the general alone in the mind.

Such language expresses correctly enough a
secondary conventional stage of conception, but it
ignores the primary fictions on which convention
itself must rest. Individual physical objects must
be discovered before abstractions can be made from
their conceived nature; the bird must be caught
before it is plucked. To discover a physical object
is to pack in the same part of space, and fuse in
one complex body, primary data like coloured form

General
qualities prior
to particular
things.
and tangible surface. Intelligence,
observing these sensible qualities to
evolve together, and to be controlled at
once by external forces, or by one's own voluntary
motions, identifies them in their operation
although they remain for ever distinct in their sensible character. A physical object is accordingly
conceived by fusing or interlacing spatial qualities, in a manner helpful to practical intelligence.
It is a far higher and remoter thing than the elements it is compacted of and that suggest it; what
habits of appearance and disappearance the latter
may have, the object reduces to permanent and
calculable principles. It is altogether erroneous,
therefore, to view an object's sensible qualities as
abstractions from it, seeing they are its original
and component elements; nor can the sensible
qualities be viewed as generic notions arising by
comparison of several concrete objects, seeing that

these concretions would never have been made or thought to be permanent, did they not express observed variations and recurrences in the sensible qualities immediately perceived and already recognised in their recurrence. These are themselves the true particulars. They are the first objects discriminated in attention and projected against the background of consciousness.

The immediate continuum may be traversed and mapped by two different methods. The prior one, because it is so very primitive and rudimentary, and so much a condition of all mental discourse, is usually ignored in psychology. The secondary method, by which external things are discovered, has received more attention. The latter consists in the fact that when several disparate sensations, having become recognisable in their repetitions, are observed to come and go together, or in fixed relation to some voluntary operation on the observer's part, they may be associated by contiguity and merged in one portion of perceived space. Those having, like sensations of touch and sight, an essentially spatial character, may easily be superposed; the surface I see and that I touch may be identified by being presented together and being found to undergo simultaneous variations and to maintain common relations to other perceptions. Thus I may come to attribute to a single object, the term of an intellectual synthesis and ideal intention, my experiences through all the senses within a certain field of association, defined by its

practical relations. That ideal object is thereby
endowed with as many qualities and powers as I
had associable sensations of which to make it up.
This object is a concretion of my perceptions in
space, so that the redness, hardness, sweetness, and
roundness of the apple are all fused together in
my practical regard and given one local habitation and one name.

Universals are concretions in discourse. This kind of synthesis, this super-
position and mixture of images into
notions of physical objects, is not, however, the only kind to which perceptions are subject. They fall together by virtue of their qualitative identity even before their spatial superposi-
tion; for in order to be known as repeatedly simultaneous, and associable by contiguity, they must
be associated by similarity and known as indi-
vidually repeated. The various recurrences of a
sensation must be recognised as recurrences, and
this implies the collection of sensations into classes
of similars and the apperception of a common
nature in several data. Now the more frequent a
perception is the harder it will be to discriminate in
memory its past occurrences from one another, and
yet the more readily will its present recurrence be
recognised as familiar. The perception in sense
will consequently be received as a repetition not of
any single earlier sensation but of a familiar and
generic experience. This experience, a spontaneous
reconstruction based on all previous sensations of
that kind, will be the one habitual *idea* with which

recurring sensations will be henceforth identified. Such a living concretion of similars succeeding one another in time, is the idea of a nature or quality, the universal falsely supposed to be an abstraction from physical objects, which in truth are conceived by putting together these very ideas into a spatial and permanent system.

Here we have, if I am not mistaken, the origin of the two terms most prominent in human knowledge, ideas and things. Two methods of conception divide our attention in common life; science and philosophy develop both, although often with an unjustifiable bias in favour of one or the other. They are nothing but the old principles of Aristotelian psychology, association by similarity and association by contiguity. Only now, after logicians have exhausted their ingenuity in criticising them and psychologists in applying them, we may go back of the traditional position and apply the ancient principles at a deeper stage of mental life.

Similar reactions, merged in one habit of reproduction, yield an idea.
Association by similarity is a fusion of impressions merging what is common in them, interchanging what is peculiar, and cancelling in the end what is incompatible; so that any excitement reaching that centre revives one generic reaction which yields the idea. These concrete generalities are actual feelings, the first terms in mental discourse, the first distinguishable particulars in knowledge, and the first bearers of names. Intellectual dominion of the conscious stream

begins with the act of recognising these pervasive entities, which having character and ideal permanence can furnish common points of reference for different moments of discourse. Save for ideas no perception could have significance, or acquire that indicative force which we call knowledge. For it would refer to nothing to which another perception might also have referred; and so long as perceptions have no common reference, so long as successive moments do not enrich by their contributions the same object of thought, evidently experience, in the pregnant sense of the word, is impossible. No fund of valid ideas, no wisdom, could in that case be acquired by living.

Ideas are ideal.   Ideas, although their material is of course sensuous, are not sensations nor perceptions nor objects of any possible immediate experience: they are creatures of intelligence, goals of thought, ideal terms which cogitation and action circle about. As the centre of mass is a body, while it may by chance coincide with one or another of its atoms, is no atom itself and no material constituent of the bulk that obeys its motion, so an idea, the centre of mass of a certain mental system, is no material fragment of that system, but an ideal term of reference and signification by allegiance to which the details of consciousness first become parts of a system and of a thought. An idea is an ideal. It represents a functional relation in the diffuse existences to which it gives a name and

a rational value.   An idea is an expression of life,
and shares with life that transitive and elusive
nature which defies definition by mere enumera-
tion of its materials.   The peculiarity of life is
that it lives; and thought also, when living, passes
out of itself and directs itself on the ideal, on the
eventual.   It is an activity.   Activity does not
consist in velocity of change but in constancy of
purpose; in the conspiracy of many moments and
many processes toward one ideal harmony and
one concomitant ideal result.   The most rudimentary apperception, recognition, or expectation, is
already a case of representative cognition, of transitive thought resting in a permanent essence.
Memory is an obvious case of the same thing; for
the past, in its truth, is a system of experiences
in relation, a system now non-existent and never,
as a system, itself experienced, yet confronted in
retrospect and made the ideal object and standard
for all historical thinking.

So-called ab-
stractions
complete facts.
These arrested and recognisable
ideas, concretions of similars succeeding one another in time, are not abstractions; but they may come to be regarded as
such after the other kind of concretions in experience, concretions of superposed perceptions in
space, have become the leading objects of attention.   The sensuous material for both concretions
is the same; the perception which, recurring in
different objects otherwise not retained in memory
gives the idea of roundness, is the same percep-

tion which helps to constitute the spatial concretion called the sun. Roundness may therefore be carelessly called an abstraction from the real object " sun "; whereas the peculiar optical and muscular feelings by which the sense of roundness is constituted—probably feelings of gyration and perpetual unbroken movement—are much earlier than any solar observations; they are a self-sufficing element in experience which, by repetition in various accidental contests, has come to be recognised and named, and to be a characteristic by virtue of which more complex objects can be distinguished and defined. The idea of the sun is a much later product, and the real sun is so far from being an original datum from which roundness is abstracted, that it is an ulterior and quite ideal construction, a spatial concretion into which the logical concretion roundness enters as a prior and independent factor. Roundness may be felt in the dark, by a mere suggestion of motion, and is a complete experience in itself. When this recognisable experience happens to be associated by contiguity with other recognisable experiences of heat, light, height, and yellowness, and these various independent objects are projected into the same portion of a real space; then a concretion occurs, and these ideas being recognised in that region and finding a momentary embodiment there, become the qualities of a thing.

A conceived thing is doubly a product of mind, more a product of mind, if you will, than an idea,

since ideas arise, so to speak, by the mind's inertia and conceptions of things by its activity.

Things con-
cretions of
concretions.
Ideas are mental sediment; conceived
things are mental growths. A concretion in discourse occurs by repetition
and mere emphasis on a datum, but a concretion
in existence requires a synthesis of disparate elements and relations. An idea is nothing but a
sensation apperceived and rendered cognitive, so
that it envisages its own recognised character as
its object and ideal: yellowness is only some sensation of yellow raised to the cognitive power and
employed as the symbol for its own specific essence.
It is consequently capable of entering as a term
into rational discourse and of becoming the subject or predicate of propositions eternally valid.
A thing, on the contrary, is discovered only when
the order and grouping of such recurring essences
can be observed, and when various themes and
strains of experience are woven together into elaborate progressive harmonies. When consciousness
first becomes cognitive it frames ideas; but when
it becomes cognitive of causes, that is, when it
becomes practical, it perceives things.

Concretions of qualities recurrent in time and
concretions of qualities associated in existence are
alike involved in daily life and inextricably in-
grown into the structure of reason. In consciousness and for logic, association by similarity, with
its aggregations and identifications of recurrences
in time, is fundamental rather than association

by contiguity and its existential syntheses; for recognition identifies similars perceived in suc-

Ideas prior in the order of knowledge, things in the order of nature.

cession, and without recognition of similars there could be no known persistence of phenomena. But physiologically and for the observer association by contiguity comes first. All instinct—without which there would be no fixity or recurrence in ideation—makes movement follow impression in an immediate way which for consciousness becomes a mere juxtaposition of sensations, a juxtaposition which it can neither explain nor avoid. Yet this juxtaposition, in which pleasure, pain, and striving are prominent factors, is the chief stimulus to attention and spreads before the mind that moving and variegated field in which it learns to make its first observations. Facts—the burdens of successive moments—are all associated by contiguity, from the first facts of perception and passion to the last facts of fate and conscience. We undergo events, we grow into character, by the subterranean working of irrational forces that make their incalculable irruptions into life none the less wonderfully in the revelations of a man's heart to himself than in the cataclysms of the world around him. Nature's placid procedure, to which we yield so willingly in times of prosperity, is a concatenation of states which can only be understood when it is made its own standard and law. A sort of philosophy without wisdom may seek to subjugate this natural life,

this blind budding of existence, to some logical or
moral necessity; but this very attempt remains,
perhaps, the most striking monument to that irrational fatality that rules affairs, a monument which
reason itself is compelled to raise with unsus-
pected irony.

Reliance on external perception, constant ap-
peals to concrete fact and physical sanctions, have
always led the mass of reasonable men to magnify
Aristotle's concretions in existence and belittle
compromise. concretions in discourse. They are too
clever, as they feel, to mistake words for things.
The most authoritative thinker on this subject,
because the most mature, Aristotle himself, taught
that things had reality, individuality, independence, and were the outer cause of perception,
while general ideas, products of association by
similarity, existed only in the mind. The public, pleased at its ability to understand this doctrine and overlooking the more incisive part of
the philosopher's teaching, could go home comforted and believing that material things were
primary and perfect entities, while ideas were only
abstractions, effects those realities produced on our
incapable minds. Aristotle, however, had a juster
view of general concepts and made in the end the
whole material universe gravitate around them
and feel their influence, though in a metaphysical
and magic fashion to which a more advanced
natural science need no longer appeal. While in
the shock of life man was always coming upon the

accidental, in the quiet of reflection he could not but recast everything in ideal moulds and retain nothing but eternal natures and intelligible relations. Aristotle conceived that while the origin of knowledge lay in the impact of matter upon sense its goal was the comprehension of essences, and that while man was involved by his animal nature in the accidents of experience he was also by virtue of his rationality a participator in eternal truth. A substantial justice was thus done both to the conditions and to the functions of human life, although, for want of a natural history inspired by mechanical ideas, this dualism remained somewhat baffling and incomprehensible in its basis. Aristotle, being a true philosopher and pupil of experience, preferred incoherence to partiality.

Empirical bias in favour of contiguity. Active life and the philosophy that borrows its concepts from practice has thus laid a great emphasis on association by contiguity. Hobbes and Locke made knowledge of this kind the only knowledge of reality, while recognising it to be quite empirical, tentative, and problematical. It was a kind of acquaintance with fact that increased with years and brought the mind into harmony with something initially alien to it. Besides this practical knowledge or prudence there was a sort of verbal and merely ideal knowledge, a knowledge of the meaning and relation of abstract terms. In mathematics and logic we might carry out long trains of abstracted thought and analyse and develop our imaginations *ad infinitum*. These speculations, however, were in the air or—what for these philosophers is much the same thing—in the mind; their applicability and their relevance to practical life and to objects given in perception remained quite problematical. A self-developing science, a synthetic science *a priori*, had a value entirely hypothetical and provisional; its practical truth depended on the verification of its results in some eventual sensible experience. Association was invoked to explain the adjustment of ideation to the order of external perception. Association, by which association by contiguity was generally understood, thus became the battle-cry of empiricism; if association by similarity had been equally in mind, the philosophy of pregnant reason could also have adopted the principle for its own. But logicians and mathematicians naturally neglect the psychology of their own processes and, accustomed as they are to an irresponsible and constructive use of the intellect, regard as a confused and uninspired intruder the critic who, by a retrospective and naturalistic method, tries to give them a little knowledge of themselves.

Rational ideas must arise somehow in the mind, and since they are not meant to be without aplication to the world of experience, it is interesting to discover the point of contact between the two and the nature of their interdependence.

This would have been found in the mind's initial capacity to frame objects of two sorts, those compacted of sensations that are persistently similar, and those compacted of sensations that are momentarily fused. In empirical philosophy the applicability of logic and mathematics remains a miracle or becomes a misinterpretation: a miracle if the process of nature independently follows the inward elaboration of human ideas; a misinterpretation if the bias of intelligence imposes *a priori* upon reality a character and order not inherent in it. The mistake of empiricists—among which Kant is in this respect to be numbered—which enabled them to disregard this difficulty, was that they admitted, beside rational thinking, another instinctive kind of wisdom by which men could live, a wisdom the Englishmen called experience and the Germans practical reason, spirit, or will. The intellectual sciences could be allowed to spin themselves out in abstracted liberty while man practised his illogical and inspired art of life.

Artificial divorce of logic from practice.

Here we observe a certain elementary crudity or barbarism which the human spirit often betrays when it is deeply stirred. Not only are chance and divination welcomed into the world but they are reverenced all the more, like the wind and fire of idolaters, precisely for not being amenable to the petty rules of human reason. In truth, however, the English duality between prudence and science is no more fundamental than the German duality between reason and understanding.* The true contrast is between impulse and reflection, instinct and intelligence. When men feel the primordial authority of the animal in them and have little respect for a glimmering reason which they suspect to be secondary but cannot discern to be ultimate, they readily imagine they are appealing to something higher than intelligence when in reality they are falling back on something deeper and lower. The rudimentary seems to them at such moments divine; and if they conceive a Life of Reason at all they despise it as a mass of artifices and conventions. Reason is indeed not indispensable to life, nor needful if living anyhow be the sole and indeterminate aim; as the existence of animals and of most men sufficiently proves. In so far as man is not a rational being and does not live in and by the mind, in so far as his chance volitions and dreamful ideas roll by without mutual representation or adjustment, in so far as his body takes the lead and even his galvanised action is a form of passivity, we may truly say that his life is not intellectual and not

* This distinction, in one sense, is Platonic: but Plato's Reason was distinguished from understanding (which dealt with phenomenal experience) because it was a moral faculty defining those values and meanings which in Platonic nomenclature took the title of reality. The German Reason was only imagination, substituting a dialectical or poetic history of the world for its natural development. German idealism, accordingly, was not, like Plato's, a moral philosophy hypostasised but a false physics adored.

dependent on the application of general concepts to experience; for he lives by instinct.

The Life of Reason, the comprehension of causes and pursuit of aims, begins precisely where instinctive operation ceases to be merely such by becom-
Their mutual involution. ing conscious of its purposes and representative of its conditions. Logical forms of thought impregnate and constitute practical intellect. The shock of experience can indeed correct, disappoint, or inhibit rational expectation, but it cannot take its place. The very first lesson that experience should again teach us after our disappointment would be a rebirth of reason in the soul. Reason has the indomitable persistence of all natural tendencies; it returns to the attack as waves beat on the shore. To observe its defeat is already to give it a new embodiment. Prudence itself is a vague science, and science, when it contains real knowledge, is but a clarified prudence, a description of experience and a guide to life. Speculative reason, if it is not also practical, is not reason at all. Propositions irrelevant to experience may be correct in form, the method they are reached by may parody scientific method, but they cannot be true in substance, because they refer to nothing. Like music, they have no object. They merely flow, and please those whose unattached sensibility they somehow flatter.

Hume, in this respect more radical and satisfactory than Kant himself, saw with perfect clearness that reason was an ideal expression of instinct, and that consequently no rational spheres could exist other than the mathematical and the empirical, and that what is not a datum must certainly be a construction. In establishing his "tendencies to feign" at the basis of intelligence, and in confessing that he yielded to them himself no less in his criticism of human nature than in his practical life, he admitted the involution of reason—that unintelligible instinct—in all the observations and maxims vouchsafed to an empiricist or to a man. He veiled his doctrine, however, in a somewhat unfair and satirical nomenclature, and he has paid the price of that indulgence in personal humour by incurring the immortal hatred of sentimentalists who are too much scandalised by his tone ever to understand his principles.

If the common mistake in empiricism is not to see the omnipresence of reason in thought, the mistake of rationalism is not to admit its variability and dependence, not to understand its **Rationalistic** natural life. Parmenides was the **suicide.** Adam of that race, and first tasted the deceptive kind of knowledge which, promising to make man God, banishes him from the paradise of experience. His sin has been transmitted to his descendants, though hardly in its magnificent and simple enormity. "The whole is one," Xenophanes had cried, gazing into heaven; and that same sense of a permeating identity, translated into rigid and logical terms, brought his sublime disciple to the conviction that an indistinguishable immutable substance was omnipresent in the world. Parmenides carried association by similarity to such lengths that he arrived at the idea of what alone is similar in everything, viz., the fact that it is. Being exists, and nothing else does; whereby every relation and variation in experience is reduced to a negligible illusion, and reason loses its function at the moment of asserting its absolute authority. Notable lesson, taught us like so many others by the first experiments of the Greek mind, in its freedom and insight, a mind led quickly by noble self-confidence to the ultimate goals of thought.

Such a pitch of heroism and abstraction has not been reached by any rationalist since. No one else has been willing to ignore entirely all the data and constructions of experience, save the highest concept reached by assimilations in that experience; no one else has been willing to demolish all the scaffolding and all the stones of his edifice, hoping still to retain the sublime symbol which he had planted on the summit. Yet all rationalists have longed to demolish or to degrade some part of the substructure, like those Gothic architects who wished to hang the vaults of their churches upon the slenderest possible supports, abolishing and turning into painted crystal all the dead walls of the building. So experience and its crowning conceptions were to rest wholly on a skeleton of general natures, physical forces being assimilated to logical terms, and concepts gained by identification of similars taking the place of those gained by grouping disparate things in their historical conjunctions. These contiguous sensations, which occasionally exemplify the logical contrasts in ideas and give them incidental existence, were either ignored altogether and dismissed as unmeaning, or admitted merely as illusions. The eye was to be trained to pass from that particoloured chaos to the firm lines and permanent divisions that were supposed to sustain it and frame it in.

Rationalism is a kind of builder's bias which the impartial public cannot share; for the dead walls and glass screens which may have no function in supporting the roof are yet as needful as the roof itself to shelter and beauty. So the incidental filling of experience which remains unclassified under logical categories retains all its primary reality and importance. The outlines of it emphasised by logic, though they may be the essential vehicle of our most soaring thoughts, are only a method and a style of architecture. They neither absorb the whole material of life nor monopolise its values. And as each material imposes upon the builder's ingenuity a different type of construction, and stone, wood, and iron must be treated on different structural principles, so logical methods of comprehension, spontaneous though they be in their mental origin, must prove themselves fitted to the natural order

and affinity of the facts.* Nor is there in this
necessity any violence to the spontaneity of reason:
for reason also has manifold forms, and the accidents of experience are more than matched in
variety by the multiplicity of categories. Here
one principle of order and there another shoots
into the mind, which breeds more genera and species than the most fertile terrestrial slime can
breed individuals.

Complement-
ary character
of essence and
existence.
Language, then, with the logic imbedded in it, is a repository of terms
formed by identifying successive perceptions, as the external world is a repository of
objects conceived by superposing perceptions that
exist together. Being formed on different principles these two orders of conception—the logical

* This natural order and affinity is something imputed to
the ultimate object of thought—the reality—by the last act of
judgment assuming its own truth. It is, of course, not
observable by consciousness before the first experiment in
comprehension has been made; the act of comprehension
which first imposes on the sensuous material some subjective
category is the first to arrive at the notion of an objective
order. The historian, however, has a well-tried and mature
conception of the natural order arrived at after many such
experiments in comprehension. From the vantage-ground
of this latest hypothesis, he surveys the attempts others have
made to understand events and compares them with the objective order which he believes himself to have discovered.
This observation is made here lest the reader should confuse
the natural order, imagined to exist before any application
of human categories, with the last conception of that order
attained by the philosopher. The latter is but faith, the
former is faith's ideal object.

and the physical—do not coincide, and the attempt
to fuse them into one system of demonstrable
reality or moral physics is doomed to failure by
the very nature of the terms compared. When the
Eleatics proved the impossibility—*i.e.,* the inex-
pressibility—of motion, or when Kant and his followers proved the unreal character of all objects
of experience and of all natural knowledge, their
task was made easy by the native diversity
between the concretions in existence which were
the object of their thought and the concretions in
discourse which were its measure. The two do
not fit; and intrenched as these philosophers were
in the forms of logic they compelled themselves
to reject as unthinkable everything not fully expressible in those particular forms. Thus they
took their revenge upon the vulgar who, being busy
chiefly with material things and dwelling in an
atmosphere of sensuous images, call unreal and
abstract every product of logical construction
or reflective analysis. These logical products,
however, are not really abstract, but, as we have
seen, concretions arrived at by a different method
than that which results in material conceptions.
Whereas the conception of a thing is a local con-
glomerate of several simultaneous sensations, logical entity is a homogeneous revival in memory
of similar sensations temporally distinct.

Thus the many armed with prejudice and the
few armed with logic fight an eternal battle,
the logician charging the physical world with

unintelligibility and the man of common-sense
charging the logical world with abstractness and
unreality. The former view is the more profound,
since association by similarity is the more elementary and gives constancy to meanings; while the
latter view is the more practical, since association
by contiguity alone informs the mind about the
mechanical sequence of its own experience.
Neither principle can be dispensed with, and each
errs only in denouncing the other and wishing to
be omnivorous, as if on the one hand logic could
make anybody understand the history of events and
the conjunction of objects, or on the other hand
as if cognitive and moral processes could have any
other terms than constant and ideal natures. The
namable essence of things or the standard of values must always be an ideal figment; existence
must always be an empirical fact. The former
remains always remote from natural existence and
the latter irreducible to a logical principle.*

* For the sake of simplicity only such ideas as precede
conceptions of things have been mentioned here. After
things are discovered, however, they may be used as terms
in a second ideal synthesis and a concretion in discourse on
a higher plane may be composed out of sustained concretions in existence. Proper names are such secondary concretions in discourse. " Venice " is a term covering many
successive aspects and conditions, not distinguished in fancy,
belonging to an object existing continuously in space and
time. Each of these states of Venice constitutes a natural
object, a concretion in existence, and is again analysable
into a mass of fused but recognisable qualities—light,
motion, beauty—each of which was an original concretion in

discourse, a primordial term in experience. A quality is recognised by its own idea or permanent nature, a thing by its constituent qualities, and an embodied spirit by fusion into an ideal essence of the constant characters possessed by a thing. To raise natural objects into historic entities it is necessary to repeat upon a higher plane that concretion in discourse by which sensations were raised to ideas. When familiar objects attain this ideal character they have become poetical and achieved a sort of personality. They then possess a spiritual status. Thus sensuous experience is solidified into logical terms, these into ideas of things, and these, recast and smelted again in imagination, into forms of spirit.

CHAPTER VIII

ON THE RELATIVE VALUE OF THINGS AND IDEAS

Moral tone of opinions derived from their logical principle. Those who look back upon the history of opinion for many centuries commonly feel, by a vague but profound instinct, that certain consecrated doctrines have an inherent dignity and spirituality, while other speculative tendencies and other vocabularies seem wedded to all that is ignoble and shallow. So fundamental is this moral tone in philosophy that people are usually more firmly convinced that their opinions are precious than that they are true. They may avow, in reflective moments, that they may be in error, seeing that thinkers of no less repute have maintained opposite opinions, but they are commonly absolutely sure that if their own views could be generally accepted, it would be a boon to mankind, that in fact the moral interests of the race are bound up, not with discovering what may chance to be true, but with discovering the truth to have a particular complexion. This predominant trust in moral judgments is in some cases conscious and avowed, so that philosophers invite the world to embrace tenets for which no

evidence is offered but that they chime in with
current aspirations or traditional bias. Thus the
substance of things hoped for becomes, even in
philosophy, the evidence of things not seen.

Such faith is indeed profoundly human and has
accompanied the mind in all its gropings and discoveries; preference being the primary principle
of discrimination and attention. Reason in her
earliest manifestations already discovered her affinities and incapacities, and loaded the ideas she
framed with friendliness or hostility. It is not
strange that her latest constructions should inherit
this relation to the will; and we shall see that the
moral tone and affinity of metaphysical systems
corresponds exactly with the primary function
belonging to that type of idea on which they are
based. Idealistic systems, still cultivating concretions in discourse, study the first conditions of
knowledge and the last interests of life; material-
istic systems, still emphasising concretions in existence, describe causal relations, and the habits of
nature. Thus the spiritual value of various philosophies rests in the last instance on the kind of
good which originally attached the mind to that
habit and plane of ideation.

We have said that perceptions must be recognised before they can be associated by contiguity,
and that consequently the fusion of temporally
diffused experiences must precede their local
fusion into material objects. It might be urged
in opposition to this statement that concrete

objects can be recognised in practice before their
general qualities have been distinguished in discourse. Recognition may be instinct-
ive, that is, based on the repetition of
a felt reaction or emotion, rather than
on any memory of a former occasion
on which the same perception occurred. Such an
objection seems to be well grounded, for it is instinctive adjustments and suggested action that
give cognitive value to sensation and endow it
with that transitive force which makes it con-
sciously representative of what is past, future, or
absent. If practical instinct did not stretch what
is given into what is meant, reason could never
recognise the datum for a copy of an ideal object.

Concretions in discourse express instinctive reactions.

This description of the case involves an application or extension of our theory rather than an
argument against it. For where recognition is
instinctive and a familiar action is performed with
absent-minded confidence and without attending to the indications that justify that action,
there is in an eminent degree a qualitative concretion in experience. Present impressions are
merged so completely in structural survivals of
the past that instead of arousing any ideas distinct enough to be objectified they merely stimu-
late the inner sense, remain imbedded in the general feeling of motion or life, and constitute in
fact a heightened sentiment of pure vitality and
freedom. For the lowest and vaguest
of concretions in discourse are the

Idealism rudimentary.

ideas of self and of an embosoming external being, with the felt continuity of both; what Fichte would call the Ego, the Non-Ego, and Life. Where no particular events are recognised there is still a feeling of continuous existence. We trail after us from our whole past some sense of the continuous energy and movement both of our passionate fancies and of the phantasmagoria capriciously at work beyond. An ignorant mind believes itself omniscient and omnipotent; those impulses in itself which really represent the inertia and unspent momentum of its last dream it regards as the creative forces of nature.

The first lines of cleavage and the first recognisable bulks at which attention is arrested are in truth those shadowy Fichtean divisions: such are the rude beginnings of logical architecture. In its inability to descry anything definite and fixed, for want of an acquired empirical background and a distinct memory, the mind flounders forward in a dream full of prophecies and wayward identifications. The world possesses as yet in its regard only the superficial forms that appear in revery, it has no hidden machinery, no third dimension in which unobserved and perpetual operations are going on. Its only terms, in a word, are concretions in discourse, ideas combined in their æsthetic and logical harmonies, not in their habitual and efficacious conjunctions. The disorder of such experience is still a spontaneous disorder; it has not discovered how calculable are its unpremedi-

tated shocks. The cataclysms that occur seem to
have only ideal grounds and only dramatic meaning. Though the dream may have its terrors and
degenerate at moments into a nightmare, it has
still infinite plasticity and buoyancy. What perceptions are retained merge in those haunting and
friendly presences, they have an intelligible and
congenial character because they appear as parts
and effluences of an inner fiction, evolving according to the barbaric prosody of an almost infant
mind.

This is the fairy-land of idealism where only
the miraculous seems a matter of course and every
hint of what is purely natural is disregarded,
for the truly natural still seems artificial, dead,
and remote. New and disconcerting facts, which
intrude themselves inopportunely into the story,
chill the currents of spontaneous imagination and
are rejected as long as possible for being alien and
perverse. Perceptions, on the contrary, which can
be attached to the old presences as confirmations
or corollaries, become at once parts of the warp
and woof of what we call ourselves. They seem
of the very substance of spirit, obeying a vital
momentum and flowing from the inmost principle
of being; and they are so much akin to human
presumptions that they pass for manifestations of
necessary truth. Thus the demonstrations of geometry being but the intent explication of a long-
consolidated ideal concretion which we call space,
are welcomed by the mind as in a sense familiar

and as revelations of a truth implicit in the soul,
so that Plato could plausibly take them for rec-
ollections of prenatal wisdom.   But a rocket that
bursts into sparks of a dozen colours, even if expected, is expected with anxiety and observed with
surprise; it assaults the senses at an incalculable
moment with a sensation individual and new.
The exciting tension and lively stimulus may
please in their way, yet the badge of the accidental and unmeaning adheres to the thing.   It is a
trivial experience and one quickly forgotten.   The
shock is superficial and were it repeated would
soon fatigue.   We should retire with relief into
darkness and silence, to our permanent and
rational thoughts.

Naturalism sad.   It is a remarkable fact, which may
easily be misinterpreted, that while all
the benefits and pleasures of life seem to be associated with external things, and all certain knowledge seems to describe material laws, yet a deified
nature has generally inspired a religion of melancholy.   Why should the only intelligible philosophy seem to defeat reason and the chief means of
benefiting mankind seem to blast our best hopes?
Whence this profound aversion to so beautiful and
fruitful a universe?   Whence this persistent search
for invisible regions and powers and for metaphysical explanations that can explain nothing,
while nature's voice without and within man cries
aloud to him to look, act, and enjoy?   And when
someone, in protest against such senseless oracu-

lar prejudices, has actually embraced the life and
faith of nature and taught others to look to the
natural world for all motives and sanctions, expecting thus to refresh and marvellously to invig-
orate human life, why have those innocent hopes
failed so miserably? Why is that sensuous optimism we may call Greek, or that industrial optimism we may call American, such a thin disguise
for despair? Why does each melt away and
become a mockery at the first approach of reflection? Why has man's conscience in the end in-
variably rebelled against naturalism and reverted
in some form or other to a cultus of the unseen?

The soul akin to the eternal and ideal. We may answer in the words of
Saint Paul: because things seen are
temporal and things not seen are eternal. And we may add, remembering our analysis
of the objects inhabiting the mind, that the eternal is the truly human, that which is akin to the
first indispensable products of intelligence, which
arise by the fusion of successive images in discourse, and transcend the particular in time, peopling the mind with permanent and recognisable
objects, and strengthening it with a synthetic,
dramatic apprehension of itself and its own experience. Concretion in existence, on the contrary,
yields essentially detached and empirical unities,
foreign to mind in spite of their order, and unintelligible in spite of their clearness. Reason fails
to assimilate in them precisely that which makes
them real, namely, their presence here and now,

in this order and number. The form and quality of them we can retain, domesticate, and weave into the texture of reflection, but their existence and individuality remain a datum of sense needing to be verified anew at every moment and actually receiving continual verification or disproof while we live in this world.

" This world " we call it, not without justifiable pathos, for many other worlds are conceivable and if discovered might prove more rational and intelligible and more akin to the soul than this strange universe which man has hitherto always looked upon with increasing astonishment. The materials of experience are no sooner in hand than they are transformed by intelligence, reduced to those permanent presences, those natures and relations, which alone can live in discourse. Those materials, rearranged into the abstract summaries we call history or science, or pieced out into the reconstructions and extensions we call poetry or religion, furnish us with ideas of as many dream-worlds as we please, all nearer to reason's ideal than is the actual chaos of perceptual experience, and some nearer to the heart's desire. When an empirical philosophy, therefore, calls us back from the irresponsible flights of imagination to the shock of sense and tries to remind us that in this alone we touch existence and come upon fact, we feel dispossessed of our nature and cramped in our life. The actuality possessed by external ex-

perience cannot make up for its instability, nor
the applicability of scientific principles for their
hypothetical character. The dependence upon
sense, which we are reduced to when we consider
the world of existences, becomes a too plain hint
of our essential impotence and mortality, while
the play of logical fancy, though it remain inevitable, is saddened by a consciousness of its own
insignificance.

That dignity, then, which inheres in logical ideas
and their affinity to moral enthusiasm, springs
from their congruity with the primary habits of
intelligence and idealisation. The soul or self or
personality, which in sophisticated social life is
so much the centre of passion and concern, is itself
an idea, a concretion in discourse; and the level
on which it swims comes to be, by association and
affinity, the region of all the more vivid and massive human interests. The pleasures which lie
Her   beneath it are ignored, and the ideals
inexperience. which lie above it are not perceived.
Aversion to an empirical or naturalistic philosophy accordingly expresses a sort of logical patriotism and attachment to homespun ideas. The
actual is too remote and unfriendly to the
dreamer; to understand it he has to learn a foreign
tongue, which his native prejudice imagines to be
unmeaning and unpoetical. The truth is, however, that nature's language is too rich for man;
and the discomfort he feels when he is compelled
to use it merely marks his lack of education.

There is nothing cheaper than idealism. It can be had by merely not observing the ineptitude of our chance prejudices, and by declaring that the first rhymes that have struck our ear are the eternal and necessary harmonies of the world.

Platonism spontaneous.   The thinker's bias is naturally favourable to logical ideas. The man of reflection will attribute, as far as possible, validity and reality to these alone. Platonism remains the classic instance of this way of thinking. Living in an age of rhetoric, with an education that dealt with nothing but ideal entities, verbal, moral, or mathematical, Plato saw in concretions in discourse the true elements of being. Definable meanings, being the terms of thought, must also, he fancied, be the constituents of reality. And with that directness and audacity which was possible to the ancients, and of which Pythagoreans and Eleatics had already given brilliant examples, he set up these terms of discourse, like the Pythagorean numbers, for absolute and eternal entities, existing before all things, revealed in all things, giving the cosmic artificer his models and the creature his goal. By some inexplicable necessity the creation had taken place. The ideas had multiplied themselves in a flux of innumerable images which could be recognised by their resemblance to their originals, but were at once cancelled and expunged by virtue of their essential inadequacy. What sounds are to words and words to thoughts, that was a thing to its idea.

Plato, however, retained the moral and significant essence of his ideas, and while he made them
ideal absolutes, fixed meanings antecedent to their changing expressions,
never dreamed that they could be natural existences, or psychological beings. In an
original thinker, in one who really thinks and
does not merely argue, to call a thing supernatural, or spiritual, or intelligible is to declare
that it is no *thing* at all, no existence actual
or possible, but a value, a term of thought, a
merely ideal principle; and the more its reality in
such a sense is insisted on the more its incommen-
surability with brute existence is asserted. To express this ideal reality myth is the natural vehicle;
a vehicle Plato could avail himself of all the more
freely that he inherited a religion still plastic and
conscious of its poetic essence, and did not have to
struggle, like his modern disciples, with the arrested childishness of minds that for a hundred
generations have learned their metaphysics in the
cradle. His ideas, although their natural basis
was ignored, were accordingly always ideal; they
always represented meanings and functions and
were never degraded from the moral to the physical sphere. The counterpart of this genuine ideality was that the theory retained its moral force and
did not degenerate into a bewildered and idola-
trous pantheism. Plato conceived the soul's destiny to be her emancipation from those material
things which in this illogical apparition were so

Its essential
fidelity to the
ideal.

alien to her essence. She should return, after her
baffling and stupefying intercourse with the world
of sense and accident, into the native heaven of her
ideas. For animal desires were no less illusory,
and yet no less significant, than sensuous perceptions. They engaged man in the pursuit of the
good and taught him, through disappointment, to
look for it only in those satisfactions which can
be permanent and perfect. Love, like intelligence, must rise from appearance to reality, and
rest in that divine world which is the fulfilment
of the human.

A geometrician does a good service when he declares and explicates the nature of the triangle,
an object suggested by many casual and recurring
sensations. His service is not less real, even if less
obvious, when he arrests some fundamental concretion in discourse, and formulates the first principles of logic. Mastering such definitions, sinking
into the dry life of such forms, he may spin out
and develop indefinitely, in the freedom of his irresponsible logic, their implications and congruous
extensions, opening by his demonstration a depth
of knowledge which we should otherwise never
have discovered in ourselves. But if the geometer
Equal rights had a fanatical zeal and forbade us to
of empiricism. consider space and the triangles it contains otherwise than as his own ideal science con-
siders them: forbade us, for instance, to inquire
how we came to perceive those triangles or that
space; what organs and senses conspired in fur-

nishing the idea of them; what material objects
show that character, and how they came to offer
themselves to our observation—then surely the
geometer would qualify his service with a distinct
injury and while he opened our eyes to one fascinating vista would tend to blind them to others
no less tempting and beautiful. For the naturalist and psychologist have also their rights and can
tell us things well worth knowing; nor will any
theory they may possibly propose concerning the
origin of spatial ideas and their material embodiments ever invalidate the demonstrations of geometry. These, in their hypothetical sphere, are perfectly autonomous and self-generating, and their
applicability to experience will hold so long as the
initial images they are applied to continue to
abound in perception.

If we awoke to-morrow in a world containing
nothing but music, geometry would indeed lose
its relevance to our future experience; but it would
keep its ideal cogency, and become again a living
language if any spatial objects should ever reappear in sense.

The history of such reappearances—natural history—is meantime a good subject for observation
and experiment. Chronicler and critic can always
approach experience with a method complementary
to the deductive methods pursued in mathematics
and logic: instead of developing the import of a
definition, he can investigate its origin and describe its relation to other disparate phenomena.

The mathematician develops the import of given ideas; the psychologist investigates their origin and describes their relation to the rest of human experience. So the prophet develops the import of his trance, and the theologian the import of the prophecy: which prevents not the historian from coming later and showing the origin, the growth, and the possible function of that maniacal sort of wisdom. True, the theologian commonly dreads a critic more than does the geometer, but this happens only because the theologian has probably not developed the import of his facts with any austerity or clearness, but has distorted that ideal interpretation with all sorts of concessions and side-glances at other tenets to which he is already pledged, so that he justly fears, when his methods are exposed, that the religious heart will be alienated from him and his conclusions be left with no foothold in human nature. If he had not been guilty of such misrepresentation, no history or criticism that reviewed his construction would do anything but recommend it to all those who found in themselves the primary religious facts and religious faculties which that construction had faithfully interpreted in its ideal deductions and extensions. All who perceived the facts would thus learn their import; and theology would reveal to the soul her natural religion, just as Euclid reveals to architects and navigators the structure of natural space, so that they value his demonstrations not only for their hypothetical cogency but for their practical relevance and truth.

Now, like the geometer and ingenuous theologian that he was, Plato developed the import of moral and logical experience. Even his followers, though they might give rein to narrower and more fantastic enthusiasms, often unveiled secrets, hidden in the oracular intent of the heart, which might never have been disclosed but for their lessons. But with a zeal unbecoming so well grounded a philosophy they turned their backs upon the rest of wisdom, they disparaged the evidence of sense, they grew hot against the ultimate practical sanctions furnished by impulse and pleasure, they proscribed beauty in art (where Plato had proscribed chiefly what to a fine sensibility is meretricious ugliness), and in a word they sought to abolish all human activities other than the one pre-eminent in themselves. In revenge for their hostility the great world has never given them more than a distrustful admiration and, confronted daily by the evident truths they denied, has encouraged itself to forget the truths they asserted. For they had the bias of reflection and man is born to do more than reflect; they attributed reality and validity only to logical ideas, and man finds other objects continually thrusting themselves before his eyes, claiming his affection and controlling his fortunes.

The most legitimate constructions of reason

Logic dependent on fact for its importance,

soon become merely speculative, soon pass, I
mean, beyond the sphere of practical application; and the man of affairs, adjusting himself
at every turn to the opaque brutality of fact, loses
his respect for the higher reaches of logic and for-
gets that his recognition of facts themselves is an
application of logical principles.   In his youth,
perhaps, he pursued metaphysics, which are the
love-affairs of the understanding; now he is wedded to convention and seeks in the passion he calls
business or in the habit he calls duty some substitute for natural happiness.   He fears to question
the value of his life, having found that such ques-
tioning adds nothing to his powers; and he thinks
the mariner would die of old age in port who
should wait for reason to justify his voyage.
Reason is indeed like the sad Iphigenia whom her
royal father, the Will, must sacrifice before any
wind can fill his sails.   The emanation of all
things from the One involves not only the incar-
nation but the crucifixion of the Logos.   Reason
must be eclipsed by its supposed expressions, and
can only shine in a darkness which does not com-
prehend it.   For reason is essentially hypothetical and subsidiary, and can never constitute what
it expresses in man, nor what it recognises in
nature.

and for its If logic should refuse to make this
subsistence. initial self-sacrifice and to subordinate
itself to impulse and fact, it would immediately
become irrational and forfeit its own justification.

For it exists by virtue of a human impulse and in answer to a human need. To ask a man, in the satisfaction of a metaphysical passion, to forego every other good is to render him fanatical and to shut his eyes daily to the sun in order that he may see better by the star-light. The radical fault of rationalism is not any incidental error committed in its deductions, although such necessarily abound in every human system. Its great original sin is its denial of its own basis and its refusal to occupy its due place in the world, an ignorant fear of being invalidated by its history and dishonoured, as it were, if its ancestry is hinted at. Only bastards should fear that fate, and criticism would indeed be fatal to a bastard philosophy, to one that does not spring from practical reason and has no roots in life. But those products of reason which arise by reflection on fact, and those spontaneous and demonstrable systems of ideas which can be verified in experience, and thus serve to render the facts calculable and articulate, will lose nothing of their lustre by discovering their lineage. So the idea of nature remains true after psychology has analysed its origin, and not only true, but beautiful and beneficent. For unlike many negligible products of speculative fancy it is woven out of recurrent perceptions into a hypothetical cause from which further perceptions can be deduced as they are actually experienced.

Such a mechanism once discovered confirms itself at every breath we draw, and surrounds

every object in history and nature with infinite
and true suggestions, making it doubly interesting, fruitful, and potent over the mind.   The
naturalist accordingly welcomes criticism because
his constructions, though no less hypothetical
and speculative than the idealist's dreams, are
such legitimate and fruitful fictions that they
are obvious truths.   For truth, at the intelligible level where it arises, means not sensible
fact, but valid ideation, verified hypothesis, and
inevitable, stable inference.   If the idealist fears
and deprecates any theory of his own origin
and function, he is only obeying the instinct of
self-preservation; for he knows very well that his
past will not bear examination.   He is heir to every
superstition and by profession an apologist; his
deepest vocation is to rescue, by some logical *tour
de force,* what spontaneously he himself would have
taken for a consecrated error.   Now history and
criticism would involve, as he instinctively perceives, the reduction of his doctrines to their pragmatic value, to their ideal significance for real life.
But he detests any admission of relativity in his
doctrines, all the more because he cannot avow his
reasons for detesting it; and zeal, here as in so
many cases, becomes the cover and evidence of a
bad conscience.   Bigotry and craft, with a rhetori-
cal vilification of enemies, then come to reinforce
in the prophet that natural limitation of his interests which turns his face away from history and
criticism; until his system, in its monstrous un-

reality and disingenuousness, becomes intolerable, and provokes a general revolt in which too often the truth of it is buried with the error in a common oblivion.

Reason and docility.   If idealism is intrenched in the very structure of human reason, empiricism represents all those energies of the external universe which, as Spinoza says, must infinitely exceed the energies of man. If meditation breeds science, wisdom comes by disillusion, even on the subject of science itself. Docility to the facts makes the sanity of science. Reason is only half grown and not really distinguishable from imagination so long as she cannot check and recast her own processes wherever they render the moulds of thought unfit for their subject-matter. Docility is, as we have seen, the deepest condition of reason's existence; for if a form of mental synthesis were by chance developed which was incapable of appropriating the data of sense, these data could not be remembered or introduced at all into a growing and cumulative experience. Sensations would leave no memorial; while logical thoughts would play idly, like so many parasites in the mind, and ultimately languish and die of inanition. To be nourished and employed, intelligence must have developed such structure and habits as will enable it to assimilate what food comes in its way; so that the persistence of any intellectual habit is a proof that it has some applicability, however partial, to the facts of sentience.

Applicable thought and clarified experience.   This applicability, the prerequisite of significant thought, is also its eventual test; and the gathering of new experiences, the consciousness of more and more facts crowding into the memory and demanding co-ordination, is at once the presentation to reason of her legitimate problem and a proof that she is already at work.   It is a presentation of her problem, because reason is not a faculty of dreams but a method in living; and by facing the flux of sensations and impulses that constitute mortal life with the gift of ideal construction and the aspiration toward eternal goods, she is only doing her duty and manifesting what she is.   To accumulate facts, moreover, is in itself to prove that rational activity is already awakened, because a consciousness of multitudinous accidents diversifying experience involves a wide scope in memory, good methods of classification, and keen senses, so that all working together they may collect many observations.   Memory and all its instruments are embodiments, on a modest scale, of rational activities which in theory and speculation reappear upon a higher level.   The expansion of the mind in point of retentiveness and wealth of images is as much an advance in knowledge as is its development in point of organisation.   The structure may be widened at the base as well as raised toward its ideal summit, and while a mass of information imperfectly digested leaves something still for intelligence to do, it shows at the same time how much intelligence has done already.

The function of reason is to dominate experience; and obviously openness to new impressions is no less necessary to that end than is the possession of principles by which new impressions may be interpreted.

CHAPTER IX

HOW THOUGHT IS PRACTICAL

Functional relations of mind and body. Nothing is more natural or more congruous with all the analogies of experience than that animals should feel and think. The relation of mind to body, of reason to nature, seems to be actually this: when bodies have reached a certain complexity and vital equilibrium, a sense begins to inhabit them which is focussed upon the preservation of that body and on its reproduction. This sense, as it becomes reflective and expressive of physical welfare, points more and more to its own persistence and harmony, and generates the Life of Reason. Nature is reason's basis and theme; reason is nature's consciousness; and, from the point of view of that consciousness when it has arisen, reason is also nature's justification and goal.

To separate things so closely bound together as are mind and body, reason and nature, is consequently a violent and artificial divorce, and a man of judgment will instinctively discredit any philosophy in which it is decreed. But to avoid divorce it is well first to avoid unnatural unions, and not to attribute to our two elements, which must be partners for life, relations repugnant to their respective natures and offices. Now the body is an instrument, the mind its function, the witness and reward of its operation. Mind is the body's entelechy, a value which accrues to the body when it has reached a certain perfection, of which it would be a pity, so to speak, that it should remain unconscious; so that while the body feeds the mind the mind perfects the body, lifting it and all its natural relations and impulses into the moral world, into the sphere of interests and ideas.

No connection could be closer than this reciprocal involution, as nature and life reveal it; but the connection is natural, not dialectical. The union will be denaturalised and, so far as philosophy goes, actually destroyed, if we seek to carry it on into logical equivalence. If we isolate the terms mind and body and study the inward implications of each apart, we shall never discover the other. That matter cannot, by transposition of its particles, *become* what we call consciousness, is an admitted truth; that mind cannot *become* its own occasions or determine its own march, though it be a truth not recognised by all philosophers, is in itself no less obvious. Matter, dialectically studied, makes consciousness seem a superfluous and unaccountable addendum; mind, studied in the same way, makes nature an embarrassing idea, a figment which ought to be subservient to conscious aims and perfectly transparent, but which remains opaque and overwhelming. In order to escape these sophistications, it suffices to revert to immediate observation and state the question in its proper terms: nature lives, and perception is a private echo and response to ambient motions. The soul is the voice of the body's interests; in watching them a man defines the world that sustains him and that conditions all his satisfactions. In discerning his origin he christens Nature by the eloquent name of mother, under which title she enters the universe of discourse. Simultaneously he discerns his own existence and marks off the inner region of his dreams. And it behooves him not to obliterate these discoveries. By trying to give his mind false points of attachment in nature he would disfigure not only nature but also that reason which is so much the essence of his life.

They form one natural life. Consciousness, then, is the expression of bodily life and the seat of all its values. Its place in the natural world is like that of its own ideal products, art, religion, or science; it translates natural relations into synthetic and ideal symbols by which things are interpreted with reference to the interests of consciousness itself. This representation is also an existence and has its place along with all other existences in the bosom of nature. In this sense its connection with its organs, and with all that affects the body or that the body affects, is a natural connection. If the word cause did not suggest dialectical bonds we might innocently say that thought was a link in

the chain of natural causes. It is at least a link in
the chain of natural events; for it has determinate
antecedents in the brain and senses and determinate consequents in actions and words. But this
dependence and this efficacy have nothing logical
about them; they are habitual collocations in the
world, like lightning and thunder. A more minute inspection of psycho-physical processes, were
it practicable, would doubtless disclose undreamed
of complexities and harmonies in them; the mathematical and dynamic relations of stimulus and
sensation might perhaps be formulated with precision. But the terms used in the equation, their
quality and inward habit, would always remain
data which the naturalist would have to assume
after having learned them by inspection. Movement could never be deduced dialectically or
graphically from thought nor thought from movement. Indeed no natural relation is in a different
case. Neither gravity, nor chemical reaction, nor
life and reproduction, nor time, space, and motion
themselves are logically deducible, nor intelligible
in terms of their limits. The phenomena have to
be accepted at their face value and allowed to
retain a certain empirical complexity; otherwise
the seed of all science is sterilised and calculation
cannot proceed for want of discernible and pregnant elements.

How fine nature's habits may be, where repetition begins, and down to what depth a mathematical treatment can penetrate, is a question for

the natural sciences to solve. Whether consciousness, for instance, accompanies vegetative life, or even all motion, is a point to be decided solely by empirical analogy. When the exact physical conditions of thought are discovered in man, we may infer how far thought is diffused through the universe, for it will be coextensive with the conditions it will have been shown to have. Now, in a very rough way, we know already what these conditions are. They are first the existence of an organic body and then its possession of adaptable instincts, of instincts that can be modified by experience. This capacity is what an observer calls intelligence; docility is the observable half of reason. When an animal winces at a blow and readjusts his pose, we say he feels; and we say he thinks when we see him brooding over his impressions, and find him launching into a new course of action after a silent decoction of his potential impulses. Conversely, when observation covers both the mental and the physical process, that is, in our own experience, we find that felt impulses, the conceived objects for which they make, and the values they determine are all correlated with animal instincts and external impressions. A desire is the inward sign of a physical proclivity to act, an image in sense is the sign in most cases of some material object in the environment and always, we may presume, of some cerebral change. The brain seems to simmer like a caldron in which all sorts of matters are perpetually transforming themselves into all sorts of shapes. When this cerebral reorganisation is pertinent to the external situation and renders the man, when he resumes action, more a master of his world, the accompanying thought is said to be practical; for it brings a consciousness of power and an earnest of success.

Cerebral processes are of course largely hypothetical. Theory suggests their existence, and experience can verify that theory only in an indirect and imperfect manner. The addition of a physical substratum to all thinking is only a scientific expedient, a hypothesis expressing the faith that nature is mechanically intelligible even beyond the reaches of minute verification. The accompanying consciousness, on the other hand, is something intimately felt by each man in his own person; it is a portion of crude and immediate experience. That it accompanies changes in his body and in the world is not an inference for him but a datum. But when crude experience is somewhat refined and the soul, at first mingled with every image, finds that it inhabits only her private body, to whose fortunes hers are altogether wedded, we begin to imagine that we know the cosmos at large better than the spirit; for beyond the narrow limits of our own person only the material phase of things is open to our observation. To add a mental phase to every part and motion of the cosmos is then seen to be an audacious fancy. It violates all empirical analogy, for the phenomenon which feeling accompanies in crude experience is not mere material existence, but reactive organisation and docility.

Artifices involved in separating them. The limits set to observation, however, render the mental and material spheres far from coincident, and even in a rough way mutually supplementary, so that human reflection has fallen into a habit of interlarding them. The world, instead of being a living body, a natural system with moral functions, has seemed to be a bisectible hybrid, half material and half mental, the clumsy conjunction of an automaton with a ghost. These phases, taken in their abstraction, as they first forced themselves on human attention, have been taken for independent and separable facts. Experience, remaining in both provinces quite sensuous and superficial, has accordingly been allowed to link this purely mental event with that purely mechanical one. The linkage is practically not deceptive, because mental transformations are indeed signs of changes in bodies; and so long as a cause is defined merely as a sign, mental and physical changes may truly be said to cause one another. But so soon as this form of augury tries to overcome its crude empiricism and to establish phenomenal laws, the mental factor has to fall out of the efficient process and be represented there by what, upon accurate examination, it is seen to be really the sign of—I mean by some physiological event.

If philosophers of the Cartesian school had taken to heart, as the German transcendentalists did, the

cogito ergo sum of their master, and had considered
that a physical world is, for knowledge, nothing
but an instrument to explain sensations and their
order, they might have expected this collapse of
half their metaphysics at the approach of their
positive science: for if mental existence was to
be kept standing only by its supposed causal
efficacy nothing could prevent the whole world
from becoming presently a *bête-machine*. Psychic
events have no links save through their organs
and their objects; the function of the material
world is, indeed, precisely to supply their linkage.
The internal relations of ideas, on the other hand,
are dialectical; their realm is eternal and absolutely irrelevant to the march of events. If we
must speak, therefore, of causal relations between
mind and body, we should say that matter is the
pervasive cause of mind's distribution, and mind
the pervasive cause of matter's discovery and
value. To ask for an efficient cause, to trace back
a force or investigate origins, is to have already
turned one's face in the direction of matter and
mechanical laws: no success in that undertaking
can fail to be a triumph for materialism. To ask
for a justification, on the other hand, is to turn no
less resolutely in the direction of ideal results and
actualities from which instrumentality and further
use have been eliminated. Spirit is useless, being
the end of things: but it is not vain, since it alone
rescues all else from vanity. It is called practical when it is prophetic of its own better fulfil-

ments, which is the case whenever forces are being turned to good uses, whenever an organism is exploring its relations and putting forth new tentacles with which to grasp the world.

Consciousness expresses vital equilibrium and docility. We saw in the beginning that the exigences of bodily life gave consciousness its first articulation. A bodily feat, like nutrition or reproduction, is celebrated by a festival in the mind, and consciousness is a sort of ritual solemnising by prayer, jubilation, or mourning, the chief episodes in the body's fortunes. The organs, by their structure, select the impressions possible to them from the divers influences abroad in the world, all of which, if animal organisms had learned to feed upon them, might plausibly have offered a basis for sensation. Every instinct or habitual impulse further selects from the passing bodily affections those that are pertinent to its own operation and which consequently adhere to it and modify its reactive machinery. Prevalent and notable sensations are therefore signs, presumably marking the presence of objects important for the body's welfare or for the execution of its predestined offices. So that not only are the soul's aims transcripts of the body's tendencies, but all ideas are grafted upon the interplay of these tendencies with environing forces. Early images hover about primary wants as highest conceptions do about ultimate achievements.

Thought is essentially practical in the sense

that but for thought no motion would be an action,
no change a progress; but thought is in no way
instrumental or servile; it is an experience realised, not a force to be
used. That same spontaneity in nature which has suggested a good must
be trusted to fulfil it. If we look fairly at the
actual resources of our minds we perceive that
we are as little informed concerning the means
and processes of action as concerning the reason why our motives move us. To execute the
simplest intention we must rely on fate: our
own acts are mysteries to us. Do I know how
I open my eyes or how I walk down stairs? Is
it the supervising wisdom of consciousness that
guides me in these acts? Is it the mind that
controls the bewildered body and points out
the way to physical habits uncertain of their
affinities? Or is it not much rather automatic
inward machinery that executes the marvellous
work, while the mind catches here and there
some glimpse of the operation, now with delight and adhesion, now with impotent rebellion? When impulses work themselves out unim-
peded we say we act; when they are thwarted we
say we are acted upon; but in neither case do we
in the least understand the natural history of
what is occurring. The mind at best vaguely
forecasts the result of action: a schematic verbal
sense of the end to be accomplished possibly hovers
in consciousness while the act is being performed;

*Its worthless-
ness as a cause
and value as
an expression.*

but this premonition is itself the sense of a process already present and betrays the tendency at work; it can obviously give no aid or direction to the unknown mechanical process that produced it and that must realise its own prophecy, if that prophecy is to be realised at all.

That such an unknown mechanism exists, and is adequate to explain every so-called decision, is indeed a hypothesis far outrunning detailed verification, although conceived by legitimate analogy with whatever is known about natural processes; but that the mind is not the source of itself or its own transformations is a matter of present experience; for the world is an unaccountable datum, in its existence, in its laws, and in its incidents. The highest hopes of science and morality look only to discovering those laws and bringing one set of incidents—facts of perception—into harmony with another set—facts of preference. This hoped-for issue, if it comes, must come about in the mind; but the mind cannot be its cause since, by hypothesis, it does not possess the ideas it seeks nor has power to realise the harmonies it desiderates. These have to be waited for and begged of destiny; human will, not controlling its basis, cannot possibly control its effects. Its existence and its efforts have at best the value of a good omen. They show in what direction natural forces are moving in so far as they are embodied in given men.

Men, like all things else in the world, are products and vehicles of natural energy, and their operation counts. But their conscious will, in its

moral assertiveness, is merely a sign of that energy and of that will's event- ual fortunes. Dramatic terror and dramatic humour both depend on con- trasting the natural pregnancy of a passion with its conscious intent. Everything in human life is ominous, even the voluntary acts. We cannot, by taking thought, add a cubit to our stature, but we may build up a world without meaning it. Man is as full of potentiality as he is of impotence. A will that represents many active forces, and is skilful in divination and augury, may long boast to be almighty without being con- tradicted by the event.

That thought is not self-directive appears best in the most immaterial processes. In strife against external forces men, being ignorant of their deeper selves, attribute the obvious effects of their action to their chance ideas; but when the process is wholly internal the real factors are more evenly represented in consciousness and the magi- cal, involuntary nature of life is better perceived. My hand, guided by I know not what machinery, is at this moment adding syllable to syllable upon this paper, to the general fulfilment, perhaps, of my felt intent, yet giving that intent an articula- tion wholly unforeseen, and often disappointing. The thoughts to be expressed simmer half-con- sciously in my brain. I feel their burden and tendency without seeing their form, until the mechanical train of impulsive association, started by the perusal of what precedes or by the accidental emergence of some new idea, lights the fuse and precipitates the phrases. If this happens in the most reflective and deliberate of activities, like this of composition, how much more does it happen in positive action, "The die is cast," said Cæsar, feeling a decision in himself of which he could neither count nor weigh the multitudinous causes; and so says every strong and clear intellect, every well-formed character, seizing at the same moment with comprehensive instinct both its purposes and the means by which they shall be attained. Only the fool, whose will signifies nothing, boasts to have created it himself.

Contemplative essence of action.

We must not seek the function of thought, then, in any supposed power to discover either ends not suggested by natural impulse or means to the accomplishment of those irrational ends. Attention is utterly powerless to change or create its objects in either respect; it rather registers without surprise—for it expects nothing in particular —and watches eagerly the images bubbling up in the living mind and the processes evolving there. These processes are themselves full of potency and promise; will and reflection are no more inconsequential than any other processes bound by natural links to the rest of the world. Even if an atomic mechanism suffices to mark the concatena-

tion of everything in nature, including the mind,
it cannot rob what it abstracts from of its natural
weight and reality: a thread that may suffice to
hold the pearls together is not the whole cause of
the necklace. But this pregnancy and implication of thought in relation to its natural environment is purely empirical. Since natural connection is merely a principle of arrangement by which
the contiguities of things may be described and
inferred, there is no difficulty in admitting consciousness and all its works into the web and woof
of nature. Each psychic episode would be heralded by its material antecedents; its transformations would be subject to mechanical laws, which
would also preside over the further transition from
thought into its material expression.

Mechanical efficacy alien to thought's essence. This inclusion of mind in nature,
however, is as far as possible from
constituting the mind's function and
value, or its efficacy in a moral and rational
sense. To have prepared changes in matter
would give no rationality to mind unless those
changes in turn paved the way to some better mental existence. The worth of natural efficacy is
therefore always derivative; the utility of mind
would be no more precious than the utility of matter; both borrow all their worth from the part
they may play empirically in introducing those
moral values which are intrinsic and self-sufficing.
In so far as thought is instrumental it is not worth
having, any more than matter, except for its prom-

ise; it must terminate in something truly profitable and ultimate which, being good in itself, may lend value to all that led up to it. But this ultimate good is itself consciousness, thought, rational activity; so that what instrumental mentality may have preceded might be abolished without loss, if matter suffices to sustain reason in being; or if that instrumental mentality is worth retaining, it is so only because it already contains some premonition and image of its own fulfilment. In a word, the value of thought is ideal. The material efficacy which may be attributed to it is the proper efficacy of matter—an efficacy which matter would doubtless claim if we knew enough of its secret mechanism. And when that imputed and incongruous utility was subtracted from ideas they would appear in their proper form of expressions, realisations, ultimate fruits.

The incongruity of making thought, in its moral and logical essence, an instrument in the natural world will appear from a different point of view if we shift the discussion for a moment to a transcendental level. Since the material world is an object for thought, and potential in relation Consciousness to immediate experience, it can hardly transcendental. lie in the same plane of reality with the thought to which it appears. The spectator on this side of the foot-lights, while surely regarded by the play as a whole, cannot expect to figure in its mechanism or to see himself strutting among the actors on the boards. He listens and is served, being at once impotent and supreme.   It has been well said that

> Only the free divine the laws,
> The causeless only know the cause.

Conversely, what in such a transcendental sense is causeless and free will evidently not be causal or determinant, being something altogether universal and notional, without inherent determinations or specific affinities.   The objects figuring in consciousness will have implications and will require causes; not so the consciousness itself.   The Ego to which all things appear equally, whatever their form or history, is the ground of nothing incidental: no specific characters or order found in the world can be attributed to its efficacy.   The march of experience is not determined by the mere fact that experience exists.   Another experience, differently logical, might be equally real.   Consciousness is not itself dynamic, for it has no body, no idiosyncrasy or particular locus, to be the point of origin for definite relationships.   It is merely an abstract name for the actuality of its random objects.   All force, implication, or direction inhere in the constitution of specific objects and live in their interplay.   Logic is revealed to thought no less than nature is, and even what we call invention or fancy is generated not by thought itself but by the chance fertility of nebulous objects, floating and breeding in the primeval chaos.   Where the natural order lapses, if it ever

does, not mind or will or reason can possibly inter-
vene to fill the chasm—for these are parcels and
expressions of the natural order—but only nothingness and pure chance.

Thought is thus an expression of natural relations, as will is of natural affinities; yet consciousness of an object's value, while it declares the
blind disposition to pursue that object, constitutes its entire worth. Apart from the pains and
satisfactions involved, an impulse and its execution would be alike destitute of importance. It
would matter nothing how chaotic or how orderly
the world became, or what animal bodies arose or
perished there; any tendencies afoot in nature,
whatever they might construct or dissolve, would
involve no progress or disaster, since no preferences would exist to pronounce one eventual state
of things better than another. These preferences
and are in themselves, if the dynamic order
transcendent. alone be considered, works of supererer-
gation, expressing force but not producing it, like
a statue of Hercules; but the principle of such
preferences, the force they express and depend
upon, is some mechanical impulse itself involved
in the causal process. Expression gives value to
power, and the strength of Hercules would have
no virtue in it had it contributed nothing to art
and civilisation. That conceived basis of all life
which we call matter would be a mere potentiality,
an inferred instrument deprived of its function, if it did not actually issue in life and con-

sciousness. What gives the material world a legitimate status and perpetual pertinence in human discourse is the conscious life it supports and carries in its own direction, as a ship carries its passengers or rather as a passion carries its hopes. Conscious interests first justify and moralise the mechanisms they express. Eventual satisfactions, while their form and possibility must be determined by animal tendencies, alone render these tendencies vehicles of the good. The direction in which benefit shall lie must be determined by irrational impulse, but the attainment of benefit consists in crowning that impulse with its ideal achievement. Nature dictates what men shall seek and prompts them to seek it; a possibility of happiness is thus generated and only its fulfilment would justify nature and man in their common venture.

It is the seat of value.   Satisfaction is the touchstone of value; without reference to it all talk about good and evil, progress or decay, is merely confused verbiage, pure sophistry in which the juggler adroitly withdraws attention from what works the wonder—namely, that human and moral colouring to which the terms he plays with owe whatever efficacy they have. Metaphysicians sometimes so define the good as to make it a matter of no importance; not seldom they give that name to the sum of all evils. A good, absolute in the sense of being divorced from all natural demand and all possible satisfaction, would

be as remote as possible from goodness: to call it
good is mere disloyalty to morals, brought about
by some fantastic or dialectical passion. In excellence there is an essential bias, an opposition
to the possible opposite; this bias expresses a
mechanical impulse, a situation that has stirred
the senses and the will. Impulse makes value possible; and the value becomes actual when the impulse issues in processes that give it satisfaction
and have a conscious worth. Character is the
basis of happiness and happiness the sanction of
character.*

That thought is nature's concomitant expression or entelechy, never one of her instruments,
is a truth long ago divined by the more judicious
thinkers, like Aristotle and Spinoza; but it has not
met with general acceptance or even consideration.
It is obstructed by superficial empiricism, which
associates the better-known aspects of events directly together, without considering what mechani-

---

* Aristippus asked Socrates "whether he knew anything good, so that if he answered by naming food or drink
or money or health or strength or valour or anything of that
sort, he might at once show that it was sometimes an evil.
Socrates, however, knew very well that if anything troubles
us what we demand is its cure, and he replied in the most
pertinent fashion. 'Are you asking me,' he said, 'if I know
anything good for a fever?' 'Oh, no,' said the other. 'Or
for sore eyes?' 'Not that, either.' 'Or for hunger?' 'No,
not for hunger.' 'Well, then,' said he, 'if you ask me
whether I know a good that is good for nothing, I neither
know it nor want to know it.'"—Xenophon, Memorabilia,
iii., 8.

cal bonds may secretly unite them; it is obstructed also by the traditional mythical idealism, intent as this philosophy is on proving nature to
be the expression of something ulterior and non-
natural and on hugging the fatal misconception
that ideals and eventual goods are creative and
miraculous forces, without perceiving that it
thereby renders goods and ideals perfectly senseless; for how can anything be a good at all to
which some existing nature is not already directed?
It may therefore be worth while, before leaving
this phase of the subject, to consider one or two
prejudices which might make it sound paradoxi-
cal to say, as we propose, that ideals are ideal and
nature natural.

**Apparent
utility of pain.** Of all forms of consciousness the
one apparently most useful is pain,
which is also the one most immersed in matter
and most opposite to ideality and excellence. Its
utility lies in the warning it gives: in trying to
escape pain we escape destruction. That we desire to escape pain is certain; its very definition
can hardly go beyond the statement that pain is
that element of feeling which we seek to abolish on
account of its intrinsic quality. That this desire,
however, should know how to initiate remedial
action is a notion contrary to experience and in
itself unthinkable. If pain could have cured us we
should long ago have been saved. The bitterest
quintessence of pain is its helplessness, and our
incapacity to abolish it. The most intolerable

torments are those we feel gaining upon us, intensifying and prolonging themselves indefinitely.
Its real impotence. This baffling quality, so conspicuous in extreme agony, is present in all pain and is perhaps its essence. If we sought to describe by a circumlocution what is of course a primary sensation, we might scarcely do better than to say that pain is consciousness at once intense and empty, fixing attention on what contains no character, and arrests all satisfactions without offering anything in exchange. The horror of pain lies in its intolerable intensity and its intolerable tedium. It can accordingly be cured either by sleep or by entertainment. In itself it has no resource; its violence is quite helpless and its vacancy offers no expedients by which it might be unknotted and relieved.

Pain is not only impotent in itself but is a sign of impotence in the sufferer. Its appearance, far from constituting its own remedy, is like all other organic phenomena subject to the law of inertia and tends only to its own continuance. A man's hatred of his own condition no more helps to improve it than hatred of other people tends to improve them. If we allowed ourselves to speak in such a case of efficacy at all, we should say that pain perpetuates and propagates itself in various ways, now by weakening the system, now by prompting convulsive efforts, now by spreading to other beings through the contagion of sympathy or vengeance. In fact, however, it merely betrays

a maladjustment which has more or less natural
stability. It may be instantaneous only; by its
lack of equilibrium it may involve the immediate
destruction of one of its factors. In that case we
fabulously say that the pain has instinctively removed its own cause. Pain is here apparently
useful because it expresses an incipient tension
which the self-preserving forces in the organism
are sufficient to remove. Pain's appearance is then
the sign for its instant disappearance; not indeed
by virtue of its inner nature or of any art it can
initiate, but merely by virtue of mechanical associations between its cause and its remedy. The
burned child dreads the fire and, reading only the
surface of his life, fancies that the pain once felt
and still remembered is the ground of his new
prudence. Punishments, however, are not always
efficacious, as everyone knows who has tried to
govern children or cities by the rod; suffering does
not bring wisdom nor even memory, unless intelligence and docility are already there; that is, unless
the friction which the pain betrayed sufficed to
obliterate permanently one of the impulses in conflict. This readjustment, on which real improvement hangs and which alone makes "experience"
useful, does not correspond to the intensity or repetition of the pains endured; it corresponds rather
to such a plasticity in the organism that the painful conflict is no longer produced.

Preformations involved. Threatened destruction would not
involve pain unless that threatened de-

struction were being resisted; so that the reaction which pain is supposed to cause must already be taking place before pain can be felt. A will without direction cannot be thwarted; so that inhibition cannot be the primary source of any effort or of any ideal. Determinate impulses must exist already for their inhibition to have taken place or for the pain to arise which is the sign of that inhibition. The child's dread of the fire marks the acceleration of that impulse which, when he was burned, originally enabled him to withdraw his hand; and if he did not now shrink in anticipation he would not remember the pain nor know to what to attach his terror. Sight now suffices to awaken the reaction which touch at first was needed to produce; the will has extended its line of battle and thrown out its scouts farther afield; and pain has been driven back to the frontiers of the spirit. The conflicting reactions are now peripheral and feeble; the pain involved in aversion is nothing to that once involved in the burn. Had this aversion to fire been innate, as many aversions are, no pain would have been caused, because no profound maladjustment would have occurred. The surviving attraction, checked by fear, is a remnant of the old disorganisation in the brain which was the seat of conflicting reactions.

To say that this conflict is the guide to its own issue is to talk without thinking. The conflict is the sign of inadequate organisation, or of

non-adaptation in the given organism to the various stimuli which irritate it. The reconstruction
Its untoward significance. which follows this conflict, when it indeed follows, is of course a new and better adaptation; so that what involves the pain may often be a process of training which directs reaction into new and smoother channels. But the pain is present whether a permanent adaptation is being attained or not. It is present in progressive dissolution and in hopeless and exhausting struggles far more than in education or in profitable correction. Toothache and sea-sickness, birth-pangs and melancholia are not useful ills. The intenser the pain the more probable its uselessness. Only in vanishing is it a sign of progress; in occurring it is an omen of defeat, just as disease is an omen of death, although, for those diseased already, medicine and convalescence may be approaches to health again. Where a man's nature is out of gear and his instincts are inordinate, suffering may be a sign that a dangerous peace, in which impulse was carrying him ignorantly into paths without issue, is giving place to a peace with security in which his reconstructed character may respond without friction to the world, and enable him to gather a clearer experience and enjoy a purer vitality. The utility of pain is thus apparent only, and due to empirical haste in collating events that have no regular nor inward relation; and even this imputed utility pain has only in proportion to the worthlessness of those who need it.

Perfect function not un- conscious. A second current prejudice which may deserve notice suggests that an organ, when its function is perfect, becomes unconscious, so that if adaptation were complete life would disappear. The well-learned routine of any mechanical art passes into habit, and habit into unconscious operation. The virtuoso is not aware how he manipulates his instrument; what was conscious labour in the beginning has become instinct and miracle in the end. Thus it might appear that to eliminate friction and difficulty would be to eliminate consciousness, and therefore value, from the world. Life would thus be involved in a contradiction and moral effort in an absurdity; for while the constant aim of practice is perfection and that of labour ease, and both are without meaning or standard unless directed to the attainment of these ends, yet such attainment, if it were actual, would be worthless, so that what alone justifies effort would lack justification and would in fact be incapable of existence. The good musician must strive to play perfectly, but, alas, we are told, if he succeeded he would have become an automaton. The good man must aspire to holiness, but, alas, if he reached holiness his moral life would have evaporated.

These melodramatic prophecies, however, need not alarm us. They are founded on nothing but rhetoric and small allegiance to any genuine good. When we attain perfection of function we lose consciousness of the medium, to become more clearly conscious of the result. The eye that does its duty gives no report of itself and has no sense of muscular tension or weariness; but it gives all the brighter and steadier image of the object seen. Consciousness is not lost when focussed, and the labour of vision is abolished in its fruition. So the musician, could he play so divinely as to be unconscious of his body, his instrument, and the very lapse of time, would be only the more absorbed in the harmony, more completely master of its unities and beauty. At such moments the body's long labour at last brings forth the soul. Life from its inception is simply some partial natural harmony raising its voice and bearing witness to its own existence; to perfect that harmony is to round out and intensify that life. This is the very secret of power, of joy, of intelligence. Not to have understood it is to have passed through life without understanding anything.

The analogy extends to morals, where also the means may be advantageously forgotten when the end has been secured. That leisure to which work is directed and that perfection in which virtue would be fulfilled are so far from being apathetic that they are states of pure activity, by containing which other acts are rescued from utter passivity and unconsciousness. Impure feeling ranges between two extremes: absolute want and complete satisfaction. The former limit is reached in anguish, madness, or the agony of death, when the accidental flux of things in contradiction has

reached its maximum or vanishing point, so that
the contradiction and the flux themselves disappear
by diremption. Such feeling denotes inward disorganisation and a hopeless conflict of reflex
actions tending toward dissolution. The second
limit is reached in contemplation, when anything
is loved, understood, or enjoyed. Synthetic power
is then at its height; the mind can survey its experience and correlate all the motions it suggests.
Power in the mind is exactly proportionate to
representative scope, and representative scope to
rational activity. A steady vision of all things
in their true order and worth results from perfection of function and is its index; it secures the
greatest distinctness in thought together with the
greatest decision, wisdom, and ease in action, as
the lightning is brilliant and quick. It also
secures, so far as human energies avail, its own
perpetuity, since what is perfectly adjusted within
and without lasts long and goes far.

Inchoate ethics. To confuse means with ends and
mistake disorder for vitality is not unnatural to
minds that hear the hum of mighty workings but
can imagine neither the cause nor the fruits of
that portentous commotion. All functions, in
such chaotic lives, seem instrumental functions.
It is then supposed that what serves no further
purpose can have no value, and that he who
suffers no offuscation can have no feeling and
no life. To attain an ideal seems to destroy
its worth. Moral life, at that low level, is a

fantastic game only, not having come in sight of humane and liberal interests. The barbarian's intensity is without seriousness and his passion without joy. His philosophy, which means to glorify all experience and to digest all vice, is in truth an expression of pathetic innocence. It betrays a rudimentary impulse to follow every beckoning hand, to assume that no adventure and no bewitchment can be anything but glorious. Such an attitude is intelligible in one who has never seen anything worth seeing nor loved anything worth loving. Immaturity could go no farther than to acknowledge no limits defining will and happiness. When such limits, however, are gradually discovered and an authoritative ideal is born of the marriage of human nature with experience, happiness becomes at once definite and attainable; for adjustment is possible to a world that has a fruitful and intelligible structure.

Such incoherences, which might well arise in ages without traditions, may be preserved and fostered by superstition. Perpetual servile employments and subjection to an irrational society may render people incapable even of conceiving a liberal life. They may come to think their happiness no longer separable from their misery and to fear the large emptiness, as they deem it, of a happy world. Like the prisoner of Chillon, after so long a captivity, they would regain their freedom with a sigh. The wholesome influences of nature, however, would soon revive their wills, contorted by unnatural oppression, and a vision of perfection would arise within them upon breathing a purer air. Freedom and perfection are synonymous with life. The peace they bring is one

> whose names are also rapture, power,
> Clear sight, and love; for these are parts of peace.

Thought the entelechy of being. Thought belongs to the sphere of ultimate results. What, indeed, could be more fitting than that consciousness, which is self-revealing and transcendentally primary, should be its own excuse for being and should contain its own total value, together with the total value of everything else? What could be more proper than that the whole worth of ideas should be ideal? To make an idea instrumental would be to prostitute what, being self-existent, should be self-justifying. That continual absoluteness which consciousness possesses, since in it alone all heaven and earth are at any moment revealed, ought to convince any radical and heart-searching philosopher that all values should be continually integrated and realised there, where all energies are being momently focussed. Thought is a fulfilment; its function is to lend utility to its causes and to make actual those conceived and subterranean processes which find in it their ultimate expression. Thought is nature represented; it is potential energy producing life and becoming an actual appearance.

The conditions of consciousness, however, are far from being its only theme. As consciousness **Its exuberance.** bears a transcendent relation to the dynamic world (for it is actual and spiritual, while the dynamic is potential and material) so it may be exuberant and irresponsibly rich. Although its elements, in point of distribution and derivation, are grounded in matter, as music is in vibrations, yet in point of character the result may be infinitely redundant. The complete musician would devote but a small part of his attention to the basis of music, its mechanism, psychology, or history. Long before he had represented to his mind the causes of his art, he would have proceeded to practise and enjoy it. So sense and imagination, passion and reason, may enrich the soil that breeds them and cover it with a maze of flowers.

The theme of consciousness is accordingly far more than the material world which constitutes its basis, though this also is one of its themes; thought is no less at home in various expressions and embroideries with which the material world can be overlaid in imagination. The material world is conceived by digging beneath experience to find its cause; it is the efficacious structure and skeleton of things. This is the subject of scientific retrospect and calculation. The forces disclosed by physical studies are of course not directed to producing a mind that might merely describe them. A force is expressed in many other ways than by being defined; it may be felt, resisted, embodied, transformed, or symbolised. Forces work; they are not, like mathematical concepts, exhausted in description. From that matter which might be describable in mechanical formulæ there issue notwithstanding all manner of forms and harmonies, visible, audible, imaginable, and passionately prized. Every phase of the ideal world emanates from the natural and loudly proclaims its origin by the interest it takes in natural existences, of which it gives a rational interpretation. Sense, art, religion, society, express nature exuberantly and in symbols long before science is added to represent, by a different abstraction, the mechanism which nature contains.

CHAPTER X

THE MEASURE OF VALUES IN REFLECTION

Honesty in hedonism. To put value in pleasure and pain, regarding a given quantity of pain as balancing a given quantity of pleasure, is to bring to practical ethics a worthy intention to be clear and, what is more precious, an undoubted honesty not always found in those moralists who maintain the opposite opinion and care more for edification than for truth. For in spite of all logical and psychological scruples, conduct that should not justify itself somehow by the satisfactions secured and the pains avoided would not justify itself at all. The most instinctive and unavoidable desire is forthwith chilled if you discover that its ultimate end is to be a preponderance of suffering; and what arrests this desire is not fear or weakness but conscience in its most categorical and sacred guise. Who would not be ashamed to acknowledge or to propose so inhuman an action?

By sad experience rooted impulses may be transformed or even obliterated. And quite intelligibly: for the idea of pain is already the sign and the beginning of a certain stoppage. To

imagine failure is to interpret ideally a felt inhibition. To prophesy a check would be impossible but for an incipient movement already meet-
ing an incipient arrest. Intensified, this prophecy
becomes its own fulfilment and totally inhibits
the opposed tendency. Therefore a mind that
foresees pain to be the ultimate result of action
cannot continue unreservedly to act, seeing that
its foresight is the conscious transcript of a recoil
already occurring. Conversely, the mind that
surrenders itself wholly to any impulse must think
that its execution would be delightful. A perfectly wise and representative will, therefore,
would aim only at what, in its attainment, could
continue to be aimed at and approved; and this
is another way of saying that its aim would secure
the maximum of satisfaction eventually possible.

Necessary qualifications. In spite, however, of this involution
of pain and pleasure in all deliberate
forecast and volition, pain and pleasure are not
the ultimate sources of value. A correct psychology and logic cannot allow that an eventual and,
in strictness, unpresentable feeling, can determine
any act or volition, but must insist that, on the
contrary, all beliefs about future experience, with
all premonition of its emotional quality, is based
on actual impulse and feeling; so that the source
of value is nothing but the inner fountain of life
and imagination, and the object of pursuit nothing but the ideal object, counterpart of the present demand. Abstract satisfaction is not pursued,

but, if the will and the environment are constant, satisfaction will necessarily be felt in achieving the object desired. A rejection of hedonistic psychology, therefore, by no means involves any opposition to eudæmonism in ethics. Eudæmonism is another name for wisdom: there is no other *moral* morality. Any system that, for some sinister reason, should absolve itself from good-will toward all creatures, and make it somehow a duty to secure their misery, would be clearly disloyal to reason, humanity, and justice. Nor would it be hard, in that case, to point out what superstition, what fantastic obsession, or what private fury, had made those persons blind to prudence and kindness in so plain a matter. Happiness is the only sanction of life; where happiness fails, existence remains a mad and lamentable experiment. The question, however, what happiness shall consist in, its complexion if it should once arise, can only be determined by reference to natural demands and capacities; so that while satisfaction by the attainment of ends can alone justify their pursuit, this pursuit itself must exist first and be spontaneous, thereby fixing the goals of endeavour and distinguishing the states in which satisfaction might be found. Natural disposition, therefore, is the principle of preference and makes morality and happiness possible.

The will must judge.   The standard of value, like every standard, must be one. Pleasures and pains are not only infinitely diverse but, even if reduced to their total bulk and abstract opposition, they remain two. Their values must be compared, and obviously neither one can be the standard by which to judge the other. This standard is an ideal involved in the judgment passed, whatever that judgment may be. Thus when Petrarch says that a thousand pleasures are not worth one pain, he establishes an ideal of value deeper than either pleasure or pain, an ideal which makes a life of satisfaction marred by a single pang an offence and a horror to his soul. If our demand for rationality is less acute and the miscellaneous affirmations of the will carry us along with a well-fed indifference to some single tragedy within us, we may aver that a single pang is only the thousandth part of a thousand pleasures and that a life so balanced is nine hundred and ninety-nine times better than nothing. This judgment, for all its air of mathematical calculation, in truth expresses a choice as irrational as Petrarch's. It merely means that, as a matter of fact, the mixed prospect presented to us attracts our wills and attracts them vehemently. So that the only possible criterion for the relative values of pains and pleasures is the will that chooses among them or among combinations of them; nor can the intensity of pleasures and pains, apart from the physical violence of their expression, be judged by any other standard than by the power they have, when represented, to control the will's movement.

Injustice inherent in representation. Here we come upon one of those initial irrationalities in the world which theories of all sorts, since they are attempts to find rationality in things, are in serious danger of overlooking. In estimating the value of any experience, our endeavour, our pretension, is to weigh the value which that experience possesses when it is actual. But to weigh is to compare, and to compare is to represent, since the transcendental isolation and self-sufficiency of actual experience precludes its lying side by side with another datum, like two objects given in a single consciousness. Successive values, to be compared, must be represented; but the conditions of representation are such that they rob objects of the values they had at their first appearance to substitute the values they possess at their recurrence. For representation mirrors consciousness only by mirroring its objects, and the emotional reaction upon those objects cannot be represented directly, but is approached by indirect methods, through an imitation or assimilation of will to will and emotion to emotion. Only by the instrumentality of signs, like gesture or language, can we bring ourselves to reproduce in some measure an absent experience and to feel some premonition of its absolute value. Apart from very elaborate and cumulative suggestions to the contrary, we should always attribute to an event in every other experience the value which its image now had in our own. But in that case the pathetic fallacy would be present; for a volitional reaction upon an idea in one vital context is no index to what the volitional reaction would be in another vital context upon the situation which that idea represents.

Æsthetic and speculative cruelty. This divergence falsifies all representation of life and renders it initially cruel, sentimental, and mythical. We dislike to trample on a flower, because its form makes a kind of blossoming in our own fancy which we call beauty; but we laugh at pangs we endured in childhood and feel no tremor at the incalculable sufferings of all mankind beyond our horizon, because no imitable image is involved to start a contrite thrill in our own bosom. The same cruelty appears in æsthetic pleasures, in lust, war, and ambition; in the illusions of desire and memory; in the unsympathetic quality of theory everywhere, which regards the uniformities of cause and effect and the beauties of law as a justification for the inherent evils in the experience described; in the unjust judgments, finally, of mystical optimism, that sinks so completely into its subjective commotion as to mistake the suspension of all discriminating and representative faculties for a true union in things, and the blur of its own ecstasy for a universal glory. These pleasures are all on the sensuous plane, the plane of levity and unintentional wickedness; but in their own sphere they have their own value. Æsthetic and speculative emotions make an im-

portant contribution to the total worth of exist
ence, but they do not abolish the evils of that experience on which they reflect with such ruthless
satisfaction. The satisfaction is due to a private
flood of emotion submerging the images present in
fancy, or to the exercise of a new intellectual function, like that of abstraction, synthesis, or comparison. Such a faculty, when fully developed,
is capable of yielding pleasures as intense and
voluminous as those proper to rudimentary animal functions,. wrongly supposed to be more vital.
The acme of vitality lies in truth in the most
comprehensive and penetrating thought. The
rhythms, the sweep, the impetuosity of impassioned
contemplation not only contain in themselves a
great vitality and potency, but they often succeed
in engaging the lower functions in a sympathetic
vibration, and we see the whole body and soul rapt,
as we say, and borne along by the harmonies of
imagination and thought. In these fugitive
moments of intoxication the detail of truth is submerged and forgotten. The emotions which
would be suggested by the parts are replaced by
the rapid emotion of transition between them; and
this exhilaration in survey, this mountain-top experience, is supposed to be also the truest vision
of reality. Absorption in a supervening function
is mistaken for comprehension of all fact, and this
inevitably, since all consciousness of particular
facts and of their values is then submerged in the
torrent of cerebral excitement.

Imputed
values: their
inconstancy.

That luminous blindness which in these cases takes an extreme form is present in principle throughout all reflection. We tend to regard our own past as good only when we still find some value in the memory of it. Last year, last week, even the feelings of the last five minutes, are not otherwise prized than by the pleasure we may still have in recalling them; the pulsations of pleasure or pain which they contained we do not even seek to remember or to discriminate. The period is called happy or unhappy merely as its ideal representation exercises fascination or repulsion over the present will. Hence the revulsion after physical indulgence, often most violent when the pleasure—judged by its concomitant expression and by the desire that heralded it—was most intense. For the strongest passions are intermittent, so that the unspeakable charm which their objects possess for a moment is lost immediately and becomes unintelligible to a chilled and cheated reflection. The situation, when yet unrealised, irresistibly solicited the will and seemed to promise incomparable ecstasy; and perhaps it yields an indescribable moment of excitement and triumph—a moment only half-appropriated into waking experience, so fleeting is it, and so unfit the mind to possess or retain its tenser attitudes. The same situation, if revived in memory when the system is in an opposite and relaxed state, forfeits all power to attract and fills the mind rather with aversion and disgust. For all violent pleasures, as Shakespeare says, are cruel and not to be trusted.

A bliss in proof and, proved, a very woe:
Before, a joy proposed; behind, a dream . . .
Enjoyed no sooner but despised straight;
Past reason hunted and, no sooner had,
Past reason hated.

Methods of control. Past reason, indeed. For although an impulsive injustice is inherent in the very nature of representation and cannot be overcome altogether, yet reason, by attending to all the evidences that can be gathered and by confronting the first pronouncement by others fetched from every quarter of experience, has power to minimise the error and reach a practically just estimate of absent values. This achieved rightness can be tested by comparing two experiences, each when it is present, with the same conventional permanent object chosen to be their expression. A love-song, for instance, can be pronounced adequate or false by various lovers; and it can thus remain a sort of index to the fleeting sentiments once confronted with it. Reason has, to be sure, no independent method of discovering values. They must be rated as the sensitive balance of present inclination, when completely laden, shows them to stand. In estimating values reason is reduced to data furnished by the mechanical processes of ideation and instinct, as in framing all knowledge; an absent joy can only be represented by a tinge of emotion dyeing an image that pictures

the situation in which the joy was felt; but the
suggested value being once projected into the
potential world, that land of inferred being, this
projection may be controlled and corroborated by
other suggestions and associations relevant to it,
which it is the function of reason to collect and
compare. A right estimate of absent values must
be conventional and mediated by signs. Direct
sympathies, which suffice for instinctive present
co-operation, fail to transmit alien or opposite
pleasures. They over-emphasise momentary relations, while they necessarily ignore permanent
bonds. Therefore the same intellect that puts a
mechanical reality behind perception must put a
moral reality behind sympathy.

Example of fame. Fame, for example, is a good; its
value arises from a certain movement
of will and emotion which is elicited by the
thought that one's name might be associated with
great deeds and with the memory of them. The
glow of this thought bathes the object it describes,
so that fame is felt to have a value quite distinct
from that which the expectation of fame may have
in the present moment. Should this expectation
be foolish and destined to prove false, it would
have no value, and be indeed the more ludicrous
and repulsive the more pleasure its dupe took in
it, and the longer his illusion lasted. The heart
is resolutely set on its object and despises its own
phenomena, not reflecting that its emotions have
first revealed that object's worth and alone can

maintain it. For if a man cares nothing for
fame, what value has it?

This projection of interest into excellence
takes place mechanically and is in the first
instance irrational. Did all glow die out from
memory and expectation, the events represented
remaining unchanged, we should be incapable
of assigning any value to those events, just
as, if eyes were lacking, we should be incapable of assigning colour to the world, which
would, notwithstanding, remain as it is at present. So fame could never be regarded as a good
if the idea of fame gave no pleasure; yet now,
because the idea pleases, the reality is regarded as
a good, absolute and intrinsic. This moral hypostasis involved in the love of fame could never be
rationalised, but would subsist unmitigated or die
out unobserved, were it not associated with other
conceptions and other habits of estimating values.
For the passions are humanised only by being
juxtaposed and forced to live together. As fame
is not man's only goal and the realisation of it
comes into manifold relations with other interests
no less vivid, we are able to criticise the impulse
to pursue it.

Fame may be the consequence of benefits con-
ferred upon mankind. In that case the abstract desire for fame would be reinforced and,
as it were, justified by its congruity with the
more voluminous and stable desire to benefit our
fellow-men. Or, again, the achievements which

insure fame and the genius that wins it probably
involve a high degree of vitality and many profound inward satisfactions to the man of genius
himself; so that again the abstract love of fame
would be reinforced by the independent and more
rational desire for a noble and comprehensive experience.   On the other hand, the minds of posterity, whose homage is craved by the ambitious
man, will probably have very false conceptions of
his thoughts and purposes.   What they will call
by his name will be, in a great measure, a fiction
of their own fancy and not his portrait at all.
Would Cæsar recognise himself in the current
notions of him, drawn from some school-history,
or perhaps from Shakespeare's satirical portrait?
Would Christ recognise himself upon our altars,
or in the romances about him constructed by imaginative critics?   And not only is remote experience thus hopelessly lost and misrepresented, but
even this nominal memorial ultimately disappears.

The love of fame, if tempered by these and similar considerations, would tend to take a place in
man's ideal such as its roots in human nature and
its functions in human progress might seem to
justify.   It would be rationalised in the only
sense in which any primary desire can be rationalised, namely, by being combined with all others
in a consistent whole.   How much of it would survive a thorough sifting and criticism, may well
remain in doubt.   The result would naturally differ for different temperaments and in different

states of society. The wisest men, perhaps, while
they would continue to feel some love of honour
and some interest in their image in other minds,
would yet wish that posterity might praise them
as Sallust praises Cato by saying: *Esse quam
videri bonus maluit;* he preferred worth to repu-
tation.

The fact that value is attributed to
absent experience according to the
value experience has in representation
appears again in one of the most curious anoma-
lies in human life—the exorbitant interest which
thought and reflection take in the form of experience and the slight account they make of its intensity or volume. Sea-sickness and child-birth
when they are over, the pangs of despised love
when that love is finally forgotten or requited, the
travail of sin when once salvation is assured, all
melt away and dissolve like a morning mist leaving a clear sky without a vestige of sorrow. So
also with merely remembered and not reproduc-
ible pleasures; the buoyancy of youth, when absurdity is not yet tedious, the rapture of sport
or passion, the immense peace found in a mystical surrender to the universal, all these generous
ardours count for nothing when they are once gone.
The memory of them cannot cure a fit of the blues
nor raise an irritable mortal above some petty
act of malice or vengeance, or reconcile him to
foul weather. An ode of Horace, on the other
hand, a scientific monograph, or a well-written

Disproportion-
ate interest in
the æsthetic.

page of music is a better antidote to melancholy than thinking on all the happiness which one's own life or that of the universe may ever have contained. Why should overwhelming masses of suffering and joy affect imagination so little while it responds sympathetically to æsthetic and intellectual irritants of very slight intensity, objects that, it must be confessed, are of almost no importance to the welfare of mankind? Why should we be so easily awed by artistic genius and exalt men whose works we know only by name, perhaps, and whose influence upon society has been infinitesimal, like a Pindar or a Leonardo, while we regard great merchants and inventors as ignoble creatures in comparison? Why should we smile at the inscription in Westminster Abbey which calls the inventor of the spinning-jenny one of the *true* benefactors of mankind? Is it not probable, on the whole, that he has had a greater and less equivocal influence on human happiness than Shakespeare with all his plays and sonnets? But the cheapness of cotton cloth produces no particularly delightful image in the fancy to be compared with Hamlet or Imogen. There is a prodigious selfishness in dreams: they live perfectly deaf and invulnerable amid the cries of the real world.

The same æsthetic bias appears in the moral sphere. Utilitarians have attempted to show that the human conscience commends precisely those actions which tend to secure general happiness and that the notions of justice and virtue pre-

vailing in any age vary with its social economy
and the prizes it is able to attain. And, if due
allowance is made for the complexity of the subject, we may reasonably admit that the precepts
of obligatory morality bear this relation to the
general welfare; thus virtue means courage in a
soldier, probity in a merchant, and chastity in a
woman. But if we turn from the morality required of all to the type regarded as perfect and
ideal, we find no such correspondence to the benefits involved. The selfish imagination intervenes
here and attributes an absolute and irrational value
to those figures that entertain it with the most
absorbing and dreamful emotions.
The character of Christ, for instance,
which even the least orthodox among
us are in the habit of holding up as a perfect
model, is not the character of a benefactor but of
a martyr, a spirit from a higher world lacerated
in its passage through this uncomprehending and
perverse existence, healing and forgiving out of
sheer compassion, sustained by his inner affinities
to the supernatural, and absolutely disenchanted
with all earthly or political goods. Christ did not
suffer, like Prometheus, for having bestowed or
wished to bestow any earthly blessing: the only
blessing he bequeathed was the image of himself
upon the cross, whereby men might be comforted
in their own sorrows, rebuked in their worldliness,
driven to put their trust in the supernatural, and
united, by their common indifference to the world,

Irrational
religious
allegiance.

in one mystic brotherhood. As men learned these
lessons, or were inwardly ready to learn them,
they recognised more and more clearly in Jesus
their heaven-sent redeemer, and in following their
own conscience and desperate idealism into the
desert or the cloister, in ignoring all civic virtues
and allowing the wealth, art, and knowledge of
the pagan world to decay, they began what they
felt to be an imitation of Christ.

All natural impulses, all natural ideals, subsisted
of course beneath this theoretic asceticism, writhed
under its unearthly control, and broke out in frequent violent irruptions against it in the life of
each man as well as in the course of history. Yet
the image of Christ remained in men's hearts and
retained its marvellous authority, so that even now,
when so many who call themselves Christians, being pure children of nature, are without the least
understanding of what Christianity came to do in
the world, they still offer his person and words a
sincere if inarticulate worship, trying to transform
that sacrificial and crucified spirit, as much as
their bungling fancy can, into a patron of Philis-
tia Felix. Why this persistent adoration of a character that is the extreme negation of all that these
good souls inwardly value and outwardly pursue?
Because the image of Christ and the associations
of his religion, apart from their original import,
remain rooted in the mind: they remain the focus
for such wayward emotions and mystic intuitions
as their magnetism can still attract, and the value

which this hallowed compound possesses in representation is transferred to its nominal object, and Christ is the conventional name for all the impulses of religion, no matter how opposite to the Christian.

Symbols, when their significance has been great, outlive their first significance. The image of Christ was a last refuge to the world; it was a consolation and a new ground for hope, from which no misfortune could drive the worshipper. Its value as an idea was therefore immense, as to the lover the idea of his untasted joys, or to the dying man the idea of health and invigorating sunshine. The votary can no more **Pathetic** ask himself whether his deity, in its **idealizations.** total operation, has really blessed him and deserved his praise than the lover can ask if his lady is worth pursuing or the expiring cripple whether it would be, in very truth, a benefit to be once more young and whole. That life is worth living is the most necessary of assumptions and, were it not assumed, the most impossible of conclusions. Experience, by its passive weight of joy and sorrow, can neither inspire nor prevent enthusiasm; only a present ideal will avail to move the will and, if realised, to justify it. A saint's halo is an optical illusion; it glorifies his actions whatever their eventual influence in the world, because they seem to have, when rehearsed dramatically, some tenderness or rapture or miracle about them.

Thus it appears that the great figures of art or religion, together with all historic and imaginative ideals, advance insensibly on the values they represent. The image has more lustre than the original, and is often the more important and influential fact. Things are esteemed as they weigh in representation. A *memorable thing,* people say in their eulogies, little thinking to touch the ground of their praise. For things are called great because they are memorable, they are not remembered because they were great. The deepest pangs, the highest joys, the widest influences are lost to apperception in its haste, and if in some rational moment reconstructed and acknowledged, are soon forgotten again and cut off from living consideration. But the emptiest experience, even the most pernicious tendency, if embodied in a picturesque image, if reverberating in the mind with a pleasant echo, is idolised and enshrined. Fortunate indeed was Achilles that Homer sang of him, and fortunate the poets that make a public titillation out of their sorrows and ignorance. This imputed and posthumous fortune is the only happiness they have. The favours of memory are extended to those feeble realities and denied to the massive substance of daily experience. When life dies, when what was present becomes a memory, its ghost flits still among the living, feared or worshipped not for the experience it once possessed but for the aspect it now wears. Yet this injustice in representation, speculatively so offensive, is practically excusable; for it is in one sense right and useful that all things, whatever their original or inherent dignity, should be valued at each moment only by their present function and utility.

Inevitable impulsiveness in prophecy. The error involved in attributing value to the past is naturally aggravated when values are to be assigned to the future. In the latter case imagination cannot be controlled by circumstantial evidence, and is consequently the only basis for judgment. But as the conception of a thing naturally evokes an emotion different from that involved in its presence, ideals of what is desirable for the future contain no warrant that the experience desired would, when actual, prove to be acceptable and good. An ideal carries no extrinsic assurance that its realisation would be a benefit. To convince ourselves that an ideal has rational authority and represents a better experience than the actual condition it is contrasted with, we must control the prophetic image by as many circumlocutions as possible.

The test a controlled present ideal. As in the case of fame, we must buttress or modify our spontaneous judgment with all the other judgments that the object envisaged can prompt: we must make our ideal harmonise with all experience rather than with a part only. The possible error remains even then; but a practical mind will always accept the risk of error when it has made every possible correction. A rational will is not a will that has reason for its basis or that possesses any other proof that its realisation would be possible or good than the oracle which a living will inspires and pronounces. The rationality possible to the will lies not in its source but in its method. An ideal cannot wait for its realisation to prove its validity. To deserve adhesion it needs only to be adequate as an ideal, that is, to express completely what the soul at present demands, and to do justice to all extant interests.

CHAPTER XI

SOME ABSTRACT CONDITIONS OF THE IDEAL

The ultimate end a resultant. Reason's function is to embody the good, but the test of excellence is itself ideal; therefore before we can assure ourselves that reason has been manifested in any given case we must make out the reasonableness of the ideal that inspires us. And in general, before we can convince ourselves that a Life of Reason, or practice guided by science and directed toward spiritual goods, is at all worth having, we must make out the possibility and character of its ultimate end. Yet each ideal is its own justification; so that the only sense in which an ultimate end can be established and become a test of general progress is this: that a harmony and cooperation of impulses should be conceived, leading to the maximum satisfaction possible in the whole community of spirits affected by our action. Now, without considering for the present any concrete Utopia, such, for instance, as Plato's Republic or the heavenly beatitude described by theologians, we may inquire what formal qualities are imposed on the ideal by its nature and function and by the relation it bears to experience and to desire.

Demands the substance of ideals.

The ideal has the same relation to given demands that the reality has to given perceptions. In the face of the ideal, particular demands forfeit their authority and the goods to which a particular being may aspire cease to be absolute; nay, the satisfaction of desire comes to appear an indifferent or unholy thing when compared or opposed to the ideal to be realised. So, precisely, in perception, flying impressions come to be regarded as illusory when contrasted with a stable conception of reality. Yet of course flying impressions are the only material out of which that conception can be formed. Life itself is a flying impression, and had we no personal and instant experience, importuning us at each successive moment, we should have no occasion to ask for a reality at all, and no materials out of which to construct so gratuitous an idea. In the same way present demands are the only materials and occasions for any ideal: without demands the ideal would have no *locus standi* or foothold in the world, no power, no charm, and no prerogative. If the ideal can confront particular desires and put them to shame, that happens only because the ideal is the object of a more profound and voluminous desire and embodies the good which they blindly and perhaps deviously pursue. Demands could not be misdirected, goods sought could not be false, if

the standard by which they are to be corrected
were not constructed out of them. Otherwise
each demand would render its object a detached,
absolute, and unimpeachable good. But when
each desire in turn has singed its wings and re-
tired before some disillusion, reflection may set
in to suggest residual satisfactions that may still
be possible, or some shifting of the ground by
which much of what was hoped for may yet be
attained.

The force for this new trial is but the old
impulse renewed; this new hope is a justified
remnant of the old optimism. Each passion, in
this second campaign, takes the field conscious that
it has indomitable enemies and ready to sign a
reasonable peace, and even to capitulate before
superior forces. Such tameness may be at first
merely a consequence of exhaustion and prudence;
but a mortal will, though absolute in its deliver-
ances, is very far from constant, and its sacrifices
soon constitute a habit, its exile a new home.
The old ambition, now proved to be unrealisable,
begins to seem capricious and extravagant; the
circle of possible satisfactions becomes the field of
Discipline of   conventional happiness. Experience,
the will.   which brings about this humbler and
more prosaic state of mind, has its own imaginative fruits. Among those forces which compelled
each particular impulse to abate its pretensions,
the most conspicuous were other impulses, other
interests active in oneself and in one's neighbours.

When the power of these alien demands is recognised they begin, in a physical way, to be respected; when an adjustment to them is sought they begin to be understood, for it is only by studying their expression and tendency that the degree of their hostility can be measured. But to understand is more than to forgive, it is to adopt; and the passion that thought merely to withdraw into a sullen and maimed self-indulgence can feel itself expanded by sympathies which in its primal vehemence it would have excluded altogether. Experience, in bringing humility, brings intelligence also. Personal interests begin to seem relative, factors only in a general voluminous welfare expressed in many common institutions and arts, moulds for whatever is communicable or rational in every passion. Each original impulse, when

Demands made practical and consistent. trimmed down more or less according to its degree of savageness, can then inhabit the state, and every good, when sufficiently transfigured, can be found again in the general ideal. The factors may indeed often be unrecognisable in the result, so much does the process of domestication transform them; but the interests that animated them survive this discipline and the new purpose is really esteemed; else the ideal would have no moral force. An ideal representing no living interest would be irrelevant to practice, just as a conception of reality would be irrelevant to perception which should not be composed of the materials that sense supplies, or should not re-embody actual sensations in an intelligible system.

The ideal natural. Here we have, then, one condition which the ideal must fulfil: it must be a resultant or synthesis of impulses already afoot. An ideal out of relation to the actual demands of living beings is so far from being an ideal that it is not even a good. The pursuit of it would be not the acme but the atrophy of moral endeavour. Mysticism and asceticism run into this danger, when the intent to be faithful to a supreme good too symbolically presented breeds a superstitious repugnance toward everything naturally prized. So also an artificial scepticism can regard all experience as deceptive, by contrasting it with the chimera of an absolute reality. As an absolute reality would be indescribable and without a function in the elucidation of phenomena, so a supreme good which was good for nobody would be without conceivable value. Respect for such an idol is a dialectical superstition; and if zeal for that shibboleth should actually begin to inhibit the exercise of intelligent choice or the development of appreciation for natural pleasures, it would constitute a reversal of the Life of Reason which, if persistently indulged in, could only issue in madness or revert to imbecility.

Need of unity and finality. No less important, however, than this basis which the ideal must have in extant demands, is the harmony with which reason must endow it. If without the one the ideal loses its value, without the other it loses its finality. Human nature is fluid and imperfect; its demands are expressed in incidental desires, elicited by a variety of objects which perhaps cannot coexist in the world. If we merely transcribe these miscellaneous demands or allow these floating desires to dictate to us the elements of the ideal, we shall never come to a Whole or to an End. One new fancy after another will seem an embodiment of perfection, and we shall contradict each expression of our ideal by every other. A **Ideals of** certain school of philosophy—if we **nothing.** may give that name to the systematic neglect of reason—has so immersed itself in the contemplation of this sort of inconstancy, which is indeed prevalent enough in the world, that it has mistaken it for a normal and necessary process. The greatness of the ideal has been put in its vagueness and in an elasticity which makes it wholly indeterminate and inconsistent. The goal of progress, beside being thus made to lie at every point of the compass in succession, is removed to an infinite distance, whereby the possibility of attaining it is denied and progress itself is made illusory. For a progress must be directed to attaining some definite type of life, the counterpart of a given natural endowment, and nothing can be called an improvement which does not contain an appreciable benefit. A victory would be a mockery that left us, for some new reason, as much impeded as before and as far removed from peace.

The picture of life as an eternal war for illusory ends was drawn at first by satirists, unhappily with too much justification in the facts. Some grosser minds, too undisciplined to have ever pursued a good either truly attainable or truly satisfactory, then proceeded to mistake that satire on human folly for a sober account of the whole universe; and finally others were not ashamed to represent it as the ideal itself—so soon is the dyer's hand subdued to what it works in. A barbarous mind cannot conceive life, like health, as a harmony continually preserved or restored, and containing those natural and ideal activities which disease merely interrupts. Such a mind, never having tasted order, cannot conceive it, and identifies progress with new conflicts and life with continual death. Its deification of unreason, instability, and strife comes partly from piety and partly from inexperience. There is piety in saluting nature in her perpetual flux and in thinking that since no equilibrium is maintained for ever none, perhaps, deserves to be. There is inexperience in not considering that wherever interests and judgments exist, the natural flux has fallen, so to speak, into a vortex, and created a natural good, a cumulative life, and an ideal purpose. Art, science, government, human nature itself, are self-defining and self-preserving: by partly fixing a structure they fix an ideal. But the barbarian can hardly regard such things, for to have distinguished and fostered them would be to have founded a civilisation.

Darwin on moral sense.   Reason's function in defining the ideal is in principle extremely simple, although all time and all existence would have to be gathered in before the applications of that principle could be exhausted. A better example of its essential working could hardly be found than one which Darwin gives to illustrate the natural origin of moral sense. A swallow, impelled by migratory instincts to leave a nest full of unfledged young, would endure a moral conflict. The more lasting impulse, memory being assumed, would prompt a moral judgment when it emerged again after being momentarily obscured by an intermittent passion. " While the mother bird is feeding or brooding over her nestlings, the maternal instinct is probably stronger than the migratory; but the instinct which is more persistent gains the victory, and at last, at a moment when her young ones are not in sight, she takes flight and deserts them. When arrived at the end of her long journey, and the migratory instinct ceases to act, what an agony of remorse each bird would feel if, from being endowed with great mental activity, she could not prevent the image continually passing before her mind of her young ones perishing in the bleak north from cold and hunger."* She would doubtless upbraid herself, like any sinner, for a senseless perfidy to her own dearest good. The perfidy, however, was not wholly senseless, because the forgotten instinct

* Descent of Man, chapter iii.

was not less natural and necessary than the remembered one, and its satisfaction no less true. Temptation has the same basis as duty. The difference is one of volume and permanence in the rival satisfactions, and the attitude conscience will assume toward these depends more on the representability of the demands compared than on their original vehemence or ultimate results.

Conscience and reason compared. A passionate conscience may thus arise in the play of impulses differing in permanence, without involving a judicial exercise of reason. Nor does such a conscience involve a synthetic ideal, but only the ideal presence of particular demands. Conflicts in the conscience are thus quite natural and would continually occur but for the narrowness that commonly characterises a mind inspired by passion. A life of sin and repentance is as remote as possible from a Life of Reason. Yet the same situation which produces conscience and the sense of duty is an occasion for applying reason to action and for forming an ideal, so soon as the demands and satisfactions concerned are synthesised and balanced imaginatively. The stork might do more than feel the conflict of his two impulses, he might do more than embody in alternation the eloquence of two hostile thoughts. He might pass judgment upon them impartially and, in the felt presence of both, conceive what might be a union or compromise between them.

This resultant object of pursuit, conceived in

reflection and in itself the initial goal of neither impulse, is the ideal of a mind occupied by the two: it is the aim prescribed by reason under the circumstances. It differs from the prescription of conscience, in that conscience is often the spokesman of one interest or of a group of interests in opposition to other primary impulses which it would annul altogether; while reason and the ideal are not active forces nor embodiments of passion at all, but merely a method by which objects of desire are compared in reflection. The goodness of an end is felt inwardly by conscience; by reason it can be only taken upon trust and registered as a fact. For conscience the object of an opposed will is an evil, for reason it is a good on the same ground as any other good, because it is pursued by a natural impulse and can bring a real satisfaction. Conscience, in fine, is a party to moral strife, reason an observer of it who, however, plays the most important and beneficent part in the outcome by suggesting the terms of peace. This suggested peace, inspired by sympathy and by knowledge of the world, is the ideal, which borrows its value and practical force from the irrational impulses which it embodies, and borrows its final authority from the truth with which it recognises them all and the necessity by which it imposes on each such sacrifices as are requisite to a general harmony.

Could each impulse, apart from reason, gain per-

fect satisfaction, it would doubtless laugh at justice. The divine, to exercise suasion, must use an
argumentum ad hominem; reason must justify
itself to the heart. But perfect satisfaction is
what an irresponsible impulse can never hope for:
Reason im- all other impulses, though absent per-
poses no new haps from the mind, are none the less
sacrifice. present in nature and have possession
of the field through their physical basis. They
offer effectual resistance to a reckless intruder.
To disregard them is therefore to gain nothing:
reason, far from creating the partial renunciation
and proportionate sacrifices which it imposes,
really minimises them by making them voluntary
and fruitful. The ideal, which may seem to wear
so severe a frown, really fosters all possible pleasures; what it retrenches is nothing to what blind
forces and natural catastrophes would otherwise
cut off; while it sweetens what it sanctions, adding
to spontaneous enjoyments a sense of moral security and an intellectual light.

Those who are guided only by an irrational
conscience can hardly understand what a good
life would be. Their Utopias have to be supernatural in order that the irresponsible rules
which they call morality may lead by miracle
to happy results. But such a magical and
undeserved happiness, if it were possible, would
be unsavoury: only one phase of human nature
would be satisfied by it, and so impoverished
an ideal cannot really attract the will. For

human nature has been moulded by the same natural forces among which its ideal has to be fulfilled,

Natural goods attainable and compatible in principle. and, apart from a certain margin of wild hopes and extravagances, the things man's heart desires are attainable under his natural conditions and would not be attainable elsewhere. The conflict of desires and interests in the world is not radical any more than man's dissatisfaction with his own nature can be; for every particular ideal, being an expression of human nature in operation, must in the end involve the primary human faculties and cannot be essentially incompatible with any other ideal which involves them too.

To adjust all demands to one ideal and adjust that ideal to its natural conditions—in other words, to live the Life of Reason—is something perfectly possible; for those demands, being akin to one another in spite of themselves, can be better furthered by co-operation than by blind conflict, while the ideal, far from demanding any profound revolution in nature, merely expresses her actual tendency and forecasts what her perfect functioning would be.

Harmony the formal and intrinsic demand of reason. Reason as such represents or rather constitutes a single formal interest, the interest in harmony. When two interests are simultaneous and fall within one act of apprehension the desirability of harmonising them is involved in the very effort to realise them together. If attention and imagination are steady enough to face this implication and not to allow impulse to oscillate between irreconcilable tendencies, reason comes into being. Henceforth things actual and things desired are confronted by an ideal which has both pertinence and authority.

CHAPTER XII

FLUX AND CONSTANCY IN HUMAN NATURE

Respectable tradition that human nature is fixed. A conception of something called human nature arises not unnaturally on observing the passions of men, passions which under various disguises seem to reappear in all ages and countries. The tendency of Greek philosophy, with its insistence on general concepts, was to define this idea of human nature still further and to encourage the belief that a single and identical essence, present in all men, determined their powers and ideal destiny. Christianity, while it transposed the human ideal and dwelt on the superhuman affinities of man, did not abandon the notion of a specific humanity. On the contrary, such a notion was implied in the Fall and Redemption, in the Sacraments, and in the universal validity of Christian doctrine and precept. For if human nature were not one, there would be no propriety in requiring all men to preserve unanimity in faith or conformity in conduct. Human nature was likewise the entity which the English psychologists set themselves to describe; and Kant was so entirely dominated by the notion of a fixed and universal human nature

that its constancy, in his opinion, was the source
of all natural as well as moral laws. Had he
doubted for a moment the stability of human
nature, the foundations of his system would have
fallen out; the forms of perception and thought
would at once have lost their boasted necessity,
since to-morrow might dawn upon new categories
and a modified *a priori* intuition of space or time;
and the avenue would also have been closed by
which man was led, through his unalterable moral
sentiments, to assumptions about metaphysical
truths.

Contrary cur-
rents of opin-
ion.

The force of this long tradition has
been broken, however, by two influences
of great weight in recent times, the
theory of evolution and the revival of pantheism.
The first has reintroduced flux into the conception

Evolution.

of existence and the second into the
conception of values. If natural species are fluid
and pass into one another, human nature is merely
a name for a group of qualities found by chance in
certain tribes of animals, a group to which new
qualities are constantly tending to attach themselves while other faculties become extinct, now in
whole races, now in sporadic individuals. Human
nature is therefore a variable, and its ideal cannot
have a greater constancy than the demands to
which it gives expression. Nor can the ideal of
one man or one age have any authority over
another, since the harmony existing in their nature
and interests is accidental and each is a transi-

tional phase in an indefinite evolution.   The crys-
tallisation of moral forces at any moment is consequently to be explained by universal, not by
human, laws; the philosopher's interest cannot be
to trace the implications of present and unstable
desires, but rather to discover the mechanical law
by which these desires have been generated and
will be transformed, so that they will change irrev-
ocably both their basis and their objects.

Pantheism.   To this picture of physical instability furnished by popular science are to be added
the mystical self-denials involved in pantheism.
These come to reinforce the doctrine that human
nature is a shifting thing with the sentiment that
it is a finite and unworthy one: for every determination of being, it is said, has its significance
as well as its origin in the infinite continuum of
which it is a part.   Forms are limitations, and
limitations, according to this philosophy, would
be defects, so that man's only goal would be to
escape humanity and lose himself in the divine
nebula that has produced and must invalidate
each of his thoughts and ideals.   As there would
be but one spirit in the world, and that infinite,
so there would be but one ideal and that indiscrim-
inate.   The despair which the naturalist's view of
human instability might tend to produce is turned
by this mystical initiation into a sort of ecstasy;
and the deluge of conformity suddenly submerges
that Life of Reason which science seemed to condemn to gradual extinction.

Reason is a human function. Though the name of reason has been applied to various alleged principles of cosmic life, vital or dialectical, these principles all lack the essence of rationality, in that they are not conscious movements toward satisfaction, not, in other words, moral and beneficent principles at all. Be the instability of human nature what it may, therefore, the instability of reason is not less, since reason is but a function of human nature. However relative and subordinate, in a physical sense, human ideals may be, these ideals remain the only possible moral standards for man, the only tests which he can apply for value or authority in any other quarter. And among unstable and relative ideals none is more relative and unstable than that which transports all value to a universal law, itself indifferent to good and evil, and worships it as a deity. Such an idolatry would indeed be impossible if it were not partial and veiled, arrived at in following out some human interest and clung to by force of moral inertia and the ambiguity of words. In truth mystics do not practise so entire a renunciation of reason as they preach: eternal validity and the capacity to deal with absolute reality are still assumed by them to belong to thought or at least to feeling. Only they overlook in their description of human nature just that faculty which they exercise in their speculation; their map leaves out the ground on which they stand. The rest, which

Instability in existences does not dethrone their ideals.

they are not identified with for the moment, they proceed to regard *de haut en bas* and to discredit as a momentary manifestation of universal laws, physical or divine. They forget that this faith in law, this absorption in the blank reality, this enthusiasm for the ultimate thought, are mere human passions like the rest; that they endure them as they might a fever and that the animal instincts are patent on which those spiritual yearnings repose.

Absolutist philosophy human and halting. This last fact would be nothing against the feelings in question, if they were not made vehicles for absolute revelations. On the contrary, such a relativity in instincts is the source of their importance. In virtue of this relativity they have some basis and function in the world; for did they not repose on human nature they could never express or transform it. Religion and philosophy are not always beneficent or important, but when they are it is precisely because they help to develop human faculty and to enrich human life. To imagine that by means of them we can escape from human nature and survey it from without is an ostrich-like illusion obvious to all but to the victim of it. Such a pretension may cause admiration in the schools, where self-hypnotisation is easy, but in the world it makes its professors ridiculous. For in their eagerness to empty their mind of human prejudices they reduce its rational burden to a minimum, and if they still continue to dogmatise,

it is sport for the satirist to observe what forgotten
accident of language or training has survived the
crash of the universe and made the one demonstrable path to Absolute Truth.

All science a   Neither the path of abstraction fol-
deliverance of   lowed by the mystics, nor that of direct
momentary
thought.   and, as it avers, unbiassed observation
followed by the naturalists, can lead beyond that
region of common experience, traditional feeling,
and conventional thought which all minds enter
at birth and can elude only at the risk of inward
collapse and extinction.   The fact that observation
involves the senses, and the senses their organs,
is one which a naturalist can hardly overlook; and
when we add that logical habits, sanctioned by
utility, are needed to interpret the data of sense,
the humanity of science and all its constructions
becomes clearer than day.   Superstition itself
could not be more human.   The path of unbiassed
observation is not a path away from conventional
life; it is a progress in conventions.   It improves
human belief by increasing the proportion of two
of its ingredients, attentive perception and practical calculus.   The whole resulting vision, as it
is sustained from moment to moment by present
experience and instinct, has no value apart from
actual ideals.   And if it proves human nature to
be unstable, it can build that proof on nothing
more stable than human faculty as at the moment
it happens to be.

Nor is abstraction a less human process, as if

by becoming very abstruse indeed we could hope
to become divine. Is it not a commonplace of the
All criticism schools that to form abstract ideas is
likewise. the prerogative of man's reason? Is not
abstraction a method by which mortal intelligence
makes haste? Is it not the makeshift of a mind
overloaded with its experience, the trick of an eye
that cannot master a profuse and ever-changing
world? Shall these diagrams drawn in fancy, this
system of signals in thought, be the Absolute
Truth dwelling within us? Do we attain reality
by making a silhouette of our dreams? If the
scientific world be a product of human faculties,
the metaphysical world must be doubly so; for the
material there given to human understanding is
here worked over again by human art. This constitutes the dignity and value of dialectic, that in
spite of appearances it is so human; it bears to
experience a relation similar to that which the arts
bear to the same, where sensible images, selected
by the artist's genius and already coloured by his
æsthetic bias, are redyed in the process of reproduction whenever he has a great style, and sat-
urated anew with his mind.

There can be no question, then, of eluding
human nature or of conceiving it and its environment in such a way as to stop its operation. We
may take up our position in one region of experience or in another, we may, in unconsciousness
of the interests and assumptions that support us,
criticise the truth or value of results obtained else-

where. Our criticism will be solid in proportion
to the solidity of the unnamed convictions that
inspire it, that is, in proportion to the deep roots
and fruitful ramifications which those convictions
may have in human life. Ultimate truth and
ultimate value will be reasonably attributed to
those ideas and possessions which can give human
nature, as it is, the highest satisfaction. We may
admit that human nature is variable; but that
admission, if justified, will be justified by the satisfaction which it gives human nature to make it.
We might even admit that human ideals are vain
but only if they were nothing worth for the attainment of the veritable human ideal.

Origins in-essential. The given constitution of reason,
with whatever a dialectical philosophy
might elicit from it, obviously determines nothing
about the causes that may have brought reason to
its present pass or the phases that may have preceded its appearance. Certain notions about
physics might no doubt suggest themselves to the
moralist, who never can be the whole man; he
might suspect, for instance, that the transitive
intent of intellect and will pointed to their vital
basis. Transcendence in operation might seem
appropriate only to a being with a history and
with an organism subject to external influences,
whose mind should thus come to represent not
merely its momentary state but also its constitu-
tive past and its eventual fortunes. Such suggestions, however, would be extraneous to dialectical

self-knowledge. They would be tentative only, and human nature would be freely admitted to be as variable, as relative, and as transitory as the natural history of the universe might make it.

Ideals functional. The error, however, would be profound and the contradiction hopeless if we should deny the ideal authority of human nature because we had discovered its origin and conditions. Nature and evolution, let us say, have brought life to the present form; but this life lives, these organs have determinate functions, and human nature, here and now, in relation to the ideal energies it unfolds, is a fundamental essence, a collection of activities with determinate limits, relations, and ideals. The integration and determinateness of these faculties is the condition for any synthetic operation of reason. As the structure of the steam-engine has varied greatly since its first invention, and its attributions have increased, so the structure of human nature has undoubtedly varied since man first appeared upon the earth; but as in each steam-engine at each moment there must be a limit of mobility, a unity of function and a clear determination of parts and tensions, so in human nature, as found at any time in any man, there is a definite scope by virtue of which alone he can have a reliable memory, a recognisable character, a faculty of connected thought and speech, a social utility, and a moral ideal. On man's given structure, on his activity hovering about fixed objects, depends the possibility of conceiving or testing any truth or making any progress in happiness.

They are transferable to similar beings. Thinkers of different experience and organisation have *pro tanto* different logics and different moral laws. There are limits to communication even among beings of the same race, and the faculties and ideals of one intelligence are not transferable without change to any other. If this historic diversity in minds were complete, so that each lived in its own moral world, a science of each of these moral worlds would still be possible provided some inner fixity or constancy existed in its meanings. In every human thought together with an immortal intent there is a mortal and irrecoverable perception: something in it perishes instantly, the part that can be materially preserved being proportionate to the stability or fertility of the organ that produced it. If the function is imitable, the object it terminates in will reappear, and two or more moments, having the same ideal, will utter comparable messages and may perhaps be unanimous. Unanimity in thought involves identity of functions and similarity in organs. These conditions mark off the sphere of rational communication and society; where they fail altogether there is no mutual intelligence, no conversation, no moral solidarity.

The inner authority of reason, however, is no more destroyed because it has limits in physical expression or because irrational things exist, than

the grammar of a given language is invalidated
Authority because other languages do not share
internal. it, or because some people break its
rules and others are dumb altogether. Innumerable madmen make no difference to the laws of
thought, which borrow their authority from the
inward intent and cogency of each rational mind.
Reason, like beauty, is its own excuse for being.
It is useful, indeed, for living well, when to give
reason satisfaction is made the measure of good.

The true philosopher, who is not one chiefly by
profession, must be prepared to tread the wine-
press alone. He may indeed flourish like the bay-
tree in a grateful environment, but more often he
will rather resemble a reed shaken by the wind.
Whether starved or fed by the accidents of fortune
he must find his essential life in his own ideal.
In spiritual life, heteronomy is suicide. That
universal soul sometimes spoken of, which is to
harmonise and correct individual demands, if it
were a will and an intelligence in act, would itself
be an individual like the others; while if it possessed no will and no intelligence, such as individuals may have, it would be a physical force or
law, a dynamic system without moral authority
and with a merely potential or represented existence. For to be actual and self-existent is to be
individual. The living mind cannot surrender its
rights to any physical power or subordinate itself
to any figment of its own art without falling into
manifest idolatry.

Human nature, in the sense in which it is the transcendental foundation of all science and morals, is a functional unity in each man; it is no general or abstract essence, the average of all men's characters, nor even the complex of the qualities common to all men. It is the entelechy of the living individual, be he typical or singular. That his type should be odd or common is merely a physical accident. If he can know himself by expressing the entelechy of his own nature in the form of a consistent ideal, he is a rational creature after his own kind, even if, like the angels of Saint Thomas, he be the only individual of his species. What the majority of human animals may tend to, or what the past or future variations of a race may be, has nothing to do with determining the ideal of human nature in a living man, or in an ideal society of men bound together by spiritual kinship. Otherwise Plato could not have reasoned well about the republic without adjusting himself to the politics of Buddha or Rousseau, and we should not be able to determine our own morality without making concessions to the cannibals or giving a vote to the ants. Within the field of an anthropology that tests humanity by the skull's shape, there might be room for any number of independent moralities, and although, as we shall see, there is actually a similar foundation in all human and even in all animal natures, which supports a rudimentary morality common to all, yet a perfect morality is

Reason autonomous.

not really common to any two men nor to any two phases of the same man's life.

Its distribution. The distribution of reason, though a subject irrelevant to pure logic or morals, is one naturally interesting to a rational man, for he is concerned to know how far beings exist with a congenial structure and an ideal akin to his own. That circumstance will largely influence his happiness if, being a man, he is a gregarious and sympathetic animal. His moral idealism itself will crave support from others, if not to give it direction, at least to give it warmth and courage. The best part of wealth is to have worthy heirs, and mind can be transmitted only to a kindred mind. Hostile natures cannot be brought together by mutual invective nor harmonised by the brute destruction and disappearance of either party. But when one or both parties have actually disappeared, and the combat has ceased for lack of combatants, natures not hostile to one another can fill the vacant place. In proportion to their inbred unanimity these will cultivate a similar ideal and rejoice together in its embodiment.

This has happened to some extent in the whole world, on account of natural conditions which limit the forms of life possible in one region; for nature is intolerant in her laxity and punishes too Natural selection of minds. great originality and heresy with death. Such moral integration has occurred very markedly in every good race and society whose members, by adapting themselves to the same external forces, have created and discovered their common soul. Spiritual unity is a natural product. There are those who see a great mystery in the presence of eternal values and impersonal ideals in a moving and animal world, and think to solve that dualism, as they call it, by denying that nature can have spiritual functions or spirit a natural cause; but nothing can be simpler if we make, as we should, existence the test of possibility. *Ab esse ad posse valet illatio.* Nature is a perfect garden of ideals, and passion is the perpetual and fertile soil for poetry, myth, and speculation. Nor is this origin merely imputed to ideals by a late and cynical observer: it is manifest in the ideals themselves, by their subject matter and intent. For what are ideals about, what do they idealise, except natural existence and natural passions? That would be a miserable and superfluous ideal indeed that was nobody's ideal of nothing. The pertinence of ideals binds them to nature, and it is only the worst and flimsiest ideals, the ideals of a sick soul, that elude nature's limits and belie her potentialities. Ideals are forerunners or heralds of nature's successes, not always followed, indeed, by their fulfilment, for nature is but nature and has to feel her way; but they are an earnest, at least, of an achieved organisation, an incipient accomplishment, that tends to maintain and root itself in the world.

To speak of nature's successes is, of course, to

impute success retroactively; but the expression
may be allowed when we consider that the same
functional equilibrium which is looked back upon
as a good by the soul it serves, first creates individual being and with it creates the possibility
of preference and the whole moral world; and it
is more than a metaphor to call that achievement
a success which has made a sense of success possible and actual. That nature cannot intend or
previously esteem those formations which are the
condition of value or intention existing at all, is
a truth too obvious to demand repetition; but
when those formations arise they determine estimation, and fix the direction of preference, so that
the evolution which produced them, when looked
back upon from the vantage-ground thus gained,
cannot help seeming to have been directed toward
the good now distinguished and partly attained.
For this reason creation is regarded as a work of
love, and the power that brought order out of
chaos is called intelligence.

**Living
stability.** These natural formations, tending
to generate and realise each its ideal,
are, as it were, eddies in the universal flux, produced no less mechanically, doubtless, than the
onward current, yet seeming to arrest or to reverse
it. Inheritance arrests the flux by repeating a
series of phases with a recognisable rhythm;
memory reverses it by modifying this rhythm itself
by the integration of earlier phases into those that
supervene. Inheritance and memory make human

stability. This stability is relative, being still a
mode of flux, and consists fundamentally in repetition. Repetition marks some progress on mere
continuity, since it preserves form and disregards
time and matter. Inheritance is repetition on a
larger scale, not excluding spontaneous variations;
while habit and memory are a sort of heredity
within the individual, since here an old perception reappears, by way of atavism, in the midst of
a forward march. Life is thus enriched and reaction adapted to a wider field; much as a note is
enriched by its overtones, and by the tensions, inherited from the preceding notes, which give it a
new setting.

Continuity
necessary to
progress.
Progress, far from consisting in
change, depends on retentiveness.
When change is absolute there remains no being to improve and no direction
is set for possible improvement: and when experience is not retained, as among savages,
infancy is perpetual. Those who cannot remember the past are condemned to repeat it. In
the first stage of life the mind is frivolous and
easily distracted; it misses progress by failing in
consecutiveness and persistence. This is the condition of children and barbarians, in whom instinct has learned nothing from experience. In a
second stage men are docile to events, plastic to
new habits and suggestions, yet able to graft them
on original instincts, which they thus bring to
fuller satisfaction. This is the plane of manhood

and true progress.   Last comes a stage when retentiveness is exhausted and all that happens is
at once forgotten; a vain, because unpractical,
repetition of the past takes the place of plasticity
and fertile readaptation.   In a moving world readaptation is the price of longevity.   The hard
shell, far from protecting the vital principle, con-
demns it to die down slowly and be gradually
chilled; immortality in such a case must have been
secured earlier, by giving birth to a generation
plastic to the contemporary world and able to retain its lessons.   Thus old age is as forgetful as
youth, and more incorrigible; it displays the same
inattentiveness to conditions; its memory becomes
self-repeating and degenerates into an instinctive
reaction, like a bird's chirp.

Limits of variation. Spirit a heritage.   Not all readaptation, however, is
progress, for ideal identity must not
be lost.   The Latin language did not
progress when it passed into Italian.   It died.
Its amiable heirs may console us for its departure, but do not remove the fact that their parent
is extinct.   So every individual, nation, and religion has its limit of adaptation; so long as the
increment it receives is digestible, so long as the
organisation already attained is extended and elab-
orated without being surrendered, growth goes on;
but when the foundation itself shifts, when what
is gained at the periphery is lost at the centre, the
flux appears again and progress is not real.   Thus
a succession of generations or languages or relig-

ions constitutes no progress unless some ideal present at the beginning is transmitted to the end and reaches a better expression there; without this stability at the core no common standard exists and all comparison of value with value must be external and arbitrary. Retentiveness, we must repeat, is the condition of progress.

The variation human nature is open to is not, then, variation in any direction. There are transformations that would destroy it. So long as it endures it must retain all that constitutes it now, all that it has so far gathered and worked into its substance. The genealogy of progress is like that of man, who can never repudiate a single ancestor. It starts, so to speak, from a single point, free as yet to take any direction. When once, however, evolution has taken a single step, say in the direction of vertebrates, that step cannot be retraced without extinction of the species. Such extinction may take place while progress in other lines is continued. All that preceded the forking of the dead and the living branch will be as well represented and as legitimately continued by the surviving radiates as it could have been by the vertebrates that are no more; but the vertebrate ideal is lost for ever, and no more progress is possible along that line.

Perfectibility.　The future of moral evolution is accordingly infinite, but its character is more and more determinate at every step. Mankind can never, without perishing, surrender its animal

nature, its need to eat and drink, its sexual method
of reproduction, its vision of nature, its faculty of
speech, its arts of music, poetry, and building.
Particular races cannot subsist if they renounce
their savage instincts, but die, like wild animals,
in captivity; and particular individuals die when
not suffered any longer to retain their memories,
their bodies, or even their master passions. Thus
human nature survives amid a continual fluctua-
tion of its embodiments. At every step twigs and
leaves are thrown out that last but one season; but
the underlying stem may have meantime grown
stronger and more luxuriant. Whole branches
sometimes wither, but others may continue to
bloom. Spiritual unity runs, like sap, from the
common root to every uttermost flower; but at
each forking in the growth the branches part company, and what happens in one is no direct concern of the others. The products of one age and
nation may well be unintelligible to another; the
elements of humanity common to both may lie
lower down. So that the highest things are communicable to the fewest persons, and yet, among
these few, are the most perfectly communicable.
The more elaborate and determinate a man's heritage and genius are, the more he has in common
with his next of kin, and the more he can transmit
and implant in his posterity for ever. Civilisation
is cumulative. The farther it goes the intenser it
is, substituting articulate interests for animal
fumes and for enigmatic passions. Such articu-

late interests can be shared; and the infinite vistas
they open up can be pursued for ever with the
knowledge that a work long ago begun is being
perfected and that an ideal is being embodied
which need never be outworn.

So long as external conditions re-
Nature and
human nature.   main constant it is obvious that the
greater organisation a being possesses
the greater strength he will have. If indeed primary conditions varied, the finer creatures would
die first; for their adaptation is more exquisite
and the irreversible core of their being much
larger relatively; but in a constant environment
their equipment makes them irresistible and
secures their permanence and multiplication. Now
man is a part of nature and her organisation may
be regarded as the foundation of his own: the word
nature is therefore less equivocal than it seems, for
every nature is Nature herself in one of her more
specific and better articulated forms. Man therefore represents the universe that sustains him; his
existence is a proof that the cosmic equilibrium
that fostered his life is a natural equilibrium,
capable of being long maintained. Some of the
ancients thought it eternal; physics now suggests
a different opinion. But even if this equilibrium,
by which the stars are kept in their courses and
human progress is allowed to proceed, is fundamentally unstable, it shows what relative stability
nature may attain. Could this balance be preserved indefinitely, no one knows what wonderful

adaptations might occur within it, and to what excellence human nature in particular might arrive. Nor is it unlikely that before the cataclysm comes time will be afforded for more improvement than moral philosophy has ever dreamed of. For it is remarkable how inane and unimaginative Utopias have generally been. This possibility is not uninspiring and may help to console those who think the natural conditions of life are not conditions that a good life can be lived in. The possibility of essential progress is bound up with the tragic possibility that progress and human life should some day end together. If the present equilibrium of forces were eternal all adaptations to it would have already taken place and, while no essential catastrophe would need to be dreaded, no essential improvement could be hoped for in all eternity. I am not sure that a humanity such as we know, were it destined to exist for ever, would offer a more exhilarating prospect than a humanity having indefinite elasticity together with a precarious tenure of life. Mortality has its compensations: one is that all evils are transitory, another that better times may come.

Human nature, then, has for its core

Human nature formulated. the substance of nature at large, and is one of its more complex formations. Its determination is progressive. It varies indefinitely in its historic manifestations and fades into what, as a matter of natural history, might no longer be termed human. At each moment it has

its fixed and determinate entelechy, the ideal of
that being's life, based on his instincts, summed
up in his character, brought to a focus in his reflection, and shared by all who have attained or
may inherit his organisation. His perceptive and
reasoning faculties are parts of human nature, as
embodied in him; all objects of belief or desire,
with all standards of justice and duty which he
can possibly acknowledge, are transcripts of it,
conditioned by it, and justifiable only as expressions of its inherent tendencies.

This definition of human nature, clear as it may
be in itself and true to the facts, will perhaps
hardly make sufficiently plain how the Life of
Reason, having a natural basis, has in the ideal
world a creative and absolute authority. A more

Its concrete
description
reserved for
the sequel.

concrete description of human nature
may accordingly not come amiss, especially as the important practical question touching the extension of a given moral
authority over times and places depends on the
degree of kinship found among the creatures inhabiting those regions. To give a general picture
of human nature and its rational functions will
be the task of the following books. The truth of
a description which must be largely historical may
not be indifferent to the reader, and I shall study
to avoid bias in the presentation, in so far as
is compatible with frankness and brevity; yet
even if some bias should manifest itself and if the
picture were historically false, the rational prin-

ciples we shall be trying to illustrate will not thereby be invalidated. Illustrations might have been sought in some fictitious world, if imagination had not seemed so much less interesting than reality, which besides enforces with unapproachable eloquence the main principle in view, namely, that nature carries its ideal with it and that the progressive organisation of irrational impulses makes a rational life.

A CATALOGUE OF SELECTED DOVER BOOKS
IN ALL FIELDS OF INTEREST

A CATALOGUE OF SELECTED DOVER
BOOKS IN ALL FIELDS OF INTEREST

CONDITIONED REFLEXES, Ivan P. Pavlov. Full translation of most complete statement of Pavlov's work; cerebral damage, conditioned reflex, experiments with dogs, sleep, similar topics of great importance. 430pp. 5⅜ x 8½.
60614-7 Pa. $4.50

NOTES ON NURSING: WHAT IT IS, AND WHAT IT IS NOT, Florence Nightingale. Outspoken writings by founder of modern nursing. When first published (1860) it played an important role in much needed revolution in nursing. Still stimulating. 140pp. 5⅜ x 8½.   22340-X Pa. $2.50

HARTER'S PICTURE ARCHIVE FOR COLLAGE AND ILLUSTRATION, Jim Harter. Over 300 authentic, rare 19th-century engravings selected by noted collagist for artists, designers, decoupeurs, etc. Machines, people, animals, etc., printed one side of page. 25 scene plates for backgrounds. 6 collages by Harter, Satty, Singer, Evans. Introduction. 192pp. 8⅞ x 11¾.
23659-5 Pa. $4.50

MANUAL OF TRADITIONAL WOOD CARVING, edited by Paul N. Hasluck. Possibly the best book in English on the craft of wood carving. Practical instructions, along with 1,146 working drawings and photographic illustrations. Formerly titled *Cassell's Wood Carving.* 576pp. 6½ x 9¼.
23489-4 Pa. $7.95

THE PRINCIPLES AND PRACTICE OF HAND OR SIMPLE TURNING, John Jacob Holtzapffel. Full coverage of basic lathe techniques—history and development, special apparatus, softwood turning, hardwood turning, metal turning. Many projects—billiard ball, works formed within a sphere, egg cups, ash trays, vases, jardiniers, others—included. 1881 edition. 800 illustrations. 592pp. 6⅛ x 9¼.   23365-0 Clothbd. $15.00

THE JOY OF HANDWEAVING, Osma Tod. Only book you need for hand weaving. Fundamentals, threads, weaves, plus numerous projects for small board-loom, two-harness, tapestry, laid-in, four-harness weaving and more. Over 160 illustrations. 2nd revised edition. 352pp. 6½ x 9¼.
23458-4 Pa. $5.00

THE BOOK OF WOOD CARVING, Charles Marshall Sayers. Still finest book for beginning student in wood sculpture. Noted teacher, craftsman discusses fundamentals, technique; gives 34 designs, over 34 projects for panels, bookends, mirrors, etc. "Absolutely first-rate"—E. J. Tangerman. 33 photos. 118pp. 7¾ x 10⅝.   23654-4 Pa. $3.00

THE AMERICAN SENATOR, Anthony Trollope. Little known, long unavailable Trollope novel on a grand scale. Here are humorous comment on American vs. English culture, and stunning portrayal of a heroine/villainess. Superb evocation of Victorian village life. 561pp. 5⅜ x 8½.
23801-6 Pa. $6.00

WAS IT MURDER? James Hilton. The author of *Lost Horizon* and *Goodbye, Mr. Chips* wrote one detective novel (under a pen-name) which was quickly forgotten and virtually lost, even at the height of Hilton's fame. This edition brings it back—a finely crafted public school puzzle resplendent with Hilton's stylish atmosphere. A thoroughly English thriller by the creator of Shangri-la. 252pp. 5⅜ x 8. (Available in U.S. only)
23774-5 Pa. $3.00

CENTRAL PARK: A PHOTOGRAPHIC GUIDE, Victor Laredo and Henry Hope Reed. 121 superb photographs show dramatic views of Central Park: Bethesda Fountain, Cleopatra's Needle, Sheep Meadow, the Blockhouse, plus people engaged in many park activities: ice skating, bike riding, etc. Captions by former Curator of Central Park, Henry Hope Reed, provide historical view, changes, etc. Also photos of N.Y. landmarks on park's periphery. 96pp. 8½ x 11. 23750-8 Pa. $4.50

NANTUCKET IN THE NINETEENTH CENTURY, Clay Lancaster. 180 rare photographs, stereographs, maps, drawings and floor plans recreate unique American island society. Authentic scenes of shipwreck, lighthouses, streets, homes are arranged in geographic sequence to provide walking-tour guide to old Nantucket existing today. Introduction, captions. 160pp. 8⅞ x 11¾. 23747-8 Pa. $6.95

STONE AND MAN: A PHOTOGRAPHIC EXPLORATION, Andreas Feininger. 106 photographs by *Life* photographer Feininger portray man's deep passion for stone through the ages. Stonehenge-like megaliths, fortified towns, sculpted marble and crumbling tenements show textures, beauties, fascination. 128pp. 9¼ x 10¾. 23756-7 Pa. $5.95

CIRCLES, A MATHEMATICAL VIEW, D. Pedoe. Fundamental aspects of college geometry, non-Euclidean geometry, and other branches of mathematics: representing circle by point. Poincare model, isoperimetric property, etc. Stimulating recreational reading. 66 figures. 96pp. 5⅝ x 8¼.
63698-4 Pa. $2.75

THE DISCOVERY OF NEPTUNE, Morton Grosser. Dramatic scientific history of the investigations leading up to the actual discovery of the eighth planet of our solar system. Lucid, well-researched book by well-known historian of science. 172pp. 5⅜ x 8½. 23726-5 Pa. $3.00

THE DEVIL'S DICTIONARY. Ambrose Bierce. Barbed, bitter, brilliant witticisms in the form of a dictionary. Best, most ferocious satire America has produced. 145pp. 5⅜ x 8½. 20487-1 Pa. $1.75

THE PHILOSOPHY OF HISTORY, Georg W. Hegel. Great classic of Western thought develops concept that history is not chance but a rational process, the evolution of freedom. 457pp. 5⅜ x 8½. 20112-0 Pa. $4.50

LANGUAGE, TRUTH AND LOGIC, Alfred J. Ayer. Famous, clear introduction to Vienna, Cambridge schools of Logical Positivism. Role of philosophy, elimination of metaphysics, nature of analysis, etc. 160pp. 5⅜ x 8½. (Available in U.S. only) 20010-8 Pa. $1.75

A PREFACE TO LOGIC, Morris R. Cohen. Great City College teacher in renowned, easily followed exposition of formal logic, probability, values, logic and world order and similar topics; no previous background needed. 209pp. 5⅜ x 8½. 23517-3 Pa. $3.50

REASON AND NATURE, Morris R. Cohen. Brilliant analysis of reason and its multitudinous ramifications by charismatic teacher. Interdisciplinary, synthesizing work widely praised when it first appeared in 1931. Second (1953) edition. Indexes. 496pp. 5⅜ x 8½. 23633-1 Pa. $6.00

AN ESSAY CONCERNING HUMAN UNDERSTANDING, John Locke. The only complete edition of enormously important classic, with authoritative editorial material by A. C. Fraser. Total of 1176pp. 5⅜ x 8½. 20530-4, 20531-2 Pa., Two-vol. set $14.00

HANDBOOK OF MATHEMATICAL FUNCTIONS WITH FORMULAS, GRAPHS, AND MATHEMATICAL TABLES, edited by Milton Abramowitz and Irene A. Stegun. Vast compendium: 29 sets of tables, some to as high as 20 places. 1,046pp. 8 x 10½. 61272-4 Pa. $12.50

MATHEMATICS FOR THE PHYSICAL SCIENCES, Herbert S. Wilf. Highly acclaimed work offers clear presentations of vector spaces and matrices, orthogonal functions, roots of polynomial equations, conformal mapping, calculus of variations, etc. Knowledge of theory of functions of real and complex variables is assumed. Exercises and solutions. Index. 284pp. 5⅝ x 8¼. 63635-6 Pa. $4.50

THE PRINCIPLE OF RELATIVITY, Albert Einstein et al. Eleven most important original papers on special and general theories. Seven by Einstein, two by Lorentz, one each by Minkowski and Weyl. All translated, unabridged. 216pp. 5⅜ x 8½. 60081-5 Pa. $3.00

THERMODYNAMICS, Enrico Fermi. A classic of modern science. Clear, organized treatment of systems, first and second laws, entropy, thermodynamic potentials, gaseous reactions, dilute solutions, entropy constant. No math beyond calculus required. Problems. 160pp. 5⅜ x 8½. 60361-X Pa. $2.75

ELEMENTARY MECHANICS OF FLUIDS, Hunter Rouse. Classic undergraduate text widely considered to be far better than many later books. Ranges from fluid velocity and acceleration to role of compressibility in fluid motion. Numerous examples, questions, problems. 224 illustrations. 376pp. 5⅝ x 8¼. 63699-2 Pa. $5.00

THE COMPLETE BOOK OF DOLL MAKING AND COLLECTING, Catherine Christopher. Instructions, patterns for dozens of dolls, from rag doll on up to elaborate, historically accurate figures. Mould faces, sew clothing, make doll houses, etc. Also collecting information. Many illustrations. 288pp. 6 x 9. 22066-4 Pa. $4.00

THE DAGUERREOTYPE IN AMERICA, Beaumont Newhall. Wonderful portraits, 1850's townscapes, landscapes; full text plus 104 photographs. The basic book. Enlarged 1976 edition. 272pp. 8¼ x 11¼. 23322-7 Pa. $6.00

CRAFTSMAN HOMES, Gustav Stickley. 296 architectural drawings, floor plans, and photographs illustrate 40 different kinds of "Mission-style" homes from *The Craftsman* (1901-16), voice of American style of simplicity and organic harmony. Thorough coverage of Craftsman idea in text and picture, now collector's item. 224pp. 8⅛ x 11. 23791-5 Pa. $6.00

PEWTER-WORKING: INSTRUCTIONS AND PROJECTS, Burl N. Osborn. & Gordon O. Wilber. Introduction to pewter-working for amateur craftsman. History and characteristics of pewter; tools, materials, step-by-step instructions. Photos, line drawings, diagrams. Total of 160pp. 7⅞ x 10¾. 23786-9 Pa. $3.50

THE GREAT CHICAGO FIRE, edited by David Lowe. 10 dramatic, eye-witness accounts of the 1871 disaster, including one of the aftermath and rebuilding, plus 70 contemporary photographs and illustrations of the ruins—courthouse, Palmer House, Great Central Depot, etc. Introduction by David Lowe. 87pp. 8¼ x 11. 23771-0 Pa. $4.00

SILHOUETTES: A PICTORIAL ARCHIVE OF VARIED ILLUSTRA-TIONS, edited by Carol Belanger Grafton. Over 600 silhouettes from the 18th to 20th centuries include profiles and full figures of men and women, children, birds and animals, groups and scenes, nature, ships, an alphabet. Dozens of uses for commercial artists and craftspeople. 144pp. 8⅜ x 11¼. 23781-8 Pa. $4.00

ANIMALS: 1,419 COPYRIGHT-FREE ILLUSTRATIONS OF MAM-MALS, BIRDS, FISH, INSECTS, ETC., edited by Jim Harter. Clear wood engravings present, in extremely lifelike poses, over 1,000 species of animals. One of the most extensive copyright-free pictorial sourcebooks of its kind. Captions. Index. 284pp. 9 x 12. 23766-4 Pa. $7.50

INDIAN DESIGNS FROM ANCIENT ECUADOR, Frederick W. Shaffer. 282 original designs by pre-Columbian Indians of Ecuador (500-1500 A.D.). Designs include people, mammals, birds, reptiles, fish, plants, heads, geometric designs. Use as is or alter for advertising, textiles, leathercraft, etc. Introduction. 95pp. 8¾ x 11¼. 23764-8 Pa. $3.50

SZIGETI ON THE VIOLIN, Joseph Szigeti. Genial, loosely structured tour by premier violinist, featuring a pleasant mixture of reminiscences, insights into great music and musicians, innumerable tips for practicing violinists. 385 musical passages. 256pp. 5⅝ x 8¼. 23763-X Pa. $3.50

TONE POEMS, SERIES II: TILL EULENSPIEGELS LUSTIGE STREICHE, ALSO SPRACH ZARATHUSTRA, AND EIN HELDEN-LEBEN, Richard Strauss. Three important orchestral works, including very popular *Till Eulenspiegel's Marry Pranks*, reproduced in full score from original editions. Study score. 315pp. 9⅜ x 12¼. (Available in U.S. only)
23755-9 Pa. $7.50

TONE POEMS, SERIES I: DON JUAN, TOD UND VERKLARUNG AND DON QUIXOTE, Richard Strauss. Three of the most often performed and recorded works in entire orchestral repertoire, reproduced in full score from original editions. Study score. 286pp. 9⅜ x 12¼. (Available in U.S. only)
23754-0 Pa. $7.50

11 LATE STRING QUARTETS, Franz Joseph Haydn. The form which Haydn defined and "brought to perfection." (*Grove's*). 11 string quartets in complete score, his last and his best. The first in a projected series of the complete Haydn string quartets. Reliable modern Eulenberg edition, otherwise difficult to obtain. 320pp. 8⅜ x 11¼. (Available in U.S. only)
23753-2 Pa. $6.95

FOURTH, FIFTH AND SIXTH SYMPHONIES IN FULL SCORE, Peter Ilyitch Tchaikovsky. Complete orchestral scores of Symphony No. 4 in F Minor, Op. 36; Symphony No. 5 in E Minor, Op. 64; Symphony No. 6 in B Minor, "Pathetique," Op. 74. Bretikopf & Hartel eds. Study score. 480pp. 9⅜ x 12¼.
23861-X Pa. $10.95

THE MARRIAGE OF FIGARO: COMPLETE SCORE, Wolfgang A. Mozart. Finest comic opera ever written. Full score, not to be confused with piano renderings. Peters edition. Study score. 448pp. 9⅜ x 12¼. (Available in U.S. only)
23751-6 Pa. $11.95

"IMAGE" ON THE ART AND EVOLUTION OF THE FILM, edited by Marshall Deutelbaum. Pioneering book brings together for first time 38 groundbreaking articles on early silent films from *Image* and 263 illustrations newly shot from rare prints in the collection of the International Museum of Photography. A landmark work. Index. 256pp. 8¼ x 11.
23777-X Pa. $8.95

AROUND-THE-WORLD COOKY BOOK, Lois Lintner Sumption and Marguerite Lintner Ashbrook. 373 cooky and frosting recipes from 28 countries (America, Austria, China, Russia, Italy, etc.) include Viennese kisses, rice wafers, London strips, lady fingers, hony, sugar spice, maple cookies, etc. Clear instructions. All tested. 38 drawings. 182pp. 5⅜ x 8.
23802-4 Pa. $2.50

THE ART NOUVEAU STYLE, edited by Roberta Waddell. 579 rare photographs, not available elsewhere, of works in jewelry, metalwork, glass, ceramics, textiles, architecture and furniture by 175 artists—Mucha, Seguy, Lalique, Tiffany, Gaudin, Hohlwein, Saarinen, and many others. 288pp. 8⅜ x 11¼.
23515-7 Pa. $6.95

YUCATAN BEFORE AND AFTER THE CONQUEST, Diego de Landa. First English translation of basic book in Maya studies, the only significant account of Yucatan written in the early post-Conquest era. Translated by distinguished Maya scholar William Gates. Appendices, introduction, 4 maps and over 120 illustrations added by translator. 162pp. 5⅜ x 8½.
23622-6 Pa. $3.00

THE MALAY ARCHIPELAGO, Alfred R. Wallace. Spirited travel account by one of founders of modern biology. Touches on zoology, botany, ethnography, geography, and geology. 62 illustrations, maps. 515pp. 5⅜ x 8½.
20187-2 Pa. $6.95

THE DISCOVERY OF THE TOMB OF TUTANKHAMEN, Howard Carter, A. C. Mace. Accompany Carter in the thrill of discovery, as ruined passage suddenly reveals unique, untouched, fabulously rich tomb. Fascinating account, with 106 illustrations. New introduction by J. M. White. Total of 382pp. 5⅜ x 8½. (Available in U.S. only) 23500-9 Pa. $4.00

THE WORLD'S GREATEST SPEECHES, edited by Lewis Copeland and Lawrence W. Lamm. Vast collection of 278 speeches from Greeks up to present. Powerful and effective models; unique look at history. Revised to 1970. Indices. 842pp. 5⅜ x 8½.
20468-5 Pa. $6.95

THE 100 GREATEST ADVERTISEMENTS, Julian Watkins. The priceless ingredient; His master's voice; 99 44/100% pure; over 100 others. How they were written, their impact, etc. Remarkable record. 130 illustrations. 233pp. 7⅞ x 10 3/5.
20540-1 Pa. $5.00

CRUICKSHANK PRINTS FOR HAND COLORING, George Cruickshank. 18 illustrations, one side of a page, on fine-quality paper suitable for watercolors. Caricatures of people in society (c. 1820) full of trenchant wit. Very large format. 32pp. 11 x 16.
23684-6 Pa. $4.50

THIRTY-TWO COLOR POSTCARDS OF TWENTIETH-CENTURY AMERICAN ART, Whitney Museum of American Art. Reproduced in full color in postcard form are 31 art works and one shot of the museum. Calder, Hopper, Rauschenberg, others. Detachable. 16pp. 8¼ x 11.
23629-3 Pa. $2.50

MUSIC OF THE SPHERES: THE MATERIAL UNIVERSE FROM ATOM TO QUASAR SIMPLY EXPLAINED, Guy Murchie. Planets, stars, geology, atoms, radiation, relativity, quantum theory, light, antimatter, similar topics. 319 figures. 664pp. 5⅜ x 8½.
21809-0, 21810-4 Pa., Two-vol. set $10.00

EINSTEIN'S THEORY OF RELATIVITY, Max Born. Finest semi-technical account; covers Einstein, Lorentz, Minkowski, and others, with much detail, much explanation of ideas and math not readily available elsewhere on this level. For student, non-specialist. 376pp. 5⅜ x 8½.
60769-0 Pa. $4.00

HISTORY OF BACTERIOLOGY, William Bulloch. The only comprehensive history of bacteriology from the beginnings through the 19th century. Special emphasis is given to biography-Leeuwenhoek, etc. Brief accounts of 350 bacteriologists form a separate section. No clearer, fuller study, suitable to scientists and general readers, has yet been written. 52 illustrations. 448pp. 5⅝ x 8¼. 23761-3 Pa. $6.50

THE COMPLETE NONSENSE OF EDWARD LEAR, Edward Lear. All nonsense limericks, zany alphabets, Owl and Pussycat, songs, nonsense botany, etc., illustrated by Lear. Total of 321pp. 5⅜ x 8½. (Available in U.S. only) 20167-8 Pa. $3.00

INGENIOUS MATHEMATICAL PROBLEMS AND METHODS, Louis A. Graham. Sophisticated material from Graham *Dial*, applied and pure; stresses solution methods. Logic, number theory, networks, inversions, etc. 237pp. 5⅜ x 8½. 20545-2 Pa. $3.50

BEST MATHEMATICAL PUZZLES OF SAM LOYD, edited by Martin Gardner. Bizarre, original, whimsical puzzles by America's greatest puzzler. From fabulously rare *Cyclopedia*, including famous 14-15 puzzles, the Horse of a Different Color, 115 more. Elementary math. 150 illustrations. 167pp. 5⅜ x 8½. 20498-7 Pa. $2.50

THE BASIS OF COMBINATION IN CHESS, J. du Mont. Easy-to-follow, instructive book on elements of combination play, with chapters on each piece and every powerful combination team—two knights, bishop and knight, rook and bishop, etc. 250 diagrams. 218pp. 5⅜ x 8½. (Available in U.S. only) 23644-7 Pa. $3.50

MODERN CHESS STRATEGY, Ludek Pachman. The use of the queen, the active king, exchanges, pawn play, the center, weak squares, etc. Section on rook alone worth price of the book. Stress on the moderns. Often considered the most important book on strategy. 314pp. 5⅜ x 8½. 20290-9 Pa. $3.50

LASKER'S MANUAL OF CHESS, Dr. Emanuel Lasker. Great world champion offers very thorough coverage of all aspects of chess. Combinations, position play, openings, end game, aesthetics of chess, philosophy of struggle, much more. Filled with analyzed games. 390pp. 5⅜ x 8½. 20640-8 Pa. $4.00

500 MASTER GAMES OF CHESS, S. Tartakower, J. du Mont. Vast collection of great chess games from 1798-1938, with much material nowhere else readily available. Fully annotated, arranged by opening for easier study. 664pp. 5⅜ x 8½. 23208-5 Pa. $6.00

A GUIDE TO CHESS ENDINGS, Dr. Max Euwe, David Hooper. One of the finest modern works on chess endings. Thorough analysis of the most frequently encountered endings by former world champion. 331 examples, each with diagram. 248pp. 5⅜ x 8½. 23332-4 Pa. $3.50

SECOND PIATIGORSKY CUP, edited by Isaac Kashdan. One of the greatest tournament books ever produced in the English language. All 90 games of the 1966 tournament, annotated by players, most annotated by both players. Features Petrosian, Spassky, Fischer, Larsen, six others. 228pp. 5⅜ x 8½.   23572-6 Pa. $3.50

ENCYCLOPEDIA OF CARD TRICKS, revised and edited by Jean Hugard. How to perform over 600 card tricks, devised by the world's greatest magicians: impromptus, spelling tricks, key cards, using special packs, much, much more. Additional chapter on card technique. 66 illustrations. 402pp. 5⅜ x 8½. (Available in U.S. only.)   21252-1 Pa. $3.95

MAGIC: STAGE ILLUSIONS, SPECIAL EFFECTS AND TRICK PHOTOGRAPHY, Albert A. Hopkins, Henry R. Evans. One of the great classics; fullest, most authorative explanation of vanishing lady, levitations, scores of other great stage effects. Also small magic, automata, stunts. 446 illustrations. 556pp. 5⅜ x 8½.   23344-8 Pa. $5.00

THE SECRETS OF HOUDINI, J. C. Cannell. Classic study of Houdini's incredible magic, exposing closely-kept professional secrets and revealing, in general terms, the whole art of stage magic. 67 illustrations. 279pp. 5⅜ x 8½.   22913-0 Pa. $3.00

HOFFMANN'S MODERN MAGIC, Professor Hoffmann. One of the best, and best-known, magicians' manuals of the past century. Hundreds of tricks from card tricks and simple sleight of hand to elaborate illusions involving construction of complicated machinery. 332 illustrations. 563pp. 5⅜ x 8½.   23623-4 Pa. $6.00

MADAME PRUNIER'S FISH COOKERY BOOK, Mme. S. B. Prunier. More than 1000 recipes from world famous Prunier's of Paris and London, specially adapted here for American kitchen. Grilled tournedos with anchovy butter, Lobster a la Bordelaise, Prunier's prized desserts, more. Glossary. 340pp. 5⅜ x 8½. (Available in U.S. only)   22679-4 Pa. $3.00

FRENCH COUNTRY COOKING FOR AMERICANS, Louis Diat. 500 easy-to-make, authentic provincial recipes compiled by former head chef at New York's Fitz-Carlton Hotel: onion soup, lamb stew, potato pie, more. 309pp. 5⅜ x 8½.   23665-X Pa. $3.95

SAUCES, FRENCH AND FAMOUS, Louis Diat. Complete book gives over 200 specific recipes: bechamel, Bordelaise, hollandaise, Cumberland, apricot, etc. Author was one of this century's finest chefs, originator of vichyssoise and many other dishes. Index. 156pp. 5⅜ x 8.
23663-3 Pa. $2.50

TOLL HOUSE TRIED AND TRUE RECIPES, Ruth Graves Wakefield. Authentic recipes from the famous Mass. restaurant: popovers, veal and ham loaf, Toll House baked beans, chocolate cake crumb pudding, much more. Many helpful hints. Nearly 700 recipes. Index. 376pp. 5⅜ x 8½.
23560-2 Pa. $4.00

AMERICAN BIRD ENGRAVINGS, Alexander Wilson et al. All 76 plates. from Wilson's *American Ornithology* (1808-14), most important ornithological work before Audubon, plus 27 plates from the supplement (1825-33) by Charles Bonaparte. Over 250 birds portrayed. 8 plates also reproduced in full color. 111pp. 9⅜ x 12½. 23195-X Pa. $6.00

CRUICKSHANK'S PHOTOGRAPHS OF BIRDS OF AMERICA, Allan D. Cruickshank. Great ornithologist, photographer presents 177 closeups, groupings, panoramas, flightings, etc., of about 150 different birds. Expanded *Wings in the Wilderness*. Introduction by Helen G. Cruickshank. 191pp. 8¼ x 11. 23497-5 Pa. $6.00

AMERICAN WILDLIFE AND PLANTS, A. C. Martin, et al. Describes food habits of more than 1000 species of mammals, birds, fish. Special treatment of important food plants. Over 300 illustrations. 500pp. 5⅜ x 8½. 20793-5 Pa. $4.95

THE PEOPLE CALLED SHAKERS, Edward D. Andrews. Lifetime of research, definitive study of Shakers: origins, beliefs, practices, dances, social organization, furniture and crafts, impact on 19th-century USA, present heritage. Indispensable to student of American history, collector. 33 illustrations. 351pp. 5⅜ x 8½. 21081-2 Pa. $4.00

OLD NEW YORK IN EARLY PHOTOGRAPHS, Mary Black. New York City as it was in 1853-1901, through 196 wonderful photographs from N.-Y. Historical Society. Great Blizzard, Lincoln's funeral procession, great buildings. 228pp. 9 x 12. 22907-6 Pa. $7.95

MR. LINCOLN'S CAMERA MAN: MATHEW BRADY, Roy Meredith. Over 300 Brady photos reproduced directly from original negatives, photos. Jackson, Webster, Grant, Lee, Carnegie, Barnum; Lincoln; Battle Smoke, Death of Rebel Sniper, Atlanta Just After Capture. Lively commentary. 368pp. 8⅜ x 11¼. 23021-X Pa. $6.95

TRAVELS OF WILLIAM BARTRAM, William Bartram. From 1773-8, Bartram explored Northern Florida, Georgia, Carolinas, and reported on wild life, plants, Indians, early settlers. Basic account for period, entertaining reading. Edited by Mark Van Doren. 13 illustrations. 141pp. 5⅜ x 8½. 20013-2 Pa. $4.50

THE GENTLEMAN AND CABINET MAKER'S DIRECTOR, Thomas Chippendale. Full reprint, 1762 style book, most influential of all time; chairs, tables, sofas, mirrors, cabinets, etc. 200 plates, plus 24 photographs of surviving pieces. 249pp. 9⅞ x 12¾. 21601-2 Pa. $6.50

AMERICAN CARRIAGES, SLEIGHS, SULKIES AND CARTS, edited by Don H. Berkebile. 168 Victorian illustrations from catalogues, trade journals, fully captioned. Useful for artists. Author is Assoc. Curator, Div. of Transportation of Smithsonian Institution. 168pp. 8½ x 9½. 23328-6 Pa. $5.00

"OSCAR" OF THE WALDORF'S COOKBOOK, Oscar Tschirky. Famous American chef reveals 3455 recipes that made Waldorf great; cream of French, German, American cooking, in all categories. Full instructions, easy home use. 1896 edition. 907pp. 6⅝ x 9⅜. 20790-0 Clothbd. $15.00

COOKING WITH BEER, Carole Fahy. Beer has as superb an effect on food as wine, and at fraction of cost. Over 250 recipes for appetizers, soups, main dishes, desserts, breads, etc. Index. 144pp. 5⅜ x 8½. (Available in U.S. only) 23661-7 Pa. $2.50

STEWS AND RAGOUTS, Kay Shaw Nelson. This international cookbook offers wide range of 108 recipes perfect for everyday, special occasions, meals-in-themselves, main dishes. Economical, nutritious, easy-to-prepare: goulash, Irish stew, boeuf bourguignon, etc. Index. 134pp. 5⅜ x 8½. 23662-5 Pa. $2.50

DELICIOUS MAIN COURSE DISHES, Marian Tracy. Main courses are the most important part of any meal. These 200 nutritious, economical recipes from around the world make every meal a delight. "I . . . have found it so useful in my own household,"—N.Y. Times. Index. 219pp. 5⅜ x 8½. 23664-1 Pa. $3.00

FIVE ACRES AND INDEPENDENCE, Maurice G. Kains. Great back-to-the-land classic explains basics of self-sufficient farming: economics, plants, crops, animals, orchards, soils, land selection, host of other necessary things. Do not confuse with skimpy faddist literature; Kains was one of America's greatest agriculturalists. 95 illustrations. 397pp. 5⅜ x 8½. 20974-1 Pa. $3.50

A PRACTICAL GUIDE FOR THE BEGINNING FARMER, Herbert Jacobs. Basic, extremely useful first book for anyone thinking about moving to the country and starting a farm. Simpler than Kains, with greater emphasis on country living in general. 246pp. 5⅜ x 8½. 23675-7 Pa. $3.50

HARDY BULBS, Louise Beebe Wilder. Fullest, most thorough book on plants grown from bulbs, corms, rhizomes and tubers. 40 genera and 335 species covered: selecting, cultivating, naturalizing; name, origins, blooming season, when to plant, special requirements. 127 illustrations. 432pp. 5⅜ x 8½. 23102-X Pa. $4.50

A GARDEN OF PLEASANT FLOWERS (PARADISI IN SOLE: PARADISUS TERRESTRIS), John Parkinson. Complete, unabridged reprint of first (1629) edition of earliest great English book on gardens and gardening. More than 1000 plants & flowers of Elizabethan, Jacobean garden fully described, most with woodcut illustrations. Botanically very reliable, a "speaking garden" of exceeding charm. 812 illustrations. 628pp. 8½ x 12¼. 23392-8 Clothbd. $25.00

MUSHROOMS, EDIBLE AND OTHERWISE, Miron E. Hard. Profusely illustrated, very useful guide to over 500 species of mushrooms growing in the Midwest and East. Nomenclature updated to 1976. 505 illustrations. 628pp. 6½ x 9¼. 23309-X Pa. $7.95

AN ILLUSTRATED FLORA OF THE NORTHERN UNITED STATES AND CANADA, Nathaniel L. Britton, Addison Brown. Encyclopedic work covers 4666 species, ferns on up. Everything. Full botanical information, illustration for each. This earlier edition is preferred by many to more recent revisions. 1913 edition. Over 4000 illustrations, total of 2087pp. 6⅛ x 9¼. 22642-5, 22643-3, 22644-1 Pa., Three-vol. set $24.00

MANUAL OF THE GRASSES OF THE UNITED STATES, A. S. Hitchcock, U.S. Dept. of Agriculture. The basic study of American grasses, both indigenous and escapes, cultivated and wild. Over 1400 species. Full descriptions, information. Over 1100 maps, illustrations. Total of 1051pp. 5⅜ x 8½. 22717-0, 22718-9 Pa., Two-vol. set $12.00

THE CACTACEAE,, Nathaniel L. Britton, John N. Rose. Exhaustive, definitive. Every cactus in the world. Full botanical descriptions. Thorough statement of nomenclatures, habitat, detailed finding keys. The one book needed by every cactus enthusiast. Over 1275 illustrations. Total of 1080pp. 8 x 10¼. 21191-6, 21192-4 Clothbd., Two-vol. set $35.00

AMERICAN MEDICINAL PLANTS, Charles F. Millspaugh. Full descriptions, 180 plants covered: history; physical description; methods of preparation with all chemical constituents extracted; all claimed curative or adverse effects. 180 full-page plates. Classification table. 804pp. 6½ x 9¼. 23034-1 Pa. $10.00

A MODERN HERBAL, Margaret Grieve. Much the fullest, most exact, most useful compilation of herbal material. Gigantic alphabetical encyclopedia, from aconite to zedoary, gives botanical information, medical properties, folklore, economic uses, and much else. Indispensable to serious reader. 161 illustrations. 888pp. 6½ x 9¼. (Available in U.S. only) 22798-7, 22799-5 Pa., Two-vol. set $11.00

THE HERBAL or GENERAL HISTORY OF PLANTS, John Gerard. The 1633 edition revised and enlarged by Thomas Johnson. Containing almost 2850 plant descriptions and 2705 superb illustrations, Gerard's *Herbal* is a monumental work, the book all modern English herbals are derived from, the one herbal every serious enthusiast should have in its entirety. Original editions are worth perhaps $750. 1678pp. 8½ x 12¼. 23147-X Clothbd. $50.00

MANUAL OF THE TREES OF NORTH AMERICA, Charles S. Sargent. The basic survey of every native tree and tree-like shrub, 717 species in all. Extremely full descriptions, information on habitat, growth, locales, economics, etc. Necessary to every serious tree lover. Over 100 finding keys. 783 illustrations. Total of 986pp. 5⅜ x 8½. 20277-1, 20278-X Pa., Two-vol. set $10.00

AMERICAN ANTIQUE FURNITURE, Edgar G. Miller, Jr. The basic coverage of all American furniture before 1840: chapters per item chronologically cover all types of furniture, with more than 2100 photos. Total of 1106pp. 7⅞ x 10¾.   21599-7, 21600-4 Pa., Two-vol. set $17.90

ILLUSTRATED GUIDE TO SHAKER FURNITURE, Robert Meader. Director, Shaker Museum, Old Chatham, presents up-to-date coverage of all furniture and appurtenances, with much on local styles not available elsewhere. 235 photos. 146pp. 9 x 12.   22819-3 Pa. $5.00

ORIENTAL RUGS, ANTIQUE AND MODERN, Walter A. Hawley. Persia, Turkey, Caucasus, Central Asia, China, other traditions. Best general survey of all aspects: styles and periods, manufacture, uses, symbols and their interpretation, and identification. 96 illustrations, 11 in color. 320pp. 6⅛ x 9¼.   22366-3 Pa. $6.00

CHINESE POTTERY AND PORCELAIN, R. L. Hobson. Detailed descriptions and analyses by former Keeper of the Department of Oriental Antiquities and Ethnography at the British Museum. Covers hundreds of pieces from primitive times to 1915. Still the standard text for most periods. 136 plates, 40 in full color. Total of 750pp. 5⅜ x 8½.
23253-0 Pa. $10.00

THE WARES OF THE MING DYNASTY, R. L. Hobson. Foremost scholar examines and illustrates many varieties of Ming (1368-1644). Famous blue and white, polychrome, lesser-known styles and shapes. 117 illustrations, 9 full color, of outstanding pieces. Total of 263pp. 6⅛ x 9¼. (Available in U.S. only)   23652-8 Pa. $6.00

ACKERMANN'S COSTUME PLATES, Rudolph Ackermann. Selection of 96 plates from the *Repository of Arts,* best published source of costume for English fashion during the early 19th century. 12 plates also in color. Captions, glossary and introduction by editor Stella Blum. Total of 120pp. 8⅜ x 11¼.   23690-0 Pa. $4.50